Seven Cents

Two stories of beating the odds

By

Lee A. Shervheim

-

-

This book is dedicated to who matters most to me, my wife and our seven great kids.

... every day is another chapter ...

Contents

-

-

-

Introduction

I can sum up a good portion of my time on planet earth with the words home and work.

First, home; I am a husband to Karen and father to Daniel, Andrew, Sam, Katie, Emie, Annie and David. Reflecting on my life, the birth of a child with Down Syndrome and the adoption of two more has stretched us, enriched us and taught us so many lessons we could never have imagined.

My work life has been about making things; I love the sounds, smells and rhythms of a factory. During a twenty-five-year career; my work has been in manufacturing plants, in a variety of roles. I consider it a true privilege to be employed in manufacturing, making useful things for people. Manufacturing is deceptively simple to the outsider; raw materials enter and products exit. In between, it is incredibly complex; an organization, technology, skilled people, machines, systems all work in an integrated environment to design, plan, build, store, ship and create things of value.

I started six years ago to write a story based on my journey; to inform, entertain and educate. What have I learned? Life is not predictable. Things come at us from all directions and at times none of it makes sense. In family life, it may be a child with a disability; at work – it might be a competitive threat so large, conquering seems impossible. I created Northern Pines Corporation and the Stanton family as a vehicle to show, especially when faced with challenge after challenge; thinking, acting and leading differently changes everything.

Are you ready to begin the journey?

Chapter 1: Bad Meetings and a Drive

"John, fix this mess or else!"

The words resonated in his ears and mind four hours after Doug spoke them. It was the tone, the urgency and bite which worried John. Normally, Doug was reserved and discrete in his criticism and did not use public forums for a thrashing. But today John could tell weightier matters loomed behind the scenes. It was the only logical explanation for the events of the day.

John felt fortunate to have a manager like Doug Walker. Doug was a mentor and after surviving workforce reductions, competitive challenges and a product recall together, they knew each other reasonably well and their skills were complementary. John was a good tactician and could implement improvements; Doug excelled at creation of the overall strategy. Doug served as the manufacturing director for the information storage division with responsibility for operations across four manufacturing sites; a big job filled with plenty of stress. Doug was having a bad day. He was having a series of bad days, and on this afternoon, John just happened to be in the line of fire.

John drove northwest; on a road, he traveled probably a hundred times during the past 15 years. I-94 would go all the way to Seattle if one would just keep following the ribbon of highway stretched out ahead. John thought, "Maybe that is what I should do, just escape." Not really an option, just a passing thought. John knew even without traveling anywhere close to Seattle, tonight was going to be a late night. The snow started just as he was leaving the parking lot of the corporate campus of Northern Pines Technology just inside the singular ring of interstate containing Minneapolis and St. Paul.

Fortunately, he left after rush hour. Not the preferred timing, but after making this trip so many times, experience taught sometimes another "hour at the office" isn't another "hour at the office." Factoring in the required time sitting stuck in traffic between Brooklyn Center and Rogers, the hour is lost anyway. John also knew once the trusty Taurus hit the open road, the February snow would probably nip 20 mph off standard speed, which quickly doing the math translated into a late night. Oh well, all in a daze work – pun intended, he thought to himself.

"Fix this mess or else!" still echoed in the car, even miles later. Lately, it seemed more meetings at headquarters ended in harsh and tense words. John knew the business was tough. He knew all too well the competitive market conditions and profit margins were shrinking. Sure, sales were now shaky and price trumped all - but everything was being done which could be done to keep the division on an even keel. His operations team created a reasonable plan, yet it seemed like patience was running thin - and John was glad most of the time he was some 220 miles removed from the epicenter.

Most days John believed he had the job of a lifetime. He commanded a plant of 450 of the best and most dedicated employees. He was in a challenging and growing industry and was able to have free reign of 'his' plant. He could lead, manage, make decisions and invest a budget greater than $100 million dollars annually. Heady stuff for someone who started his working career by detasseling corn during sweltering Iowa summers. To run a plant was one of his life goals; and here it was, the opportunity to make his mark on the industry, technology and corporation.

The site housed five major production lines and included a research and development area outfitted with world-class, state of the art equipment. Nearly anything could be conceived, designed and fabricated in house. Ideas could be turned into reality quickly. This strategy was so valuable, the previous site manager created a contract manufacturing business, selling integrated services to those demanding speed, precision and flexibility. It made sense; many of the technologies used in data and information storage are complementary to other industries. So, as part of the autonomy of being a remote site, a small skunkworks operation was established. It started slowly, but recently, with several new customers, the operation generated sales approaching one million dollars a month.

The site received recognition globally for excellence in development, manufacturing and quality. John knew this site very well, as he spent nearly all his career here; the only exception being the time in the engineering and management- training program when he joined one of the Fortune 50 – Northern Pines Technology.

When John was hired, he enrolled as one of the first members of the Northern Pines Technology department called Optimized Operations. Northern Pines developed a progressive program where newly hired engineers were trained to be experts in Just-In-Time (JIT) practices and quality improvement.

JIT was an approach developed and used widely by Toyota to synchronize their manufacturing operations by reducing waste in the process. The focus on waste reduction produces lower cost and better responsiveness to customer needs. Excellent implementation of JIT brings quality improvement; by stressing one-piece flow and operator empowerment.

These high potential, well-educated, leadership candidates worked as internal consultants within Northern Pines Technology facilities. The program graduates provided project leadership and worked closely with existing plant resources to identify opportunities, create pilot projects and bring rapid change. These teams were a catalyst for rapid innovation.

In the early 1990s when John joined the program, manufacturing in the United States was in flux. The late 1970s and 1980s were turbulent times for industry. Quality of workmanship began to substantially differentiate the global markets. For years, consumers perceived Japan as producing low cost, poor quality goods. In a rapid turnaround, brands like Sony, JVC and Seiko demonstrated to the US consumer Japan knew how to build high quality, reliable goods. This prowess extended to the auto industry as well. In short, Detroit car manufacturers had been arrogant and not listened to their customers. To be blunt, Detroit had the keys handed to them and they started Toyotas, Hondas and Nissans, not Fords, Chryslers and Chevys. Said another way, American manufacturing was in deep trouble and sadly did not realize the severity of the situation until it was almost too late.

During this time, the American auto industry looked for anything to provide answers. All industry tried to find the secret to achieve rapid improvement. Whether it was quality circles, quality squares or quality rectangles, it didn't matter. What resulted was a proliferation of authors, professors and consultants hawking single-point solutions such as World Class Manufacturing by Schonberger and theory of constraints by Goldratt in The Goal. Lean Six Sigma was still very much in its infancy, incubated by the likes of Motorola and GE, but the concept had yet to mature and be widely accepted across industry.

John felt fortunate to be in a reasonable career trajectory. Early on he had come to terms, he was not ever going to be CEO; but at age 42, he really did not aspire to the C-level anymore. Years in the trenches created a more realistic goal. John wanted to: keep advancing upwards, make a difference, do great work and be successful at leading people through tough challenges. He was perhaps a reformed Type A, recognizing he didn't need to be Alpha in every pack. His competitive juices still flowed fast and deep, John didn't like to come in second place.

Tempering this ambition in his work life was his wife, Kristin, and a busier and busier family life as the years advanced. He met his wife at Iowa State University, married the proverbial farmer's daughter and launched into a corporate career. After finishing graduate school, getting married and during the first two years of his career, he worked in four plants, including a short stint overseas focused in a Spanish distribution center. There, he worked on transportation optimization and supply chain management to help distribution center operations become more competitive. Two and half years into his career, John traveled up the map to North Dakota.

On the interview trip, John recalled being highly impressed by the caliber of people, the size of the operation and the wide use of leading edge technology. Recruiting trips always result in a sell job on both parties' part; but when the interview was over, John knew this was where he wanted to be. He did not even play poker to get a higher offer. They offered a nice package, and the deal was done. Kristin and John Stanton arrived at Twin Ports, North Dakota in the summer of 1993, and he began work as a quality engineer. They were settling after a nomadic few years and looking forward to the next stages of life, including starting a family.

John was maybe unique in today's world. He had only worked for Northern Pines Technology. No job-hopping for him. He was a committed 'one-company' man and for good reason. Northern Pines Technology is a powerhouse within the industry. It excelled in fundamental research, industry relationships, educational partnerships and possessed superior manufacturing prowess. There were few product categories in information, electronic data storage and management systems where it did not dominate.

The origins of Northern Pines Technology are deeply rooted in the upper Midwest, with a 100-year history of always innovating and advancing new technology. The pathway into information technology had been a little rockier than previous technologies and continued to be a challenge with the rate of change and mounting competitive pressure, mostly from Asia.

When John searched for his first engineering job, he created a list of factors and used a logical engineering methodology to narrow the search. When all the data was in, Northern Pines Technology was at the top of the list. Although based in the Midwest, the company emerged as a global presence, remained strong in technology and most importantly, manufactured almost all their own products. John reasoned he would have many options with this one unique and special company: a challenging career, potential for growth, ability to raise kids in a small town; and maybe someday, transition to a staff role at corporate headquarters.

Northern Pines Technology had been good to him and he was not going to let them down; the employer/employee relationship resulted in a union of shared values, endearing one to the other.

"Fix this mess or else!" The snow hit the windshield almost calling out a drumbeat of Doug's words. The message pounded with a renewed force. As the lights of the Twin Cities faded behind and the darkness of western Minnesota loomed ahead, John repeatedly played back the meeting in his head. The production numbers were good. Costs were just slightly above plan, but the topic which seemed to be the most problematic was the three-year outlook.

Budget time was never fun. The scarcity mindset seemed to rule over logic, facts and data. There was never enough money to go around, so there ended up being a fight for limited resources, which escalated with each year. It seemed like a 'cut way past the bone mentality' was starting to dominate current executive management thinking. This was the third year of zero-based budgeting, starting from scratch and justifying every element, line by line. John encountered an extra challenge in explaining the development, more challenging to offset the rising rate of development costs versus the direct production costs.

It was tough to run a plant, but John knew he and the team were up to the challenge. They had been in this situation before with the business and knew what was ahead was comparable to a bare-knuckle street fight.

Northern Pines Technology is a complicated intersection of products, technology and solutions. It was fundamentally run differently than many other companies. It enjoyed good margins and growth from many of its previous business endeavors. In the past, nearly everything the company touched turned to gold. When one division's sales were lower, another was there to balance out the loss. Northern Pines Technology enjoyed respect on Wall Street, because diversity delivered consistent and predictably good results. However, with the latest global economic woes slowing growth, it seemed the business was in uncharted waters. The balance of power and the rate of change of the technology driven by overseas competitors was changing business dynamics.

Fundamentally, what was happening? The sales department was fearful to forecast numbers they could not attain. Without growth, the sites struggled to put together a positive operating scenario. Over the years, John learned to take a pragmatic approach. His mentors, the three previous plant managers trained him well. The site must commit to what it can deliver, but always save a little for the rainy day fund. John was sure every member of the staff could recite that little truism by heart: Commit and Deliver. Those who committed and could not deliver quietly disappeared.

The spirit of success and the mantra ran deep. In fact, there was a rumor the staff was going to gift a tattoo of "commit and deliver" to John as a retirement gift, that is, if he survived to experience that day, very long into the future.

John had only been in the role of plant manager five months. Time flies; but having been an engineer, general supervisor and technical manager, he knew nearly every crack in the floor and water stain on the ceiling. Whether the problem was with budgets, safety issues, strategic planning or day-to- day operations, this was not his first rodeo.

In preparation for John's meeting at headquarters, the staff analyzed data and mapped a reasonably aggressive plan. The leadership tackled two, tough technology challenges. Numbers were scrubbed repeatedly; and to top it all off, the site committed to a 3.4% annualized cost down plan, including a planned reorganization of the entire operations to drive 3 to 4% productivity improvement. This was on a baseline budget which site operations committed to reduce direct operating expense (minus materials) by 2%. But after today, John wasn't confident of two things. First, was it enough; and second, did anyone care? It seemed as if something else was going on.

One of the perks of being remote is one doesn't get drawn into the day-to-day politics. However, there is also a downside, in that one is unaware if you are the subject of the day-to-day politics. John decided the first order of business on Thursday was to do a little sleuthing. Something just did not add up, and John needed to figure out what was going on.

The Taurus almost by habit pulled into the usual mid-trip stopping point. A quick fill with gas and a cup of trucker's coffee was about all that was available in Sauk Center, Minnesota. This was the home of Sinclair Lewis, as the sign John had passed at least a hundred times proclaimed. Starbucks and Caribou had not yet made it to rural Minnesota, which was fine by John. He could pay for coffee with a dollar and still get change. Try doing that in an upscale Twin Cities java joint! He was thankful for the break and for the coffee. Caffeine wasn't what the mind needed, but it would probably keep the body going for the next two hours.

It was ninety minutes later as John turned west to leave the interstate when his phone vibrated. Kristin called, and the exchange was quick

- just wondering when John would be home. John happily reported he was on the home stretch, having just left the interstate with only 20 miles of two-lane, straight as an arrow road remaining. Soon he would be pulling into Twin Ports.

Twin Ports is an old river town; although the river most of the time is unimpressive. Back in pioneer days, it was also somewhat of a gateway to the west being on a main route to the Pacific Northwest. Even James J Hill knew the strategic value of Twin Ports as the headwaters of the Red River of the North. Early in Hill's career, he established riverboat commerce on the Red, and later charted his railroad empire right across these fertile plains.

Most people are familiar with the Red River of the South. It is memorialized in song, legend and stories of the Wild West. John happened to live near the one a thousand miles north, formed by an ancient glacial lake and splits the states of North Dakota and Minnesota. The Red River was the defining feature between the rolling farmlands on the east and the vast prairie opening to the west.

The Red River of the North represents a geological oddity in the sense it one of the few rivers in the country which does not flow from north to south. The flow reverses, flowing from south to north. In southern climates, this is fine; however, where there are four distinct seasons, a not so subtle problem exists in this land is flat as a granite countertop. When ice melts in the southern valley and flows up to the frozen lakes and rivers to the north, there is no place for the water to go. The only remaining option is flowing over land; the net result is large areas can be rapidly covered with overland flooding.

The last miles went by fast. Because of the lack of contours in the bottom of the ancient lakebed, John could see the lights of town at least ten miles outside of Twin Ports. It was not like there were many to see, but the streetlights and a small industrial park on the north side of town had just enough to create a glow. The recent

9

snow cover perhaps magnified the effect, because tonight it somehow looked brighter than usual. The snow subsided and the roads covered in white, but no wind and a temperature of -5 F degrees ensured the last few minutes would be uneventful. John pulled the Taurus into the driveway at 11:20 PM, quickly parked, opened the trunk to grab his suitcase and briefcase and headed into the house.

The snow crunched under his feet as he stopped by the mailbox and grabbed a stack of bills before opening the front door. John purposely tried to be quiet as he dropped his bags by the front door. John first went to the boy's room. David and Eric had just moved downstairs. They were twins, born just over ten years ago and they had taken over the only main floor bedroom in their Cape Cod style house. They had lofted bunks Kristin built for them and they felt more grown up because they moved downstairs, further away from the nightly oversight and earshot of mom and dad.

Funny, when the Stanton's bought their starter house, 2,400 square feet seemed like a lot. In fact, there were rooms they hardly ever used because there was no need. Years later, with the addition of five kids, the house was busting at the seams.

Next stop was Seth's room. Seth was six and bunking with his baby brother Mark upstairs. Okay, not actually bunking. Seth was in his bed and the crib had been rolled into his room to sit in the corner. Seth was a sport and truly loved his baby brother, so sharing wasn't yet a burden. John closed the shade as the old windows sometimes let in more cold air than it seemed like they kept out. At least another thin barrier would provide some extra help to keep out the winter air.

With this house, no one worried about new house problems of too tightly sealed. The larger concern was the growing monthly natural gas bill to keep the drafty, old place warm. The last stop was the home office combined with what used to be a nursery and now post-toddler room.   In here was the princess, the only girl in the Stanton clan.   Caroline was now officially past the toddler stage.   Caroline just moved into a girlie fairy tale, princess bed.   John frankly wasn't sure exactly what to call it, but Kristin was excited because she had found it on Craigslist and enjoyed refinishing it.   The bed looked awesome and Caroline loved it.   John kissed her gently on the forehead and just watched her for a moment.

When John and Kristin saw their first daughter, it was love at first sight.   However, it was obvious their little baby girl had some distinct features.   After the initial consultation with the doctors, a decision was made she should be tested for several genetic conditions.   The results were not a surprise; the tests only confirmed the obvious: Trisomy 21, more commonly known as Down Syndrome.

Somewhere early in Caroline's development an extra 21st chromosome split in a unique way.   Both John and Kristin had a lot to absorb during the first few days of her life.   Their research indicated the syndrome can cause mental delays, physical challenges and internally, potential issues with heart abnormalities.   Historically, life expectancy is significantly shorter; a very scary thought for any parent.

While those first weeks were of a jumble by taking care of three boys at home, juggling work and contemplating the future for Caroline. John recalls going through his own period of shock, grief and anger. There were days of soul searching and asking God why, as any person might be inclined to do.

The memory most distinctly in John's mind was simply thinking, "I am not going to walk this girl down the aisle on her wedding day." As time passed, joy has replaced the grief, with hope and an absolute confidence this girl is going to do great things.   John had already seen his precious daughter impact their life and the lives of many others, so who knows what the future will bring?

As with any other challenge life puts in their path, John and Kristin clung to faith, friends and family helping them through the tough times. The experience of raising their boys and girl bonded them together as a family.

"I have a good life," John thought to himself as he walked down the short hallway to the last bedroom. The final stop for a tired, middle-aged guy was bed. John undressed, tossing his clothes on the closet floor, walked to the bed and crawled in. Kristin asked, "John, how did it go today?" John responded, "Tough drive, brutal day." She understood. John kissed Kristin goodnight and he rolled over to go to sleep.

Chapter 2: The Plant

The alarm on the bedside table buzzed at a crazy early hour. John turned to look outside and remembered last night the few inches of snow blanketing the driveway and sidewalk. He surmised more had fallen since he arrived home.   He reluctantly decided it would be an excellent time to be a good neighbor and shovel before all the school kids used the sidewalk on their walk to Lincoln Elementary.   Lincoln was the older of the two local elementary schools, but well used yet well loved.

The Stanton family lived in an aging neighborhood. Fifty years ago, the homes lining Seventh Street were some of the nicest in town. Now they were in various states of repair or disrepair, depending on the homeowner. John felt thankful their block remained well kept. In fact, an old-timer told John their street used to be called "silk stocking row." During the Second World War, the only women in town who had silk stockings lived on this stretch of Seventh Street.

Over the years, the town's population grew slowly; Twin Ports emerged as a regional hub for shopping and commerce. This was not as much a statement about its size as an indication this is where the prairie started to separate; first the towns and then farms and ranches by many, many miles. Much of the commerce in Twin Ports was affiliated with agriculture, equipment and storage of crops. The bottom of this prehistoric river valley contained some of the most fertile soil in the world, known for its sugar beets, sunflowers and row crops.

As John stepped outside, the drone of snowblowers filled the early morning air. The sun had yet to make an appearance but after 30 minutes of brisk "sweoveling" (that is, a cross between sweeping and shoveling). If done correctly, a rapid sweeping motion will clear most of the snow; and provide an acceptable path for the many snow boots passing by on the way to school.

"Sweoveling" allowed for thinking time, and the conversations and demands of the recent trip were fresh on John's mind. He had to formulate a game plan; John needed to figure out if something else lurked beneath the surface or if this was more of the usual politics and posturing. His gut told him there was something much deeper; however, the tricky part was how to sort through a messy series of events.

After completing the task, the smell of coffee filled the lower level of the house. The dwelling was still quiet, but he knew a few short minutes could change all that. In fact, by the time he had showered and come back downstairs, more than half the family was awake. Kristin was doing her best to take breakfast orders.

An Average North Dakota Winter

How she manages the morning routine is nothing short of amazing - waffles, pancakes, toast, eggs, cereal. When did the yellow house become a diner and Kristin a short-order cook? John scooped a few scrambled eggs onto a large spoon, downed them, grabbed his insulated mug and headed out the door once more into the chill of a February morning.

John often joked with his coworkers in the Twin Cities he had a one-song commute; maybe two if it was a Johnny Cash song. Oftentimes, John could leave the house and the song on the radio would not finish by the time he arrived at work. Two stop signs and slightly less than two miles to drive. Kenny Chesney was wrapping up "Another Friday Night" before John eased into an empty parking spot at the plant.

A fundamental difference between the plant and headquarters was the site had no designated parking spots. They still did at headquarters. This site used to; but after some of the employee empowerment discussions at the plant ten years ago, the leadership team decided preferred parking spots set the wrong tone. Offering a designated parking spot based on virtue of job title seemed presumptuous. Workers occupied spots at the plant 24/7. It was more logical to think some of them deserved the closest parking spot if it was open. This morning John was returning the lease car anyway, so by practice, lease vehicles always parked somewhere on the east side of the parking lot. Parking in the east lot at least saved the time of wandering around trying to figure out what Ford Taurus was the lease vehicle.

The observable variances between HQ and the plant didn't end with parking spots. The differences were more fundamental.

One area where this was most prevalent was how costs were managed at the plant. Product cost and maintaining margins was a constant focus at Northern Pines and the plant took the role of cost management very seriously.

One simple, but illustrative example is how the plant at Twin ports decided to lease cars for travel to the Twin Cities. It could be summed up in a four-letter acronym: QICR.

Quality Improvement/Cost Reduction. The plant fine-tuned this concept over the years, trying to find a better, faster or cheaper way to work. There is no mysterious code or secret, really. It boiled down to discipline and thoroughness in understanding and managing costs. Each year, the departments undergo a structured analysis process to figure out how they can both improve quality and reduce costs. All departments participate and through the years, this process has saved Twin Ports and Northern Pines hundreds of millions of dollars in cost.

It might seem as if reducing costs and improving quality objectives conflict somewhat, but data consistently showed many cost savings ideas satisfy both outcomes. And nothing is off limits – this being one, and arguably the most important tenet of the process.

The lease cars illustrate the concept beautifully; one of the engineers ran a quick calculation and brought the data to the monthly engineering meeting. The site averaged 17 trips a month to the Twin Cities. Each trip averaged two days and often three nights. The analysis showed the local auto dealership charged a car rental rate of $35/night with unlimited mileage. $35/night * 3 nights average * 17 * 12 = $21,420 spent per year renting cars which only went down and back to the Twin Cities. The bottom line surprised the engineers and managers equally.

The analysis only calculated the cost of one rental car. Often, two cars travelled to the Twin Cities because of scheduling conflicts. Ouch. No long drawn out process, no committee formed. The engineering manager brought it to the Plant Leadership Team meeting; and after five minutes of discussion, the decision made. It took the sourcing manager about two hours to line up two new lease vehicles from a fleet service in Fargo. The expense now costs

$400/month and two cars are available in the east lot for site travel and use. That simple idea saved just under $12,000 each year. With an annual operating budget in excess of one hundred million dollars, it might seem like a drop in a bucket, but the idea fits the quality improvement/cost reduction culture. $12k in annual repeating savings generated a solid return on investment.

The entire initiative served as a win:win from any angle, except maybe the local auto dealership. John felt very little sorrow for them; they had made their money, going forward, there was a much better way.

One of the key lessons learned from the leasing analysis is nothing should be sacred or off limits for scrutiny. Obviously, the big wins in savings come from reducing material costs, where spending is in the millions of dollars. However, plenty of other areas exist where a large operation spends significant dollars.

The beauty of QICR is not all savings needs to come from direct product cost. Even small savings results in lower cost to the plant. Whether it is electricity, supplies, cutting the grass or plowing snow; saving cash affects the cost of goods sold, both directly and indirectly.

Some might view QICR as a progressive new thing, but to Twin Ports, it was common sense. If there is a better, faster, cheaper way of doing something; why not analyze and consider implementing? It is not an overstatement to say the resulting culture helped support the very survival of the plant.

John breezed past Stacey Baltz, at the front desk and dropped off the keys behind the receptionist's desk. He made a beeline for his office, craving just a few minutes alone to think before the rest of the day unfolded.

John walked briskly down the hall to his office passing the empty offices of Grant Richards, Supply Chain Manager, Mary Ann Tackett,

Engineering and Technology Manager, and Jeff Alberts, Human Resources.

This morning, the offices remained empty and John breathed a sigh of relief. He knew if the managers were there, they would ask how the prior day's meetings went. He could imagine their questions. Who got chewed out? What was said? What decisions were made? All valid questions and John didn't want to purposely withhold things. He prided himself on being transparent amidst the challenges; however, this was different. John wasn't sure he was ready to tip his hand, at least not yet. There was too much uncertainty running through his mind to begin communicating any of it outwardly.

As John settled into his chair behind his desk, the first thing to catch his eye was a note taped to the computer monitor. It was from Becky Tanner, the production supervisor on the A crew. They had just wrapped up the night shift. The note announced a new production record on Line 12: 134,564 diskettes produced in 24 hours!

One of the things John loved about this plant was the energy and the drive of its employees. This site had been making diskettes for nearly 20 years, and the people on the line took such pride, ownership and responsibility in their work, it made managing the factory more fun than work. The employees set the bar very high, tracking line performance on their own. Daily output became a source of personal pride. No manager could force that behavior. It came from the quality and caliber of the people. John's thinking may be jaded; but in his mind, these are the best, most dedicated and skilled employees in the world. This was his plant and he was a proud leader; recognizing the results do not come from edicts from the top, but everyone doing their own job in an excellent way.

John remembered the first time a line produced 100,000 parts in a day. He was the production general supervisor at the time. The entire department celebrated across all crews with pizza, pop and ice cream. This was to celebrate an accomplishment by the entire diskette department working as a team.

The team concept best explains why Twin Ports operates at high efficiency. No one part is more important than any other; it is an interdependent system. The roles are well defined. Engineers drive utilization and line speed improvements. The maintenance crews implement line changes and manage the equipment runtime and utilization. The final element is the operators who reach for excellence by following procedures in responding quickly to alarms and following the established quality practices.

John was not surprised the record was broken on Line 12. Line 12 is Reggie's line. Reggie Pitarski, is one very driven and skilled operator, who maybe has taken personal accountability to a new level. When on shift, his line has made over 75,000 diskettes in a single shift, even more than actual machine capacity! His line ranks as the fastest of all the 14 diskette lines, running at 103 parts per minute [PPM].

103 PPM * 60 min/hr * 12 hours/shift = 74,160.

To account for the remaining 840 parts, Reggie minimized the downtime on a constrained resource and figured out how to manually introduce parts ahead of where there was slightly more capacity that is excess and used those extra one or two parts per minute differences to achieve 101.13% productivity. Unusual? Maybe, but Twin Ports knew the harsh reality of competitive pressure and it was just the standard way of doing things. Reggie believed with the extra 840 parts he made; Twin Ports was one-step closer to winning the battle to be the lowest cost diskette producer in the world.

Reggie exemplified the drive and determination that years of optimization, engineering, and just plain hard work have been put into this product line. Each time John stepped onto the factory floor, he stood in amazement watching the synchronous machines churn out product. He knew this was a global battle. The continuum ranged from low-cost labor and manual operations in Mexico and China to modern automated plants, similar to Twin Ports. John had the opportunity to see a range of global plants – from very manual to semi-automated to fully automated; very different in approach – but all sharing the exactly the same goal. To produce the best quality, lowest cost product in the world.

John was the steward of a high performing plant working in a fast paced, ever-changing area of technology. The plant existed today because of the growth of the personal computer. In the mid-1980s, the personal computer market was in its infancy. DOS 2.0 was the operating system of choice; hard drives were very expensive and only in the high-end machines. Consumers had a choice of media between a 5¼" floppy disk or a new hard-shelled, robust 3½" diskette holding almost triple the information of the old floppy.

Back then, most personal data storage needs were modest. Northern Pines Technology was just beginning to see the promise in this new personal computer market. In 1988, the company invested heavily in molding, assembly, and test equipment. Over the next ten years, the investment paid off nicely; with the business growing from $10 million in annual sales to over $400 million dollars. While some manufacturers were regionalizing production, Northern Pines saw the size of the market and opted to centralize, looking for synergy in high-volume, dedicated lines pumping out diskettes by the millions.

With rapid growth also came the entrance to very new market dynamics for the company, bringing competitive retail pricing and shrinking margins. Northern Pines, up until now, made most of its money in the industrial sector. This brave new world of retailers was an eye-opening experience. Retailers were ruthless in their pricing often using the diskette as the 'lost leader' to get people into their stores. This resulted in continuous pressure to drive down costs. Competition was continuous and relentless. John loved being a part of this landscape and hoped the plant would be a driving force in the future of Northern Pines.

Most people look at a diskette and think of it as a cheap way of storing or file transferring, but it is much more than that. It is one of the greatest cost reduction stories of all time. It is the story of American manufacturing competitiveness on the world stage; and not only competitive but leading the world in terms of technology, intellectual property and fundamental product understanding. This represents a true path to competitive advantage and a story to be replicated across other industries and products.

It is easy to point out the failed industries and lost competitiveness over the past 40 years: garments, textiles, furniture, automobiles, machine tools, televisions, consumer electronics and computers are all industries which lost. The jobs, technology and investments have gone to economies outside the United States.

Through the life of the product, diskettes have been able to fight the rising tide. John's plant, the most profitable diskette factory in the world was located in the upper Midwest. It was highly automated, paid good wages to its employees, and John believes, in large part, was due to the results and success of QICR and the spirit of competitiveness that drove the overall business.

To give one an idea of the size of the Northern Pines operation at Twin Ports, the front plant has 31 molding presses, two high-speed metal stamping machines, 15 high-speed automated assembly lines and four packaging lines which, on a good day, can make almost two million diskettes. Since the beginning of production back in the late 1980s, the site has manufactured more than 6 billion diskettes. Few technology products run on this scale. To put it into perspective, if all the diskettes made were put end to end, they would circle the earth 13 times.

The site also contains two other buildings on site filled with equally impressive technology. The scale of the production operation is massive and the technical knowledge and horsepower required to stay at the front of technology is significant and never-ending.

The phone rang, yanking John back from his thoughts. It was Sarah Bergstrom, Operations Manager in the North building. An 8:00 AM meeting had been scheduled after John checked the calendar last night.

Thinking time was over. He grabbed his notebook, safety glasses and headed through the plant to the back door for a short walk to the north building.

The next time John checked his watch it was 1:30. Where had the morning gone? John grabbed a Diet Coke from the vending machine and two bags of peanuts from Diane's snack stash. Diane was John's administrative assistant and he thought she was a genius. She had evolved in her role as administrative assistant nicely. John was the youngest plant manager the site had, and one of the first who would be described as technologically savvy. Old school managers needed assistants to make overheads or send out memos. Diane joked, in the old days, her time was spent making coffee, typing memos and creating overheads. Now she was John's proverbial right hand. She was an awesome proofreader, seemed to have a sixth sense about watching out for the plant, well connected in the community and generally made John's life ten times easier. John didn't know what he would do without her.

Today, she reminded him there was Cub Scout field trip day on the calendar and John was on deck to take the troop to the Red River Valley Railroad at 3:00 PM.

Between now and then, there was just time to punch out a few emails, run the weekly staff meeting and follow up on 500 rolls of production material on hold with Lenny Garst. Lenny was the site quality manager. A great guy with a driest sense of humor on the planet. However, Lenny was humorless today; the Glacier product line received a new shipment of computer tape and was running poorly, yielding worse and exhibiting high bit rate errors. Lenny was a by-the-numbers manager; don't deviate from the process type of quality manager. John liked that characteristic and respected him for his steady approach. The two agreed to a conference call with the media supply plant located in Oregon.

The phone beeped at 2:45 - time to go, just enough time to swing by home and pick up the twins. The rest of the day consumed with an operations tour at the local rail yard and trying to keep twelve 10-year-olds from being squished by a massive 205-ton diesel train engine; the weight of a SD-70 locomotive. The tour was fascinating. As the tour concluded, the boys climbed in the locomotive as it drove slowly through the yard. Each boy was handed the throttle for a short time, so they could feel the raw power.

John loved the engineering magic behind the massive diesel engines and the intricate complexity of the network on which they are scheduled and run. John recalled his two years of graduate school. His educational background was engineering and operations research, solving many network problems based on examples from the railroad. The professors drilled in the never-ending challenge of trying to get the freight through the network with the least possible cost in the fastest way possible. It was anything but easy, especially without access to the computing and simulation tools available today.

Being at the railroad seeded another reminder of the plants' QICR process. A few years ago, the plant worked with the local economic development board to add a rail spur on the north end of town. John didn't remember all the details, but he thought it was something like a 50/50 cost split. Other businesses used it periodically, but his site was the primary beneficiary.

The purchasing department figured out a long time ago rail transportation was the most cost effective method of transportation to rural North Dakota. The two or three cents per pound saved on transportation really adds up. Most of the plastic resin suppliers were in the industrial region between Ohio and Michigan.

There was good rail demand and velocity through Chicago to the west coast. The site processed a rail car of polystyrene every few days, so saving a few thousand dollars every week was more than just good business. It gave the operation a competitive advantage over everyone else who was bringing in material in semis or pallet quantities.

It is all about competitive advantage; doing something either your competitor can't or won't. Early in John's career, he was naïve enough to think all manufacturers did things using QICR, like Twin Ports.

The results were not just evident to the plant, they were recognized globally. The plant was seasoned in: benchmarking against the Baldrige criteria as well as frequent auditors from ISO to survey the quality system. As a capstone, a few years ago, the plant was recognition by Industry Week as a Top Ten Plant in the United States. Twin Ports was recognized for world class accomplishments in the areas of: safety, quality, customer service, cost management and technology application.

To the site, driving to this level of excellence and results was common sense. John had been taught well by previous site leaders the important of disciplined operations. He now learned firsthand, at least with the approach to cost management, what seemed to him to be common sense was not very common. Even with the reminder from the railroad visit with the Cub Scouts, John resolved even more, to use QICR for competitive advantage during his tenure.

Chapter 3:   This Site Knows How to Manufacture

It had been a long week.   Weeks with travel always seem to be extra tiresome; time in the car, different bed, food and overall lack of routine with a disrupted schedule.   Monday was at the plant, Tuesday and Wednesday at headquarters, home late on Wednesday and Thursday at the plant.   John was glad it was Friday.

He arrived at the office early and sat down at his desk.   He liked his current office arrangement because the window looked out toward the east.   He could see the first hint of dawn; tinged of orange and yellow as the night faded and the sky started to brighten across the prairie.

Sunrise Across the Prairie

Today, John came to work with a mission; to think about next steps. Some quiet time; alone in his thoughts and watching the day begin was his plan. Things seem clearer in the morning; perhaps less clutter. As he sat and his eyes scanned books on the bookshelf.

The Goal caught John's attention. He remembered it as a great read on how to manage bottlenecks and material scheduling and flow. However, was it relevant now? The book was over 20 years old; much had changed in the world since its first printing. The Machine that Changed the World defined lean within the context of Toyota. The book was cutting edge at the time, because prior to Womack's seminal work, a definition of lean didn't exist.

Since graduation from college almost 20 years ago, John vowed he would read a book a month. For many years, he could keep up the pace. Lately with five kids and a busy life, reading had slowed down some. Finding time to sit down and pick up a book provided insights and knowledge to him not available anywhere else. For quick knowledge, it was hard to beat Google. Nevertheless, the difficult questions requiring thought and idea fermentation seemed best found in a book.

One of John's personal favorites was My Life and Work by Henry Ford. Ford possessed a broad vision for humanity, and whatever one's thoughts on the man's politics, he was a genius in the art and science of manufacturing systems. He truly saw the enterprise as a system and pioneered such techniques as vertical integration, minimization of cycle time, standard work, the assembly line production, single piece flow and many more innovations. In fact, the early pioneers at Toyota visited Fords' plants in the 1930s to understand and innovate based on Ford's assembly line concept. Kiichiro Toyoda was responsible for the family sewing machine manufacturing business, which wasn't going very well. It was lessons learned from Ford that created what would become the mighty Toyota Motor Company.

The phone rang interrupting the solace. It was a strange and unexpected call. Megan, Doug Walker's administrative assistant initiated the call and the words seemed scripted. "All direct reports of Doug Walker are to be at the Northwestern Lodge and Conference Center in Maple Grove, MN at 9:00 AM on Monday, February 22nd." The directive ended with a clandestine statement this was a highly confidential meeting. If anyone asks, "You will be offsite for a business meeting on Monday."

As he hung up, John wondered, "Who else was getting this call?" He had just spent two days with Doug and a second meeting was not mentioned. Was this the answer to the question from the difficult discussion on Wednesday? Is this why John seemed to get a cool reception to the three-year plan? The day's demands began in earnest at 7:45; so for now, these questions were unanswerable. John speculated in another 72 hours or so, he would find out.

The rest of the morning offered an array of production meetings. John's highly talented employees ran the day-to-day operations of Northern Pine Technology. Periodically, he enjoyed attending the production meetings, mostly to keep his ear to the rail. There is no better way to get a pulse of the operation than attending the daily meetings. The good, the bad and the ugly all show-up.

The diskette department highlights involved the continued outstanding performance of the lines. Department maintenance recently audited all the lines in assembly and increased the speed of 2-3 parts per minute. A bit of a settling period always occurred after a round of speed ups. The lines were closely monitored for signs of fatigue after major changes.

Despite the best predictive maintenance work, a machine usually cracked a cam follower or broke a rod during line speed ups. The extra stress and cycles would strain the weakest point and create a failure. Learning those lessons resulted in the team becoming proactive in trying to prevent problems early based on data, signals and previous experience. John was proud of the skills and talents of the maintenance team.

Of the multiple assembly lines purchased more than 15 years ago, the engineering and maintenance team had been able to:

> Double their speed by incremental improvement efforts
> Maintain an effective utilization of 92%
> Error proof 20 stations on the line (cameras, sensors)

John knew Hitachi, the original equipment manufacturer (OEM), would love to come to Twin Ports and see the modifications. Many of these changes were trade secrets and were even more impressive because the OEM said they could not be done.

One of the keys to success is sustained competitive advantage. Just like in auto racing, the other team is not invited into the garage to see how the engine is fine-tuned. In fact, John would never allow it because of the significant number of novel modifications developed and implemented on the lines.

Other manufacturers simply added capacity by buying more lines. Twin Ports saw the benefit in making the existing lines run better; creating a sustained competitive advantage. While the competition invested $10 million dollars for a new line, Twin Ports invested just a fraction of that amount in speeding up the existing lines and driving machine utilization to near theoretically perfect levels. The work required to speed up the lines was technically challenging, but the investment was more than worth it. One of John's favorite quotes was from a Chinese Proverb, "Those who say it can't be done should get out of the way of those who are doing it."

Midmorning, John trekked over to the other building. The north building houses the data tape operations. The site employs a focused factory model. While John has overall site responsibility, two separate operations managers run each building. The operations are mostly self-sustaining, with their own operators, maintenance, engineering staff and materials control. Resources are combined when it makes sense financially and drives common decisions and policy across the site; areas such as sourcing, quality, and human resources are shared and utilized across all site operations.

Sarah Bergstrom is the operations manager and does a great job of managing costs, productivity and morale in her operations. She ranks on the list as a high potential candidate, and as John passes her with a wave, he mentally records a thought for him to mention Sarah's accomplishments in her new assignment to Doug. Plant a few seeds for the future; Sarah is going to go places.

Northern Pines Technology, Twin Ports

As John breezed past, a small maintenance team was huddled over new automation for inserting a door and spring assembly on a tape cartridge line. The manual operation was an ergonomic nightmare, both in terms of dexterity needed and repetitive motions. Maintenance designed and developed the automation in-house, to eliminate the risk of injury. The techs responsible for the build continued their involvement in the project by working to get the machine to run at its designed rate.

They were making good progress, so John just walked by, smiled and said, "Everything under control? Need any engineering help?" The crew knew this was mostly in jest; this work was largely being done without engineering. The talents existing in the maintenance department were honed and well respected. They knew the lines, knew the need, and knew what it took to make a robust process. John knew, not too many more shifts from now, the site would be reaping the benefits of cost savings, improved quality and the reduced risk of repetitive motion injuries to the workers.

The program was difficult to justify to corporate finance, aka the bean counters, but inherently John knew it was the right thing to do. He did not want anyone to get hurt at work whether an accident requiring stitches, a broken arm, or an overuse injury. Any injury meant bad news for the site; driving up costs and impacting the workforce negatively.

The last stop before heading home for a quick lunch was in the technology area. Northern Pines Technology invested a small fortune back in the late 1980s to put a complete molding design center and pilot fabrication area. John was now the beneficiary of this, and he vowed to fully exploit its advantages. Competitive tool shops existed in the area; however, it proved tough to achieve the turnaround time needed. John always felt better when designs stayed in the facility, shielding product or process secrets from entering the public domain.

The techs busied themselves on the EDM machine, making a new set of inserts for one of the diskette prototype molds. They were testing out a concept to remove the lifter and replace it with a molded feature.

The project was high risk, but also high reward, both financially and in terms of blocking replicating the new feature with patent protection.

The idea was truly genius, replacing a multi-step process with a simple molded in feature. In the current process, a small piece of crimped, polyethylene film is dispensed from a roll. A bead of adhesive is placed on the plastic shell and the lifter applied. The lifter provides two critical functions; it aids in cleaning as it pushes against the liner, a nonwoven cleaning fabric. Secondly, the lifter provides constant torque on the drive motor. Both functions are required for reliable data writing and retrieval.

The new design concept removes the lifter and replaces it with a molded- in feature much like a rib with a mating depression on the opposite side. As the media traveled over the rib and through the mated gap, it provided torque effectively creating an S-curve for the media to travel through. Early results had been promising, and provisional patent application filed. This concept was one of those million dollar ideas – literally.

Ultimately patent number EP0912977 was granted to the inventors for an idea which changed the game for Northern Pines Technology. The business now had something others could not use to gain competitive advantage. The patent provided American, European and broader global protection. If needed, Northern Pines would defend the invention rigorously.

Taking the time to understand the true requirements and explaining, modeling and developing solutions based on first principles proved even more valuable to the company. In cases where the engineers and designers gained true first principles understanding they attained a depth of knowledge in the performance critical to the continuous improvement effort. With first principles, the knowledge builds and the path making it much more difficult for others to follow. The engineers' nirvana is when they reach this breakthrough and then create the models or simulation predicting the performance and results.

John doubted anyone else would ever invest the time and energy to get to the level of understanding over this simple, yet critical componen

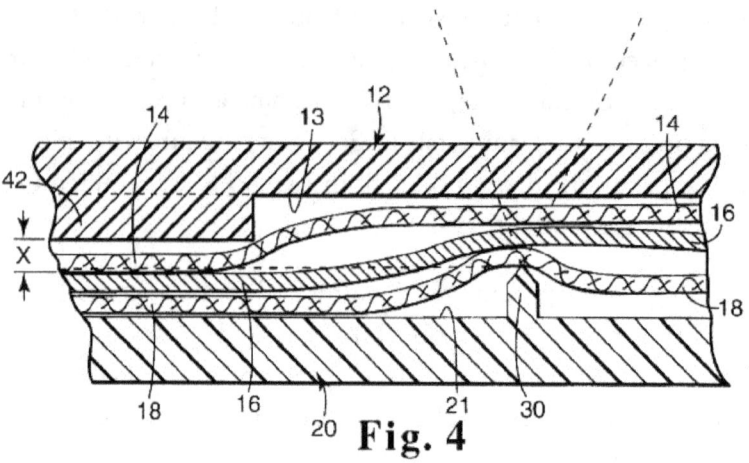

Patent EP0912977 *Diskette Lifter Tab Elimination*

One thing many people do not understand about high volume manufacturing is the idea of a little number multiplied by a very large number is still a lot of money.

In this case, each lifter was $0.0078 and the adhesive was $0.0003/ unit for a total cost of $0.008, less than a penny per diskette. However, multiply the number by the 500 million diskettes made each year and suddenly the idea jumps to a $4.0 million annual dollar payback. Those numbers get even the most jaded accountants and business people interested and excited. The math was simple. The shop could retrofit the molds and tooling for less than $250,000, so payback was weeks.

The site always had a small portfolio of 'stretch' programs. These were not committed, in terms of the official plan required to meet the financial commitments. The projects were high risk, and often need significant technology discovery for commercialization. The programs are managed as a contingency; or upside to the plan. The lifter program had been on the stretch program list for several years. Seeing the recent progress John was confident the engineering and design team would solve the technical challenges and bring it to completion.

John walked out into the mid-winter air. It was a standard 'one-song commute' to arrive at home. John tried to go home most days for lunch. It was a good break and the kids loved to see dad during the day. Kristin prepared piping hot soup and grilled cheese sandwiches.

Lunch talk was casual, the conversation briefly touching upcoming weekend plans. Other than the usual catch up activities, it promised to be a relatively uneventful couple of days. John mentioned he had to be in the Cities again on Monday with the caveat of it being a 'secret' meeting.

John could read the look on Kristin's face was one of concern. After slurping his soup, and feeding Caroline and chasing Mark upstairs, John stood at the front door. Kristin asked, "Is something big going on?" John did not really know how to respond. He was new at this too; it could be nothing. He said, "I am sure it will be fine; probably just some topic which cannot be discussed on a conference call."

Kristin was still adjusting to life as the wife of the site manager at Northern Pines. In a small town, this was a visible position. People knew how important the plant was to the local economy and lives of people. Some residents assumed Kristin must also be "in the know" on everything at the plant. John loved Kristin and wanted to shield her from these difficult discussions. He himself was still wading through all this. He knew they needed to be cautious about any comments about the plant, as people may make erroneous assumptions about what might seem to be a benign comment.

John drove back to the plant and returned with a relatively light afternoon schedule. Only two meetings scheduled for the balance of the afternoon. The first meeting involved sitting in on the employee club meeting. The site has a volunteer staffed committee who plans and hosts the annual Christmas party, various children's events and even does selected charity sponsorship. The funds to support the employee club activities come via vending machine sales. Working in a 24/7-hour operation, caffeine consumption is high. The profits from vending machines provide roughly a thousand dollars or so per month of operating funds for the club. The employees manage the fund with limited oversight from John and the human resources department.

Today's agenda included the primary topic of discussion was the upcoming Bunny Day. Around Easter, the site hosts an egg hunt for employee's children and grandchildren, which includes a visit from the Easter Bunny. One of the site employees lives on a hobby farm and usually brings in a herd of baby bunnies. The kids love to see and handle the tiny bunnies, and miraculously, so far, all the animal babies have survived.

John's mind wandered to the early morning topic. When brought back to reality, somehow, he had been nominated, seconded, and approved to be the guy who dresses up in the rabbit costume. John didn't argue because it was pointless; a known hazard of being a member of the management team. He enjoyed the job, but did remember from the last time he had been in the suit; it was hot and stuffy inside.

The second meeting of the afternoon was a conference call with members of Dakota Manufacturing Partnership. The Partnership exists to provide companies with services and access to public and private resources that enhance growth, improve productivity, and expand capacity. The organization offered training and consultants to help with projects, and established networks of professionals who assist businesses to be more competitive. Steve Swift acted as the

CEO. John served as a board member for the past two years. The partnership provided John an outlet in helping to meet a great need within the manufacturing community.

One of the recent focus areas encouraged students to consider careers in manufacturing. The businesses in the upper plains suffered from recent demographic trends: migration of young people from rural to urban areas, aging of the workforce, and less interest in manufacturing careers.

The teleconference was to expand on the idea of hosting a manufacturing boot camp to educate high school students about the skills and opportunities for individuals trained in wiring, machine fabrication, Programmable Logic Computer [PLC] programming, welding and other skilled trades.

After the call, Grant Richards showed up around 4:30, mostly just to chat. Grant and John worked for Northern Pines Technology about the same amount of time. Grant earned his business degree and started as temporary production employee. It didn't take long for the supervisors to figure out Grant had much more to offer. Grant was promoted to supply planner and over time developed his skills and advanced to Supply Chain Manager. Grant had two sons and was busy most winter weekends serving as coach for his younger sons' hockey team; his wife taught math at the local college. Their family was headed to Grand Forks early on Saturday for a three-state tournament.

Out came the peanuts, a bag reserved for these impromptu meetings, and the chairs were circled around the garbage can. Before John knew it, Jeff and Mary Ann joined, and the banter was light. It was a good way to decompress after a hectic week.

John felt blessed with such a dedicated and hardworking group of managers. These three were his peers until his recent promotion; even with the promotion, little had changed. The group worked together for years, genuinely liked each other and more importantly trusted each other. This was a tough business, what made it palatable was the respect, professionalism, and shared purpose and camaraderie. Moments of posturing and politicking rarely reared its ugly head. Most of the time, this team was busy figuring out how to get diskettes out the door or how to get more tape from the sister production facilities to worry too much about stepping on a friend's ego.

Grant scratched his newly crew-cut hair and led off with a hypothetical question, "If money was no object, what would you like to do?" Interesting line of question, John thought. After a brief pause, answers began to float around the room. Grant and Mary Ann both shared the dream or desire to 'be their own boss'. To make or own something uniquely of their own creation.

When it was Jeff's turn, he said, "I would like to be a rancher and sideline as a rodeo clown." A few chuckles ensued, but actually, it fit; Jeff grew up in the western part of the state and ranching and a love of wide open spaces was a part of his psyche.

As shells cracked, John thought, he shared many of the same dreams, to be free of structure, a boss and be independent. The conversation circled back and all agreed they were grateful to Northern Pines for the stability, opportunity and income. Northern Pines operations put money in people's pockets and funded: braces on kid's teeth, furniture for living rooms and kept the economy of Twin Ports chugging along.

Despite different trajectories, it was more than fate that John and this group of talented managers landed in the same office on a Friday afternoon. As the last of the peanut shells made its way to the garbage can, it was time to call it a week. The paging system remained quiet indicating things were running smoothly throughout the plant, and it was time to get out of Dodge.

John quickly vacuumed the evidence of the impromptu gathering from the floor, gathered his laptop, grabbed two files, stuffed them in his briefcase for Monday, and headed for the parking lot.

Chapter 4: An Unplanned Trip

The directness of Doug's comments, were just a little over four days old, but they still resonated in John's head, "Fix this mess or else!" John felt a little perplexed as he drove down to Maple Grove, because truthfully, the more he thought about Dougs' directive; the less sense it made. Why had Doug lashed out at him? It did not fit. He knew something was brewing, but little did he expect when he walked into the Northwestern Lodge and Conference Center his fate and the fate of literally hundreds of people teetered on a very slippery slope.

John entered the lobby and immediately found his peers. Three other plant managers made the trek to the Twin Cities: Ray Molter, Charlie Cordero and Tom Wikner, each representing their portion of the manufacturing might of Northern Pines Technology. Ray was a few years from retirement and was not shy about expressing his desire to slow down. He was still current with technology, well respected and engaged, but definitely thinking more about his future after Northern Pines. His senior member status was evident on the deep tanned creases on his face. They also defined the fact he is actively working on his golf handicap during his off hours. Charlie Cordero came to the information technology division from research and technology; John had only met him a few times. Charlie is about the same age as John and he earned master's degree in analytical chemistry from Purdue. Tom Wikner and John had a long history, starting with the company at the same time in the Optimized Operations department. They were never on the same project teams, but have kept in contact over the past few years. When schedules permit they'll have lunch or dinner, so John knows enough to catch up on family news and happenings at the Wikner home. The families share the joint experience of raising twins; although theirs came at the end of their family; rather than at the beginning. They have had a few good laughs over parenting; especially when the number of kids exceeds the number of parents. Both Tom and John have lost children at the mall.

John's plant was different than the other facilities, because Twin Ports did not coat tape, only converting finished goods such as diskettes and tape cartridges. Each has its own complexities and unique challenges. The other operations output supplied large quantities of coated rolls of tape to Twin Ports. Twin Ports used the tape supplied as an input and transformed it into millions of diskettes and tape cartridges by assembling, testing and packaging for sale.

Coating is the process of uniformly spreading slurry (in this case magnetic pigments suspended in solvents) across a moving roll. The roll consists of film, called the web. The process is done at high speed and travels from an unwind station, through coating heads, around rollers through a massive drying oven and back up on a take-up reel. The speeds can exceed 1000 ft. / min. The economics are simple: machine speed equals money. If everything is working right, coating is uniform at specification and dried adequately, the money is income. If quality is poor, lots of money is being wasted and product is scrapped.

An average person commonly utilizes many things made via a web coating process. Paper and cardboard boxes incorporate roll coating. Newspapers and magazines are printed on rolls, adhesive tapes, as well as data storage and video/audio tapes. Coating serves as a core technology platform utilized by Northern Pines Technology and employed across a wide and growing set of product applications.

The group cordially shook hands, but no one dared to launch the question on everyone's mind, "Why are we here on a Monday morning under a cloud of secrecy? What could possibly be of such critical importance it could not wait until the monthly staff meeting?" Small talk ended in the hallway and the atmosphere turned tense.

One source of tension was always promotion and upward mobility. These four men were always in competition to have the best plant, to get the best results and vying for the next promotion. It was a longstanding fact Northern Pines Technology promoted from within and the pyramid gets smaller at the top. The next "Doug" likely would be one of the three men, as Ray had excused himself from the 'next boss' race. Who and when, kept them on their toes and guessing.

Northern Pines Technology's current approach to career development appeared a bit Darwinian. It was survival of the fittest. Those employees, who didn't develop their skills, improve their business acumen, or gain new certifications, their careers were metaphorically eaten by the stronger.

The landmines were many. Employees, who crossed the wrong people, made some career- damaging blunder or did not deliver the expected and required results were released to "pursue other opportunities." This happened with regular frequency. The corporate announcements always sounded sterile. Between the lines, all knew the individual was canned and probably had less than 20 minutes to clean out their desk before the security guards escorted him or her and their few boxes out of the building.

Doug Walker's opened the closed door of the Ottertail room. He invited his managers into the meeting. John shot a quick glance at Doug and he looked conflicted. John scanned the room and he could see Dougs' boss, someone else with a Northern Pines Technology badge, whom he didn't recognize and a gentleman who looked to be of Indian descent. They were the only occupants in the room. Doug asked the new arrivals to find a seat.

He systematically circled around the room, introducing each of his reports and the plants each represented. Doug introduced his boss, Lucinda Marshall, Vice President of Operations; John had attended one meeting previously where she presided. The unknown individual with the Northern Pines Technology badge introduced herself as Melyssa McDonald, Assistant to Chief Legal Counsel for Northern Pines Technology. The visitor from afar was introduced as Anil Gupta, Vice President of Operations for Mendal Enterprises, an Indian manufacturing conglomerate with operations throughout the Far East. Their holdings included optical disk manufacturing, USB devices, diskettes as well as a broad reach into telecommunications including servers, routers, IP switching devices and other IT infrastructure.

Doug began, sounding nervous. His comments seemed scripted. "The information we are going to disclose to you is privileged and confidential. As you know, with this type of information you will be required to sign non-disclosure agreements, due to the sensitive nature of its content. The non-disclosure is a legally binding agreement, which placed all on a blackout list; no stock trading allowed as well as any breach of the confidentiality would have serious consequences, up to and including termination."

John smiled as a thought entered his head, if only for the irony. Unsure about his counterparts, John encountered two or three of these meetings before. The first was a joint venture when John was recruited to be part of the investigation or due diligence team. It also happened to be in India, coincidentally, and was codenamed Gold Fish. The second named Red Robin, a proposal he was not sure even his coworkers seated next to him knew. Red Robin's intent two years ago was to consolidate all manufacturing operations into two plants – mega sites. Twin Ports was destined to be one, because the site had capacity, capability and enough space to shoehorn in some additional lines. The operating theory was Twin Ports would do all converting. The media / coating plant consolidation was much more difficult. Three plants involved, all with different capabilities. The project assessed which site showed the most rapid path to qualification of the other types of media, how much time would it take, and cost.

With a dramatic drop in the stock price, perhaps accelerated by the financial crisis, Red Robin was ultimately shelved as the company endured two quarters of sales misses, and on-boarded a new CEO who promised to take the company "in a new direction".

His explanation of the new direction did not satisfy the shareholders or Wall Street; so, to use a sailing term, Northern Pines was in the doldrums, and his ideas did not create any wind. There was no desire to spend the type of money consolidation would cost with a stock price 40% off historic highs, and frankly, moving in the wrong direction. Those conditions and limited return potential quickly threw the proverbial anchor on the Red Robin initiative, never to be heard chirping again.

Doug pushed a crisp white sheet of paper in front of John and each of his peers. He glanced at it. "The information you are about to hear is confidential... no disclosure... punishment... hit squads . . . phone bugged..." Okay, maybe not that severe, but one gets the idea. John's mind flashed, what if he didn't sign it and got up and walked out? A one-man protest? What could they do?

John's rational mind concluded walking out was a career ending move. Usually throughout John's life, in a few milestone events, he focused like radar on what needed to be done. In contrast, sometimes his mind scurried like a squirrel trying to avoid cars on a busy highway. John felt more like a squirrel in the moment than a confident professional. He had one more of these quick mind-flashes, reached for the pen in his pocket and scribbled a signature on the non-disclosure form. Done. He was now committed.

John's co-workers signed the paper. Melyssa collected the signed documents, placed them in an official-looking manila envelope and sealed it. She quickly tucked the package into her briefcase. The leather bag appeared to be finely tooled leather; perhaps even rich Corinthian leather. John still carried the Land's End briefcase from college. Apparently, he hadn't reached the big leagues. His $50 canvas bag hardly compared to the fancy and expensive Berluti leather bag Melyssa was toting.

Doug began his story by recapping Gold Fish and even touched on Red Robin, which was interesting. By now, Doug appeared to have found his voice and cadence as he continued, "Two quarters of tough sales, and this one was not looking too much better, a financial crisis impacted not only Northern Pines, but our: business partners, financial institutions, government and large IT enterprises significantly." In summary, dramatic and significant changes were needed.

Doug paused, maybe for effect, or maybe as a way of transitioning to Ms. Marshall. John was interested in her presentation today. In the first meeting, she proved to be smart, perceptive and ruthless all at the same time. John witnessed her take apart a finance director piece by piece with her command of the details around product development cost. John had been sitting in on the meeting for Doug, and it was quite an introduction to Ms. Lucinda Marshall.

Ms. Marshall was a 30-something hotshot who had come from the IT infrastructure giant, Norwood. Most of the time, Northern Pines promoted management from within the company, but Lucinda represented a rare exception, an external executive hire. Early on, the rumor mill circulated Lucinda Marshall was brought in specifically to light a fire under a bunch of complacent long-term directors and drive some new behaviors. She was not only an outsider, but a change agent who was shaking up a normally conservative company.

Lucinda possessed a solid pedigree. Her resume impressed with a Bachelor's of Science in Electrical Engineering from Stanford, Masters of Business Administration from Michigan and 10 years of employment at Norwood. She quickly rose through the ranks and her accomplishments well publicized in the trade journals. It was clear her presence in this meeting involved shaking up the status quo.

Lucinda spoke the words of Marshall Tucker, Northern Plains CEO, but inserted the familiar "we," as she spoke.

"We are convinced the best course of action for Northern Pines Technology is to: first, launch into new adjacent markets; areas where our technology is complimentary. Second, move to a tiered brand management strategy – good, better and best. Lastly, outsource manufacturing; to reduce product costs. Off-shoring manufacturing is what all savvy companies are doing and Northern Pines needs to exploit this strategy to stay competitive."

This was the first-time John had heard a plan, let alone "the plan." John's stomach turned when he heard two words he despised more than any other in the English language: "outsource manufacturing." As far as John was concerned, the meeting could stop; he knew exactly where this was going to end.

It made sense now; no wonder the meeting received the "secret" label. Today marked the beginning of the end for the manufacturing plants at Northern Pines Technology.

He had not seen this coming.

John stole a glance at both Tom and Charlie. Charlie was stoic. John only caught Tom's face for a fraction of a second, but eyes were squinted and jaw was set. Tom was angry. Tom was like John; both had spent their entire career in manufacturing and had a passion to make things better. John too felt anger rising.

The idea of outsourcing manufacturing operations hit John in the gut. It was personal; he joined Northern Pines Technology for a very distinct reason. Northern Pines shared his values, praised for innovation, and was a run by smart, ethical people who valued a pipeline of new products and strong technology investments. The company respected its employees. In fact, Northern Pines prided itself as one of the oldest companies in the United States. Its legacy was originally service to enable other businesses to succeed. It had nurtured other industries, often supplying them with the basic products needed to be successful.

Back in the earliest days, Northern Pines began as a logging operation in the Arrowhead region of Minnesota. The company slowly diversified into lubricants, mining tools and transportation. The automobile, created Americas first true mega-industry, and early on, Northern Pines transportation division helped Ford, Dodge and Chevrolet grow and prosper.

Data storage, IT and automation equipment came later, but remain part of the fabric of Northern Pines Technology. The beauty of the company is its diversification; Northern Pines does a little bit of everything, across many business sectors. The result is a remarkably stabilizing effect of diversifying the risk and the impact of a financial downturn in any one area. Northern Pines generally made their investors happy because the company consistently met its numbers, remained stable, provided nice dividend income; and even though it had some lean early years, performed predictably.

John's second thought was for the employees; not just in Twin Ports, but all over America. John immediately felt the sinking weight of his responsibility for a plant of 450 people, the single largest employer in Twin Ports and probably one of the top five high-tech employers in the state of North Dakota.

Emotions rose unchecked until John fumed inside. This affects individuals, families, the community and the state; do they have any idea what they are doing? This is going to screw up families, hopes, dreams and promises, whether spoken or implied to hundreds of people.

Doug took over, "The plan is a multi-staged initiative and only a small part is to be disclosed now. The primary phase is the announcement of the joint agreement between Northern Pines

Technology and Mendal Enterprises." The public relations announcement would tell the world both companies would be jointly developing and manufacturing solutions for the IT industry. Northern Pines will have technical exchanges, share intellectual property and leverage the global manufacturing capability of Mendal Enterprises.

Doug proceeded with more information, "The second phase will not be announced for three quarters, but aligns manufacturing operations to take advantage of synergy created by the joint agreement."

Doug concluded the outline with, "Phase three is the closure of US manufacturing operations and involved another step in the relationship - cobranding – taking advantage of the Mendal brand in China, India and Russia – all large and emerging markets. The Northern Pines Technology brand would be used in the rest of the world."

The timeline Doug mapped out seemed especially painful. John watched what happened in other businesses and industries. Manufacturing companies ramp down in many ways. The most extreme way involves closing the plant and workers finding out about it only as they showed up for work on Monday morning with a sign attached to the door. Closed.

Everyone has heard a story or two about the draconian shock method. Northern Pines Technology chose the exact opposite approach. This closure would not be publicly announced for nine to twelve months, but certainly speculation would start immediately. Both methods were extremely painful; one for the immediacy and one for the deception.

It wasn't clear if this was a meeting where you could ask questions, but the formality bypassed Tom's thinking. The interruption seemed to catch everyone off-guard. Tom's question was pointed and simple, "Isn't this deception on the broadest of scales?"

Silence filled every corner, until Melyssa, who up until now had been quiet answered, "The Board of Directors has approved and authorized this plan; it has been reviewed and approved by legal and it is our responsibility to carry out their wishes." Not exactly an answer, but Lucinda nor Doug stepped in to offer additional insights.

Spot on Tom, John thought, sharing the same opinion of this underhanded approach. Where was this great company's moral compass? The early founders would have never envisioned these actions. Their worries involved how to get the trees skidded over frozen land and transport them to the river when the river was high enough for the lumber to get down to the mills and shipped out. Never in a million years would those early pioneers of industry have thought of taking good jobs and shifting them for the sake of low cost labor.

In the coarsest of terms, once Northern Pines employees helped the new overseas partners reach a critical mass of transition; the more costly branch severed; factories would close and people left without employment. John saw right through the scheme; this wasn't about technology exchange nearly as much as it was about manufacturing competitiveness. This was offshoring of jobs in search of low cost labor. This game contained stacked deck, loaded dice and a crooked dealer.

Doug recapped – so the attendees could check notes. In one way, it was ironic as an unforgettable piece of news was unloaded; it was not likely anyone would forget it soon.

It continued as a somber review – and rehashing it only made it worse. Doug began his recap at the top and painfully worked his way through each point on the outline:

- ✓ Three strategic objectives reviewed
- ✓ Corporate announcement on Thursday the 25th of February–after markets closed – check
- ✓ Mr. Anil Gupta – initial plant visits next week, team of 3 engineers – study trip to learn about operations

Doug's words really didn't matter – John was only hearing the Charlie Brown teacher version, "whaa whaa wahh wahh." Doug continued, "Northern Pines Technology is committed to its employees and knows fully well our company has the best employees in the world. The company will offer transitional services as they move into the next phase of their lives and career."

Mr. Gupta walked to the podium and outlined his plans. He began, "I will be visiting each of your plants and spending two or three days with a small team of engineers and my production manager learning the operations. Our objectives are to understand: material flow, key process steps, critical equipment needed and begin the planning process to replicate the operations." Mr. Gupta turned to Doug to confirm, "The visits start next week, correct?" Doug nodded affirming the timing. As karma dictated, Twin Ports plant was first.

The meeting agenda allocated time for questions, but the rawness of the information and the shock of those in attendance did not allow adequate time to formulate anything of value. Other than the earlier interruption by Tom and the question not answered, all the site managers sat in stunned silence.

Ray Mullins, site manager for the Arizona facility, finally mustered a question about capital expenses. Coaters are massive, complex and not something one moves every day. What is the strategy or plan to move a coater?" Doug mapped out the thinking, "We will analyze and see which coater is the most feasible for movement; the site will then coat ahead six months of material and only then would the coater be systematically taken apart – loaded into crates and shipping containers and reassembled in its new home."

Doug sounded confident, but Ray was not convinced. John thought back to his experience and Northern Pines had moved a lot of equipment, but he could not recall anything as massive or complex as one of the coaters.

Ray looked shaken as Doug explained. In Ray's mind, the operating assumption was coaters were a little like Mount Rushmore; they are monuments and once built, they did not move. A coater reaches two or three stories high, considering the roll handling and drying ovens. It can stretch longer than a football field.

Each of the three site managers of the coating plants stared blankly – John knew a harsh reality had just hit all of them at the same time. This new reality is simply nothing is off limits; even large equipment previously thought of as fixed monuments now were candidates to be moved to a low labor cost area of the world.

Twin Ports did not coat the tape. This fact doesn't diminish the role of Twin Ports. Converting was still huge. The primary difference was the equipment was much more easily moved. The technology of winding, testing, packaging and customization was probably as complex; converting was done on smaller, more mobile equipment.

John had always known that unlike the massive coaters, the equipment at Twin Ports was relatively mobile. His equipment was much smaller and in fact, much of what was running at his facility had been moved over the past fifteen years. Power, air, water, vacuum and a good project plan will relocate most of Twin Ports equipment to a new location in less than two weeks. John's mission has been to try to stay a step ahead of the competition with cost, quality and service and thus avoiding any discussion of moving Twin Ports equipment. To date, the site had been effective in meeting this objective.

As the meeting wrapped up, Doug asked, "Anyone want to stay for lunch?" John had no appetite. John didn't think the other three would stay either. If they felt anything like John, he simply wanted to be alone. He assumed the others would head back to the airport and wait for the next flight home. Since John drove a car, he politely excused himself.

He opened the car door and threw his Lands' End briefcase in the back seat. As he got behind the wheel, he glanced at his watch – it was only 11:45 AM. At this moment, he wanted to get away, the direction he drove didn't matter. He wanted as much distance as possible between him and the hotel. The first turn to enter the interstate was ahead and John turned left to the on-ramp. Destination was unknown.

John rubbed his eyes with his left hand as he steered with his right, hoping the rubbing would clear his thoughts as well as his eyes. He needed time to think, time to clear his head. John felt blindsided. More concerned with the plants day-to-day challenges, John didn't anticipate a problem of this magnitude coming.

John mulled in his mind, this can't be happening.

John said to an empty car, "I've got create a plan to not let Mendal take away jobs from Twin Ports."

The gas tank was half-full and thirty minutes went by. Without thought, driving had taken him east; he merged onto I-35 and was now heading due north. Although not planned, he would be taking the long way home today.

Once he realized he was on the way to Duluth instead of Twin Ports, he knew his destination. He was heading to Duluth, then along the North Shore and to his retreat, the cabin; one of the best places for him to think. It was a three-hour drive from the Twin Cities; and if John spent a few hours there, he could still be home by 10. Driving back to the plant in Twin Ports to arrive at 4:30 in the afternoon, just in time to see his coworkers walk out the door made John shudder.

He stopped the car at a rest area and pecked out two texts. The first one to Kristin stated, "Be home by 10." The second to Diane, – "Busy the rest of the day." Once the texts delivered, John turned off the phone.

He needed solitude and he was not available.

Chapter 5: Long Way Home

The car headed north, gray clouds replaced bright February sun, a fitting backdrop to John's day. The farmlands of central Minnesota gradually gave way to the lakes and trees, creating the boreal forests known as the arrowhead region. Years ago, trappers made their living from the bounty of these woods. Early Scandinavian settlers drew on their knowledge and thriftiness, crafting a hardscrabble life among the pines. Some engaged in fishing, trapping, logging and later mining along with other pursuits to survive. In the last 50 years, tourism replaced much of the industry drawing visitors from around the world to the natural beauty and calm enveloping the region.

Northern Pines began here, first as a paper and pulp manufacturer, hence, the name Northern Pines. During the 1920s and through the depression, Northern Pines diversified and survived by being on the front end of the production value chain. Their stock and trade was raw materials, timber and chemicals used by other manufacturers. After the war, demand for all types of goods rose to an all-time high. Northern Pines found its true niche in being a material supplier to a variety of industries, including chemical processing and coatings. They also developed their own unique technologies. It was through value created in those endeavors and strategic acquisitions, which created the Data Storage and Information Management [DSIM] products group; of which John was now fully immersed in a very competitive, cut-throat global business.

John and Northern Pines shared a deep respect for this unique land. In fact, it was because of his affinity John began looking for a piece of land to call his own. The cabin is a relatively new endeavor for the Stanton's and it happened somewhat by accident. Growing up, his family traveled to the area and explored and canoed in the Boundary Waters. John returned with his church youth group annually during high school. It was then he fell in love with the forest and vowed someday to return.

The Boundary Waters is a unique area, one of the largest untouched regions in the US. It is part of the Superior National Forest, managed by the US Forest service and contains over 400,000 acres of pristine wilderness. Two congressional acts in 1964 and 1978 effectively preserved this area as a wilderness region; thus significantly limiting visitor counts and use. One can hike and canoe, but no motors allowed, and of course, leave no trace. It is available for all and owned by no one.

The opportunity to buy land and a cabin in the north woods came somewhat by happenstance. The family had not been looking for a cabin. In fact, John had plenty of work keeping one old house in functioning order. Owning a second old home, remotely located was not first on the priority list.

John was surfing the Internet and saw information on a land sale in northeast Minnesota. The page opened to an official notice of the Isabella Ranger Station staff homes to be sold at auction. There were seven dwellings, several outbuildings and a visitor's center being offered. The auction structured the sale by splitting the land and buildings into nine parcels. Two of the properties piqued John's interest, the guard cabins and the assistant ranger house. All three dwellings were built in the 1930s under the guidance of the WPA program and by men in the Civilian Conservation Corps, also known as the CCC.

Part of the appeal to John was historical. These properties were a unique part of history. The CCC, established by Roosevelt in the 1930s during the height of the depression, provided men work and prevented an even worse outcome than the depression created. The organization contributed much in the areas of conservation, enhancing state and national parks and forest areas and other good works. While many of the structures built during that time no longer exists, a few state and national parks bear the distinct marks of a job well done by the members of the CCC.

Local artisans, many first-generation immigrants from Norway, Sweden, Finland and Denmark, built these dwellings. They brought with them skills in the areas of building, wood crafting and a work ethic beyond compare. These homes represented a piece of the nation's past and are historically significant.

Despite all the work, expense, and effort, the cabin provided solitude and peace, especially now when John was facing his biggest crisis. Time passed quickly, it was 2:45 PM as he arrived at the cabin. He noticed someone must have been up recently because the few roads leading up to the cabin were nicely plowed. John drove right up to the garage and parked the car. The minute he stepped out, his nostrils inhaled the familiar pine scent. One of the best parts of any trip; the mixed aroma of cold air, pine and a faint hint of burning wood; likely from a distant wood burning furnace.

It was cold at 1,923 feet above sea level. The trip took John 1,200 feet above Lake Superior. In fact, this ridge measures as one of the higher elevations in Minnesota. Only Eagle Mountain, about 50 miles east-northeast, is higher, with a geological altitude at 2,301 feet. John guessed the temperature was maybe mid-teens, and two or so hours of sunlight remained. He opened the cabin and looked at the thermometer at 50 degrees. This was a quick trip, so John didn't even turn up the thermostat. He went down in the basement and checked the water and furnace. Everything looked in order. John changed into warm clothes and grabbed the snowshoes from the garage. He needed – a mind clearing cross-country trek through the woods.

As he strapped on the snowshoes, he decided to head east, to the familiar path to the forest. The cabins reside adjacent to the Tomahawk trail, a popular cross- country, snowshoe and snowmobile path. John hooked up with the rough trail and trekked vigorously through the silent winter wonderland.

Cabin, at the Arrowhead in northern MN

He scared up a snowshoe hare a few paces ahead. His mind thought of the tough people who homesteaded here – the miners, loggers and even further back – those who made their living trapping; in days past, the snowshoe hare would have likely been in a stew for supper.

Great stories exist about local trappers who would run a circuit sixty or more miles, managing their trap lines. These tough individuals would often overnight in either a crude tent or lean-to with temperatures easily plunging to -20 below zero. The trappers caught mink, beaver and hares as well as fox and wolf. They could make a survivalist living on trapping in the winter and living off the bounty of the land during the other seasons. Their return was selling the hides to outfits such as Hudson's Bay Company or Northwest Fur Company.

John's could not shake the bombshell from the morning. It is an understatement to say this day turned out very differently than expected. He thought about the consequences of the conversations in the meeting. He contemplated the next 18-24 months; he would preside over the slow death of the plant, a way of life and the dissolving dreams of great workers and people.

During the morning discourse and subsequent drive, John vowed he could not allow the plant to die; the concept was unthinkable. He brainstormed ways to avoid it, civil disobedience or shareholder activism. All seemed crazy and nothing was likely to move the needle far enough or even be practical to make an impact, especially at his level.

Slowly, the flicker of an idea began to emerge. John's first intuition was trying to beat Mendal at their own game. This required proving to his executive team that moving his plant would not save them money; in fact, just the opposite, it would cost them money. The only way to disrupt the chain of events was to demonstrate the plan and logic was flawed. Not only flawed from a risk perspective, but the basic assumptions were flawed. The best hope for saving Twin Ports was to raise the performance of the plant to a level no competitor could replicate.

John knew exactly what that meant – in the lifeblood of a factory – there are relatively few metrics which ultimately matter. Safety, service and cost performance generally define the "make or break" metrics. In John's factory; there was no bigger focal point than diskettes and within diskettes the biggest target was unit cost; the calculated monthly cost of producing the diskette. John's eureka moment came down to two words, seven cents.

Theoretically, seven cents equaled the lowest cost ever projected for a single packed out diskette. It was the "all in" number. This morning, Doug himself presented a target cost of 8.25 cents per diskette – when the moves were complete and the dust had settled; Mendal had committed to 8.25 cents. John's 7 cent target bested their target performance by over a full penny. Quickly doing the math, 1.25 cents over 500 million per year – a number was north of six million dollars. John knew the team had to pull out all the stops – the site had to deliver a sub-seven cent diskette and do it in a way which could not be replicated in India, China or anywhere else in the world.

As John passed the familiar fork in the trail, the one leading the loop back around versus the trail which heads down to the river, John was reminded of the Robert Frost poem studied and analyzed in a humanities class 20 years ago.

The theme of the poem reminded John of a reasonable metaphor for his predicament. The words solidified his thinking; he needed to blaze his own trail, one less traveled. It would take long hours, careful thought, deliberate actions and a healthy dose of leadership to achieve his goal. The promise was at the end, making a difference. When it is all done, John knew what he wanted most, simply to make a difference.

The Road Not Taken

Two roads diverged in a yellow wood,
And sorry I could not travel both
And be one traveler, long I stood
And looked down one as far as I could
To where it bent in the undergrowth;

Then took the other, as just as fair,
And having perhaps the better claim
Because it was grassy and wanted wear,
Though as for that the passing there
Had worn them really about the same,

And both that morning equally lay
In leaves no step had trodden black.
Oh, I marked the first for another day!

Yet knowing how way leads on to way
I doubted if I should ever come back.

I shall be telling this with a sigh
Somewhere ages and ages hence:
Two roads diverged in a wood, and I,
I took the one less traveled by,
And that has made all the difference.

Robert Frost

John realized his moment of truth. The plant reached its proverbial fork in the road. John set his course and determined not to go down without a fight.

Right there in the middle of a stand of Norway pines, rock solid for 100 years, John experienced his one glimmer of hope; maybe a multi-faceted approach to rapidly improve operations. This wouldn't be a message the site was bad, but a positive message the site had to demonstrate immediate and dramatic improvement; the future of the plant likely depended upon results. The ability to focus in a few key areas, maybe three or four seemed to make sense and based on the successes of the last 15 years – yes, it seemed to be a logical step.

The approach was not perfect but hopefully, adequate, at least, as a start. John knew time was of the essence. Tomorrow morning when he returned the site, he had to start on this new mission and journey. John knew a familiar approach would be a way to focus the teams efforts, create a shared sense of ownership, and hopefully have a few successes to celebrate in the process. If everything worked right, it just might be enough to save the plant from inevitable doom.

To achieve the goals, and more importantly the financial results, Twin Ports had to run QICR programs like never before. QICR pepped up on steroids, so to speak. The site needed strong accountability. The team needed to make decisions lightning fast, and forge every decision with ownership. Leadership and speed – John and his team needed to be decisive and act with conviction.

He felt slightly better as he returned from the snowshoe circuit. He had done a few miles, worked up a sweat and set the framework which might put the site on a course which might disrupt the plans of the executive team at Northern Pines Technology and Mendal Industries.

His mind continued to work over these thoughts and strategies as John drove west across northern MN. John realized since passing up Doug's offer for lunch, he had not eaten anything all day. In fact, he did not even remember if he ate breakfast. John stopped in Brainerd for a quick drive through McDonalds. He splurged on a Big Mac combo meal – as John rationalized it was the only meal of the day and he had just burned off at least a few calories on the trail; and the Diet Coke balanced off some of the calories from the burger and fries.

Halfway home, John spotted a sign along the road for training for rural Minnesota workers at Superior Technical College. Early in his career; John had done a stint as a project manager and worked with Superior Tech to deliver Just-In-Time training to the workforce at a Northern Pines supplier. Seeing the sign rattled a loose thought needing follow-up. John mentally noted he had to radically change the thinking process with relationship to workforce training.

At the top of the list, John needed a more flexible and diverse workforce, skilled people, able to run various types of equipment. The site needed to train for knowledge. John recalled the Training Within Industry book on his shelf. Perhaps, the book held the answer he was looking for. The book outlined strategies used in the 1940s when skilled industries needed to replace those who had gone off to war. If those strategies worked then, maybe he could make them work now.

John arrived home at 10:26 PM and was still wound up from the day, thanks to both the drive and the Coke. John shared the day with Kristin. She was attentive and highly engaged, and of course, surprised John had been tramping around the Superior National Forest.

She said, "What are you going to do?" John shared the outline of his plan and explained the basics. He had to rally the team to deliver results way beyond what was expected, disrupt the plans and hopefully create an opening wide enough to save the plant. Kristin said, "How much are you going to share with your staff?" John had been thinking about that exact question, but didn't yet have an answer. After a long discussion, she wrapped up with, "John, this is brilliant and I have every confidence you are the man for this job." That was all the encouragement John needed to keep going.

John and Kristin shared everything related to the day's events, despite a signed piece of paper in Melyssa's briefcase. There were no secrets; their commitment to honesty with each other began long before work at Northern Pines Technology. Their marriage commitment would long outlast John's tenure at Northern Pines Technology. If this plan was going to work, he needed all support and allies he could muster.

John didn't usually share the day to day routine work stuff with Kristin, simply because he really did not want to rehash work at home after living it all day. The respite of coming home was an important separation and Team Stanton agreed with this. On the flipside, on big issues, having Kristin's sympathetic ear provided John the only sane sounding board in navigating these troubled waters.

John knew he needed Kristin's steady support and understanding. This was not what he signed up for just a few months ago, when he was named plant manager. John felt a bit overwhelmed by the enormity of the day, the meeting, the drive, the brainstorming, and the plan he concocted.

He wished the decision makers down at headquarters could walk in his shoes for just a few hours. In this community, the Northern Pines plant is considered part of the structure; foundational to the town. Years ago, Twin Ports lobbied aggressively for Northern Pines Technology to build a plant. Two and sometimes three generations of families worked at this site. John can't go to church, the grocery store, Cub Scouts, or the park without seeing co-workers.

The town didn't don't know it yet, but its fate now rests in the ability to pull off a miracle. Somehow, John needs to deliver results to convince some nameless, faceless autocrats it is going to cost too much to relocate US-based operations.

As John tossed and turned in bed, he thought of his team and the dilemma they posed within Northern Pines outsourcing plan. Everything about the plan was wrong. Wrong for employees, wrong for Twin Ports and wrong for Northern Pines. This site was capable of meeting seven cents and more. It just needed a little time; it had a record of accomplishment and the drive to succeed. John hoped for a chance to let the plant show what it could do.

If the decision makers completed a comprehensive study including true payback, John was confident the result would come out not nearly as favorably as the current ginned up analysis.

In his role as a director at the Dakota Manufacturing Partnership – the Partnership had just contributed to a national study on the true costs of outsourcing. In general, companies ended up spending between 10 and 20% more by the time all factors were considered. This does not match published results by the major business press because the short-term allure is very strong. CFOs and CEOs see the technical cost and labor cost at 15-20% of the cost of a US worker and they think immediately, it does not matter if I must hire twice as many, I can capture a significant benefit on these costs, just by outsourcing. Simplistic thinking and a few strokes of the pen are all that is required to capture a labor and overhead benefit.

It didn't surprise John the executive team's inability to grasp this relatively simple flaw. The devil is in the details. The thoughts continued to churn in John's head, offering him slow and shallow sleep.

Tomorrow is a new day.

Chapter 6: Moral Dilemma

As morning light lifted in the east, John was back at his desk. The office was quiet and he treasured a few minutes alone. He faced a significant dilemma upon signing the confidentiality agreement. These were not just words on paper, but rather a conflict of loyalties. He had to decide where to place his loyalty; was it to his corporation and employer or to the people who he was directly responsible? This conflict created a greater battle than he expected. Usually, he did not have much trouble discerning what to do. His compass used: data, facts and logic, driven by moral guidance to do the right thing.

John's mind drifted back to the Northwestern Lodge and Conference Center and the hesitation experienced just a moment before scribbling the signature on the official confidentiality document. His pause reflected the decision he had to make now. Did a signature mean anything or not?

In his mind, the fundamental question came down to where his loyalties reside. Was he obligated to maintain the complete and absolute confidence a sheet of white paper demanded, signed on the spur of the moment, without warning? If so, the plant would slowly die.

The other option was to violate the agreement and begin a process to disrupt the plans of Northern Pines Technology and Mendal Industries with the goal of ultimately saving the plant.

John could see both sides with clarity; however, he had to decide quickly, what was he going to do? Strangely, John was not overly concerned about himself and family. John was at peace with his family's future. His family could weather whatever consequences.

In vexing situations such as this, John usually processed his position by listing out the pros and cons. In absence of any better ideas, he took out a pencil and began to create the list:

Null Hypothesis: Maintain the loyalty to Northern Pines Technology and not thwart the Mendal plan.

Pros:

- ✓ Most linear decision (do what you say and say what you do).
- ✓ Best for career with Northern Pines Technology
- ✓ Would not violate the chain of command; my respect for authority
- ✓ Team player; maybe there is a role after the plant closes?
- ✓ This was inevitable; if not now, it would be later. Why spend energy fighting the inevitable conclusion?

Cons:

- ✓ Many families, people and businesses in Twin Ports negatively affected by my lack of action.
- ✓ Loss of jobs for the city, state and lack of opportunity will exist in the future and impact my co-workers and friends.
- ✓ Traitor – what will co-workers say/do act; knowing no steps were taken to act?
- ✓ Is this deal best for the shareholders? Were there risks to success that could cost more money?
- ✓ Living with the consequences of action? Living with the consequences of not doing anything?

Thinking ahead, John already knew he was going to have to be cagey to his team about the plan announced at the Northwest Inn and Conference Center; Gupta & Associates are visiting next week. He will have to explain why these people are at the facility, what they are doing and what information the site is obligated to provide. He realized the first of many dilemmas starts now.

Considering all this, John could sense the compass was starting to move off center; and his direction was emerging.

John knew he did not have long to figure this out; public information in the form of corporate announcements were coming soon. He recalled the announcements were to be released after markets closed on Thursday night. He went back to check his notes for certainty. Today was Tuesday. John scanned his phone quickly to see his daily meeting calendar. Today was booked – all morning QICR meeting for tape products in the north building and afternoon – the same in the front plant. It was going to be a busy week.

In addition to all the day-to-day activities managing a factory requires; John needed time to come up with a rational story. His staff was not naïve. He could put himself in their place: In the last week, John had been to corporate headquarters to present the three-year plan, had been to an unplanned offsite, corporate announcements coming and a visit / study trip by four people from an international manufacturer; with some complimentary technology. They would quickly see this was not business as usual and something significant was brewing.

John knew, perhaps one single event would likely not arouse much curiosity, but three factors combined began to raise logical questions. John realized he had a problem with providing a good explanation for these events. Someone inevitably would ask, "Why all of a sudden so much cloak and dagger?" These thoughts were going to have to ruminate a little longer, as the tyranny of the urgent was well, urgently waiting. There was just enough time to walk between buildings to attend the QICR meeting. John grabbed laptop, coat, safety glasses and headed for the door.

The data from the morning site review was mixed; kind of like a partly cloudy weather forecast. Yields were good, however preliminary indications from suppliers hinted they were planning to pass off increases to the site, leaving Northern Pines to absorb higher prices for metal and plastic. One of John's least favorite roles was the raw material purchasing side. John did not think of himself as a good negotiator and didn't really enjoy the 'cat and mouse' game of contract negotiations. He likened it to natural selection at its best; when the weak don't survive. Who is going to blink first? Generally, the party who blinked first ended up absorbing the cost increase. The site always played the card of being in a tremendously competitive environment and needed the advantage to stay ahead. The vendor argued the plant was already getting preferred pricing and needed to absorb the increase just to stay profitable. In the end, the site probably split increases 50/50. Some games won by the cat; some by the mouse; and much energy was spent just to achieve a divided outcome.

The site was more advanced than many manufacturing locations. Over the years, it developed advanced analytical capability. It included a complete materials characterization lab. A Ph.D. chemist ran it and employed two technicians for support, who could do many of the advanced analytical tests like FTIR, IR and X-ray scans. Even though last year's capital budget was rough, the site was successful in securing a scanning electron microscope to further enhance capability. Engineers had analytical tools at their disposal of which most manufacturing sites can only dream.

This capability became a site core competency and was critical for operations. It allowed the site to generate unbiased data about the quality of raw materials. With data, the lab drove a new level of credibility with suppliers. Jason Strong, Ph.D., served as the analytical chemist since his hiring three years ago.

Jason proved a great addition. Most importantly, Jason gave Twin Ports the ability to diagnose a problem, analyze the source, and get to root cause. If it was due to a supplier or a recent change, Jason put together a compelling case the material was 'their' problem and not fixable at the site. Not every problem was supplier related. Twin Ports managed to induce plenty of its own issues; but when the data could show the root cause, it was hard information for suppliers to refute.

John and Jason shared another common bond. Jason served as the co-Den Leader for Cub Scouts. Despite his long hours in the lab, Jason was a devoted dad. John shared the leadership duties with Jason, so they had a unique relationship built on mutual respect and trust both in the workplace and outside.

John glanced back down at the scribbled notes –

		Changes	
Product	**Cost**	**% – QTD**	**% YTD**
5476	$43.21	down 2.3%	down 5.6%
Keystone	$12.42	flat	down 3.1%
Glacier	$77.32	down 6.1%	new

He was pleased by the improvements in Glacier. The product launch was six short months ago and the product was now seeing some of the best volumes yet, and growing ahead of plan. Costs were starting to move as well once the production system stabilized. Eventually, the Glacier cartridge was to obsolete Keystone, which the site had been making for over ten years. In the data cartridge business, companies invest in a platform and generally need a compelling reason (improved security, capacity, speed) to make a change as a platform change involves significant hardware expense and is time-consuming.

Keystone had a good run, but early sales results showed a healthy initial migration from Keystone to Glacier, which was good for both margin and morale. The Glacier cartridge increased capacity more than 25 times with only a moderate rise in manufacturing cost; so for those spending IT infrastructure dollars, with extra leverage, it was a good time to be investing in new technology. This new product dropped the cost per GB [$/GB] by a factor of over ten. Business used this ratio as a primary justification in their IT spending. Cartridge cost was one element; drive and system cost was another.

The local Chinese restaurant delivered lunch as the team continued work into the afternoon putting together interim plans for extra capacity for Glacier. "I am really pleased with the progress this team has made," John said as the meeting ended. Sarah led the entire department now after her promotion from the engineering ranks only a year ago. She transitioned seamlessly from a technical contributor to the department head. John was proud of the talent and the opportunities available at Twin Ports. Sarah worked at Twin Ports for five years, coming straight from the University of North Dakota. She possessed drive, good people skills and already led with unlimited potential.

Sarah brought out the best in her engineers; and John knew if anyone could focus them on doing the right things, it was Sarah. She figured out, contrary to popular belief, engineers are passionate people. They are just passionate about things most take for granted.

John was proud of her. Truth be told, she might be the lead candidate to be his successor in due time. He hoped that date was still years away; but in reality, this is corporate America. Easy come and easy go; loyalty has nothing to show. John knew if he didn't deliver the goods for a quarter or two, he would be replaced and it would be done without delay.

What struck John most as he reflected on the morning was the way the team shared their results during the meeting. He sensed an energy for customers, products, and pride of accomplishments and results. Although it had been nearly 15 years since he arrived at the plant, the spark, drive and dedication never waned. If anything, it reinforced itself with each new crop of recruits joining the Northern Pines team.

As John dropped off his laptop and coat in his office, his realized his head ached from wrestling with the moral dilemma. Seeing the energy, talent and knowledge existed on data cartridge products made his decision even more difficult.

John stopped by the vending machine, popped two aspirin and washed them down with a Diet Coke. He walked into Training Room A just as the diskette QICR meeting was starting.

Chapter 7: Good News and Bad News

As much as the morning meeting encouraged John, the afternoon meeting discouraged. The diskette unit cost results were unimpressive, which in the competitive diskette market meant the business lost valuable time and ground. The product managers knew their operations were the lowest cost producers in the world. Twin Ports benchmarked the competition aggressively. However, all knew this favorable position was tenuous as a change in pricing, a new innovative approach or another low-cost labor facility coming on line could disrupt the delicate balance.

Northern Pines Technology employed a large sales force around the world; and during his time with the company, John developed relationships with a number of the sales staff, especially in emerging markets. This was a benefit when it came time to benchmark the competition. These sales associates bought product in their respective regions, usually Japan, Latin America, Europe, South Asia and India. They would send the product to the plant and technicians and analysts completed an extensive reverse engineering analysis. Product features, materials, methods were just some of the items investigated.

In an academic kind of way, the managers and engineers looked forward to a preview of the results; it was about as close to detective work as the site was able to do. Over time, rich knowledge was developed about the product, capability, materials and methods used to manufacture. One simple example, the tooling ID or injection molding markings for a variety of the manufacturers were tracked. Through database analysis and spreadsheets, a sophisticated matrix was created about who was manufacturing; who was branding for others and who was not the business anymore.

The competitive analysis and reverse engineering, coupled with costing and accounting by component, allowed the site to develop a methodology to assess the value of its QICR programs. From the data and detailed analysis, the site built robust and remarkable accurate 'should cost' models for all major competitors.

It was always interesting to see who was experimenting with new approaches and technology. Another component included relative labor rates around the world. Based on best estimates, the site was still between $0.005 and $0.006 better than Shen-Wa in Taiwan, the closest cost competitor at the time.

John quickly learned a new kind of math or, at least, an appreciation for significant digits. Every month, the site manufactured a huge number of diskettes, somewhere between 50 and 60 million. The site also spent a significant amount of money, usually somewhere between four and five million dollars in materials, wages, overhead and other expenses. A big number divided by another big number equals going pretty far into the decimals and significant digits to understand cost performance. Movements of a tenth of a cent in unit cost made huge differences in financial analysis between suppliers. The scale of reference measured to the hundredth of a cent to manage effective cost reduction programs. The site celebrated movements of literally a few hundredths of a penny in unit cost on diskettes.

Strangely, two accounting systems evolved at the plant site. The 'official' enterprise/ERP system, implemented about six years ago, unfortunately, took things which were once easy to do and made them hard. John quickly learned to despise it. It was traditional accounting based on standard costs. Not that John didn't get it. On the contrary, he understood it just fine. It was just so much non-value, added time determining the standard costs, deciding if they were right, adjusting them. Someone always had a plug or variance to explain everything, turning it into meaning nothing. It was a nightmare to accurately cost the production operation.

The site utilized a 'home grown' system one of the engineers developed back in the late 90s which actually worked better. It gave better resolution, and results were available in nearly real time. Sure, it was spreadsheet based and needed maintenance; but in a competitive business, Twin Ports needed a simple temperature gauge for performance, not an elaborate standard cost analysis based on variances to standards not easily defined, whose information was at best two weeks aged.

The enterprise system always lagged, usually available the 8th or 9th working day of the month, which practically meant the month was almost half over before any tangible knowledge became available. In this business, as well as other highly cost sensitive ones, half a month is an eternity and not an acceptable way to manage a product line.

The homegrown system incorporated local real-time spending data and made projections based on the current yield data, historically relevant department spending, and other factors added over time. During the early part of the month, because it used an algorithm and extrapolation, variable projections emerged; but by the time mid-month arrived, it was starting to estimate an accurate number. Many aspects of cost were somewhat predictable, and barring an anomaly, the tool worked remarkably well.

Last month's data troubled John. Molding and metal stamping crept up a little. Gains made in both assembly and packaging offset the other numbers. On the 21st day of last month, the department encountered a large material write off, of which no one seemed to have any details. The same punch in metal stamping broke twice in the month. Between the downtime and the costs of repairing the die tooling twice in less than 30 days, the department spent about $7,000 more than the previous month. John asked Geoff Schneider, the engineer responsible for metal stamping, to get the master operators to together, and complete an A3 to get to the root of the problem. John needed answers by the end of the week.

The engineering department started using A3s recently as a problem-solving methodology. John called in a favor for some free training from Steve at Dakota Manufacturing Partnership (DMP). The site utilized the A3 for training, coaching and mentoring with the staff. The benefits of the investment in training and methodology standardization were emerging quickly. Recent success from operations included production supervisors using the process to optimize the production break schedule. With the involvement of the operators, supervisors and just a bit of oversight from HR, they came up with a novel plan insuring line coverage, but also allowing some flexibility resulting in a win for the production operators.

John continued to be amazed at the talent and creativity of people when allowed to do their best work. Generally speaking, for many years, the message to manufacturing workers (not just at Northern Pines Technology, but everywhere) stated, "Come. Do your time. Run your machine." The not so subtle message was, "Let the engineers do the thinking and park your brain at the door." Not too rewarding; sounding more like a prison than a job. Now more than ever, the site needed everyone rowing in the same direction, all brainpower available and focused to establish innovative solutions to the business challenges.

The site benefits from a great educational system in North Dakota. High school graduation rates rank high. Many students go on to college or trade schools, and in fact, Twin Ports is privileged to have a two-year technical and pre-professional school supplying a constant roster of excellent and talented workers. Over the years, the site developed a close working relationship with the school. North Dakota Science College remains proactive and progressive in their approach to the students, which has helped the site highly competitive.

John's mind wandered away from the QICR meeting; he had heard enough for now. He thought to himself, "I'll look over the cost data myself after the meeting." He discretely web-surfed a little to get onto LinkedIn. He had not done this for a week or so. John enjoyed keeping up with colleagues from Iowa State, and it was always interesting to see what they were up to, as well as others around Northern Pines.

John noticed an invite from Doug Walker, his boss. "Good to see Doug had entered the 21st century by joining LinkedIn," John thought. John happened to notice Doug linked to Lucinda. Interesting connection, so John clicked. His eyes quickly scanned her page and focused on a contact John recognized – Anil Gupta and Ramnath Gupta.

That was interesting. John looked at Ramnath, a consultant at Blackhill & McGrath LLC. Ramnath Gupta attended Michigan, MBA Class of 2001. Ramnath looked a lot like Anil. Relative? Son, maybe? John never claimed to be the sharpest knife in the drawer, but it was obvious he needed to conduct some digital sleuthing to try and put a few things together.

It seemed possible if not even logical; Lucinda driving to secure her place on the C-level executive team at Northern Pines, and Anil Gupta, making a play for Northern Pines products would be connected. However, the twist, of Ramnath, may be related to Anil, and a previous history both being classmates at Michigan, seemed more than coincidental.

John scanned further; Ramnath and Lucinda worked together at Blackhill & McGrath right after business school. John wasn't aware of this interesting fact. Making just a few assumptions, John could not rule out a spinoff from Northern Pines Technology could potentially be the sights of Blackhill & McGrath as the acquisition. The data and information management portion of Northern Pines would be well suited. It struggled with technology and the competitive nature, short product lifecycles, and high investments costs. It would be logical if Northern Pines could return to its core businesses of 20 years ago. The balance sheet would look much better. That could be accomplished by a joint venture, take advantage of low-cost labor and then spin off the businesses which didn't make much money.

Blackhill & McGrath were well known in the technology space during the high-flying dot com age. Their reputation was they minted millionaires quarterly. Their formula seemed simple: buy a company, ready the technology/software/product for launch, take it public; and between the investment bankers and the highly cultivated deals, ride the stock up to astronomical levels and then sell. Take the proceeds and repeat. During the dot-com days, no visible downside existed. The nature of the market was everything kept appreciating.

During the economic downturn, Blackhill & McGrath changed its modus operandi slightly. They were now known as the 'acquire, gut and cut' capital management advisory firm. They sought out companies with brand value, asset value or some combination of the two and brokered a merger. None of it ended well for the acquired companies. Jobs were lost and profits moved overseas.

Each step of his digital journey caused John's stomach to churn. Unfortunately, this ache in his gut could not be blamed on bad Chinese at lunch. He began to see a clearer picture emerge as the pieces of the puzzle may be starting to come together. If this connection was true, and John's hunch right, this was a total game changer for Northern Pines.

As the meeting wrapped, John asked Lee Swenson, the operations manager for the personal storage business, to send him the unit cost files. John was going to work on the files tonight.

For John, even though this was still speculative, he knew he could not wait. Beginning with Doug's blow up, the meeting at the Northland Inn, the connections between players in this merger, all pointed to details he had to first understand and then derail.

	A	B	C	AN	AO	AP
1						
2						
3	**Diskette - Unit Cost Performance**					
4	2 MB OEM Black					
5						
6						
7						
8				Nov	Dec	Jan
9	Item / Department	Description		Act Ext Cost	Act Ext Cost	Act Ext Cost
10	4200B027822	2MB OEM MEDIA		$0.01443	$0.01356	$0.01530
11	11F01816625	LIQUID A RING		$0.00024	$0.00033	$0.00016
12	1120000K508	OVOH LINER MATERIAL (new)		$0.00041	$0.00042	$0.00040
13	78801W98169	SPRING TORSION		$0.00111	$0.00128	$0.00094
14	78809821M01	3.5" HUB		$0.00382	$0.00376	$0.00387
15	788077R7200	SHUTTER OEM		$0.00675	$0.00722	$0.00627
16	78811R22256	2MB BLACK RESIN SHELL MOLDED		$0.03223	$0.03199	$0.03246
17	1675 LBR	MN TECH TwinPort 5432-1 3 HALF INCH		$0.00985	$0.00876	$0.01095
18	3171	MN TECH TwinPort 5432-1 ADMIN		$0.00385	$0.00415	$0.00355
19	3571	MN TECH TwinPort 5432-1 ENGINEERING		$0.00148	$0.00166	$0.00130
20	3272	MN TECH TwinPort 5432-1 INVENTORY MGMT		$0.00072	$0.00077	$0.00066
21	3271	MN TECH TwinPort 5432-1 RM SF REC AND W		$0.00222	$0.00244	$0.00199
22	1875 VOH	MN TECH TwinPort 5432-1 3 HALF INCH		$0.01213	$0.01439	$0.00987
23			Unit Cost	$ 0.0892	$ 0.0907	$ 0.0877
24			Units	52,341,844	48,945,707	55,737,981
25						

Figure 1: *Diskette Unit Cost Performance*

In his mind, John's course of action was now set. He concluded this resembled more of an ambush than a technology partnership. John knew in his mind what he had to do: engage his team, disrupt the plans to try to save the plant at all costs.

He would have to accept this might be career suicide. He was resolute. Knowing what he knew now, John could not let this happen to the plant. He had to demonstrate Twin Ports brought much more value (financial and intangible) than analysts who had never seen Twin Ports calculations could possibly have factored in.

Closing the plant was the wrong thing to do. John concluded he had been lied to, and closing manufacturing was not in the best interests of Northern Pines, especially if Blackhill & McGrath were anywhere close to the deal.

After leaving the training room, John scribbled a note on Diane's desk. "Please call an emergency staff meeting for 4:00 PM on Thursday afternoon."

Chapter 8: 4:00 PM Sharp

John hurriedly jotted a few notes for the staff discussion at four. He was not ready to lay out all his detective work, largely because he did not have enough solid data. Nonetheless, he did have a growing hunch, suspicion, whatever one might call it.

John prided himself on being very careful and precise with his analysis. False data is worse than no data, John learned. People carry a mental bias and take solace in data as presented. People deal with no data, but data that turns out to be factually wrong; it is generally more damaging. John wanted to make sure the facts were right; he did not dare step out of bounds in the comments he made to his staff. He needed to be verbally precise; he knew his words mattered.

John thought about his team. How would they handle the information? He did not have any concerns about the confidentiality; they had proven themselves trustworthy on a variety of other issues. Granted, this ranks as one of the weightiest pieces of information his leadership team had dealt with, but John knew most of these people for over ten years. The trust level was high, both ways.

One way the mutual trust had been built was a shared sense of community. This team celebrated their successes together and shed a few tears during their losses. This went beyond all of that. These people represented more than coworkers; they were truly friends.

This was shown by keeping an unwritten tradition or practice. When and where appropriate, they tried to attend significant events in each other's lives. John recalled going to funerals for over half of the staff family members, sometimes traveling hundreds of miles. They learned, in times like this, actions meant more than words. Grant lost his older brother to cancer last fall and the entire team came together and made the drive out to Bismarck to be there for Grant and his family. Several of the staff with farming in their backgrounds volunteered on subsequent weekends to help with unfinished harvesting. These were people who did this not because they had to; they did it because they wanted to help their friend.

These bonds created a sense of family and unity of purpose. Over time, respect had been built of each other's thought process, decision making and valued opinions. Like an infantry unit, this team was forged into a combat ready unit by some shared experiences during challenging times.

As a sanity check, John knew the next months would be taxing; he was already thinking about whom he could lean on for the various aspects of the program. John pulled up the spreadsheet on skills/attributes of the Twin Ports leadership team. The group participated in an offsite about a month ago and taken StrongLink – an assessment tool to identify key areas of an individual strengths.

John Stanton	Discipline, Analytical, Learner, Focus
Grant Richards	Learner, Input, Individualization, Analytical,
Mary Ann Tackett	Context, Analytical, Learner, Achiever,
Jeff Alberts	Harmony, Restorative, Analytical, Learner,
Lee Swenson	Analytical, Learner, Deliberative, Context,
Sarah Bergstrom	Focus, Achiever, Learner, Strategic,
Lenny Garst	Analytical, Deliberative, Focus, Learner

John's thoughts returned to the task at hand; preparing for a very difficult announcement and conversation. How do you begin to convey the magnitude of what is about to happen? How do you anticipate reactions, questions and start the process of leading through the challenge?

John had been sent an advanced copy of the press release. He used the prepared words as a baseline. John figured the announcement would probably come out over the dinner hour. Recently, that is how most information was deployed; at least, those updates deemed material by the legal team. These kinds of things were generally reserved for hours when the stock was not being traded.

At the appointed hour, with staff gathered in the conference room, John began his remarks, "Team, we have been through some real challenges together, and I am afraid we have another one coming up which will test us even more than anything in the past. As you know, I was called down to the Twin Cities on Monday to be made aware there is going to be a joint venture announced between Northern Pines Technology and Mendal Industries."

John then proceeded to read a draft of the announcement.

Thursday, February 22, 2007

Draft Press Release: Not to be released prior to close of markets on Thursday.

Today, Northern Pines Technology (NPT) is announcing a joint technology and development agreement between NPT and Mendal Enterprises. The agreement will be a sharing of technology in the area of IT infrastructure and storage solutions. Lucinda Marshall, Vice President of Operations for NPT, "We hope to bring the synergistic entrepreneurial spirit of Mendal and the stature and depth of technological understanding from Northern Pines Technology into a new level of collaboration which will benefit both companies in the markets we serve. Ultimately it will be our customers and shareholders who will benefit from this unique partnership."

Mendal Enterprises is a leading provider of new applications across the entire spectrum of information technology and infrastructure and has an established and growing presence in Asia.

The technology agreement will allow for technical exchange, shared intellectual property and joint development on new product platforms for both Northern Pines Technology and Mendal Enterprises.

Marshall Tucker, Northern Pines Technology CEO, "We look forward to a long and prosperous working relationship with Mendal Enterprises, we have admired their technology and innovation and now look forward to combining the best resources at Northern Pines Technology with the best at Mendal and creating solutions for our customers that will accelerate growth, leverage our intellectual property and provide new opportunities for the future."

It was foot noted in small font with the following:

Certain information contained in this statement relates to historical information may be not constitute forward-looking statements within the meaning of the Private Securities Litigation Reform Act of 1995. Such statements are subject to varied risks, uncertainties and variability that may our actual performance in the future to differ materially from our historical results and those presently anticipated or projected. Northern Pines Technology cautions investors not to overly rely on any such forward-looking statements. Any statements speak only as of the date on which statements are made, and we neither plan nor are obligated to provide update to information to reflect activities arising after date of publication.

John finished at the bottom of the prepared text, paused and waded past the point of no return.

He cleared the throat and continued, "There is more to this than is being announced. As it was explained to me on Monday, the plan is to announce the joint development agreement and let this continue for a few quarters, followed by the announcement of a joint manufacturing agreement."

Right away, Sarah interrupted, "What does this mean for the plant?" John said, "It is not good for Twin Ports or any of the manufacturing facilities in our division. The intent is to begin to outsource all manufacturing in the next two years and to close up shop in the US." John paused and looked out at everyone, after letting the words he hoped he would never have to speak, hang in the room. There were looks of confusion, bewilderment, betrayal and listlessness, which John read also as a form of shock.

Silence lasted for probably close to a minute; no words were spoken, none needed.

Looking at the expressions on familiar faces, John continued, "Since Monday, I have been racking the brain trying to figure out what to do. I am upset, angry and confused. We don't have much time as next week we have a visit Mr. Anil Gupta and a team from Mendal." He continued, "They are supposed to learn absolutely everything they can about our entire operation: suppliers, documentation, process, technology, development programs…everything. This is under the guise of the joint technology agreement, but in reality has more to do with the subsequent plans to shutter US manufacturing."

John continued in a somber tone, "I did not talk to the other managers. I think, like you, we were all in shock. You have my commitment I am going to do everything in my power to undermine this and make sure the results coming from this plant are so good, they cannot be replicated anywhere and people would be fools for trying."

Lenny spoke up first, "Can we all just take vacation next week?" There were a few chuckles, but no one seriously thought the option was available, and that was not the intent. Lenny had a unique ability to break tension with humor and his spot-on insights.

John reiterated the confidentiality of this additional information. He needed this time to fully understand the intent and the strategic direction as defined by Marshall Tucker and Lucinda Marshall, and what it meant to Twin Ports.

John said, "I have gone out on a limb to tell you this; which is an indication of the trust I have in each one of you and this entire team. However, if or when you are asked by anyone at corporate, I do not want you to lie about me sharing this information. Tell the truth and I will take whatever consequences there might be."

John finished with, "I strongly doubt other plant managers are having this discussion with their staff, and I cannot speak for them. I have spent the last three days trying to figure out what to do. In the end, we must put our heads together, figure out a plan, execute and let the plant performance speak for us."

John continued, "It goes without saying, we have an obligation to keep this within our team. This information is privileged, confidential; and if this information were to leak to the plant or community, we would have a public relations mess on our hands. At this time, I would appreciate it if you would not even share this with your spouses. I know that is hard, but I am worried a thoughtless word might leak out."

It was Lenny again who interrupted the silence, "John, what are we going to do?" John shared he had an outline of a plan. Lenny quickly retorted, "This isn't operation 'Lighting Strike', is it?" The group chuckled. Lighting Strike was a code name for a proposed change in organization structure someone paid lot of money to get; and it proved to be a bad idea, through and through.

John paused for a moment and shared his very basic outline of a plan with the staff. It was easy to see there was a healthy dose of skepticism. John benefited from a few days to process all this. They were getting the information as rapidly as if they were standing under a waterfall.

As the initial shock began to fade, the team listened as John mapped out the principles important to the site's success over the next 9-12 months. John shared the rough outline of what he had come up with so far, explained it was very much a work in progress and he needed their full support and help.

John continued his pitch to achieve the site goals, and financial results. "We are going to have to run our QICR process like never before. We must drive strong accountability deep into the organization. We must make decisions like this is our own money; every penny counts, now more than ever before. Leadership and speed. We have to act decisively and with conviction."

"How were we going to create that overnight?" John threw out the question somewhat rhetorically. The answer may be a lesson from the past.

John admitted he did not have all the answers, but he knew somehow training for knowledge, the Training Within Industry kind could help make the site more flexible. Every person, every day was going to be a part of the solution to keep Twin Ports a thriving manufacturer. The leadership team had been slowly introduced to Training Within Industry over the past few months, as managers already started looking for more ways to create flexibility and accountability in the plant operations.

The meeting ended with a quick brainstorming about how to handle next week. The announcement had done a nice job of explaining the joint venture, so they could talk freely with the plant employees about the high-level message. It was more challenging when detailed questions started to be asked, such as:

> Why are these people going into so much detail?
> Why do they need to spend an entire week?
> Is it acceptable to share machine cycle time?

John did provide one piece of advice that everyone agreed upon. "Let's treat this like an audit. We will answer the question asked, offer no more and no less, be factually accurate but guarded in our information."

The team all agreed this was a reasonable course of action and broke up. It was 4:55 PM. It has been a stressful day; John knew; this was only the beginning of a very long journey.

As John walked back to his office, he wondered about the eight previous plant managers. Twin Ports had been blessed with very good leaders. Each made their own mark. John wondered; what would they do? In a quick moment, he chose to believe they would be initiating the same actions as he was beginning to put in place.

John wanted to take a quick look at the diskette numbers and then he was ready to go home to the five noisy, rambunctious (maybe spirited is a better word) kids and his longsuffering wife. Kristin planned a shopping trip out with Laura, her best friend, so John needed to be home for the kids.

It would be pizza for all, bath and bed early for the three little ones and either Wii or a John Wayne movie with the twins. John was trying to teach them a sense of cinematic discernment. Lesson #1: Basically, anything with John Wayne was a worthy way to spend hard-earned relaxing time. Later John would introduce them to Chevy Chase and Steve Martin comedies, but best to start with the classics first.

However tonight, John could use a little comedy in his life.

Chapter 9: Vegetarians & Ice Fishing

The visitors from Mendal Industries arrived on Tuesday precisely at 9:00 AM. The site hosted dozens of visitors during the course of a year, so routines were well established. The presentations, tour route, clean up, where to stash the things that did not need to be seen – the whole drill was executed with near military precision.

The introductions and the plenary session began in the Medora Room, the site 'showcase' conference room and one most commonly used for hosting customer visits. This room contained the latest technology and perfectly showcased the company's products. John began the meeting with introductions. First, Mr. Gupta introduced himself. John didn't realize it, but he had been educated in England and had spent about five years in the US during previous acquisitions. He also mentioned he was the father of two children, a daughter with a family in India and a son who had been educated in the US and now worked as a consultant with a firm in Silicon Valley. Mr. Gupta worked for Mendal in the US when they acquired a hard disk drive manufacturer based in California.

The rest of the team consisted of:

Mayank Puri – engineering manager of Mendal's hardware business
Agarwal Rajesh – chief engineer
Shah Rukeshkalamida – supply chain and operations director

John clicked through the 22 site overview slides; having done this enough he could do it in his sleep. Purposefully, he stopped to linger on a few key slides. John reinforced the site's vertical integration. This was critical; concept, design, development, prototyping and production could all be done inside the four walls of this very building. The one-stop-shop competency showed a marked distinction, and John knew it. John shared with the group a recent example of how the engineers were able to capture an idea, prototype it in-house, make the necessary adjustments, run the tooling in the development press and fully vet the idea for feasibility inside of 30 days. Outside involvement would require triple the time and cost.

The Mendal personnel also spoke of their deep integration and how they were able the same. John smiled. Without saying, he expected gamesmanship, after all, this was business. Inside, he had serious doubts they really understood vertical integration and the tremendous competitive advantage it afforded, especially in the context of time to market speed and guarding intellectual property.

John was a practical person, and tried to give the benefit of the doubt, but in this case, he knew a thing or two about business negotiations. From previous experiences – he had seen organizations boast about their capability and then ultimately not be able to deliver.

John was not savvy across all regions; but in his business dealings and exposure, he had an appreciation for the role culture and values bring to business discussions. Back in 2001, John had been asked to be part of a joint venture investigation called Royal Flush. He was asked to assess the operational and technological capability of a flash disk manufacturer called Kingfisher Industries, located outside Bangalore. Kingfisher, at the time, was one of the early flash memory producers using the 16 nm wavelength technology.

John travelled to India to see Kingfishers' operation. They built a factory and hired over 1,300 workers to operate the facility. The size of the factory was impressive. However, the site lacked basic infrastructure, or at least what one would consider necessities to run a large manufacturing operation. The facility ran a site back-up power generation and water treatment, because their mean time between failures of both municipal systems was less than one month. Power/water could be out for anywhere from a few hours to a day or more, depending on when someone from the municipal utilities was available to fix the problem. Also, some of the basic infrastructure lacked the presence to run a high-tech facility. In the six months prior to John's visit in 2001, The high-speed fiber optic cable had been cut twice due to some rogue construction somewhere between the city and the plant. One of the service disruptions happened during John's visit. None of these were necessarily complete showstoppers; however, they were certainly competitive disadvantages compared to locations with a more reliable power grid and supporting infrastructure.

The primary takeaway John observed during the trip was Kingfisher's tremendous desire to drive a hard bargain, but an open question on their ability to subsequently deliver. The people seemed knowledgeable in technology and quality systems, but they could not consistently produce solid evidence when pressed for details. John specifically asked Kingfisher about incoming material inspection and corrective and preventive action. They all confirmed their involvement in doing preventive action; however, when pushed, their system was not available for inspection. They eluded actually producing A3's, 8D's or any other form of hard evidence.

This left doubt in John's mind about everything in Kingfisher's quality system really working exactly as described. At the time, they did not have ISO 9001 Quality System registration, but did claim their certification audit was imminent. Six months passed, and while the story changed slightly, the fact remained Kingfisher had yet to be certified to the international quality standard. These indicators, were maybe a signal or sign, at least in John's mind, something was not quite right.

During the Kingfisher negotiations, John witnessed their tactics at work; first, negotiate everything, never concede a single point. Second, claim parity, but when pressed for details, state it would take time to get the data. And lastly, anything offered by negotiators would be topped by minimum of 5% and maybe even more if that's what it took to close the deal. It seemed to be Kingfisher's modus operandi.

In the end, Northern Pine Technology opted not to do a deal with Kingfisher Industries. The whole experience gave John valuable perspective on international business and more importantly how negotiations really work.

John's trip to India in 2001 provided more than an encounter with Kingfisher. John experienced something deeply personal seared in his memory forever. It happened as the team was driving back from the plant to the city after work one evening. They maneuvered through the animal dodge; that is, waiting for the cattle or goats or whatever to move to the side of the road. The car stopped for a brief moment. John rode in the comfort of a Mercedes with air conditioning. Outside, the temperature raged towards 110 degrees with a near blinding sandstorm charged through the streets.

John peered through the dusty window. In the foreground, a small Ferris wheel came into focus. The whole thing reached only eight feet high, powered by a cheap electric motor whose cord somehow disappeared into a maze of tangled wires.

A few other vendors stood nearby. It wasn't clear if this was a small-scale carnival or what exactly was going on. Sites such as this proved common from what John had observed in India. People milled about the vendors as if in a carnival-like atmosphere. Alongside the road adjacent to the Mercedes, a five or six-year-old young boy sat on the curb, not two feet from the car. He cradled what appeared to be his sister as she cried. The little girl was maybe two or three. The girl's matted hair complemented the dirty, tear-stained cheeks. She looked inconsolable as if she had been crying for a long time. Their clothes looked dirty. No adults in sight took responsibility. John felt a helpless compassion. He wondered about these children. Is the little girl in pain? Does she have a home? Does she have family other than her brother? Who cares for them? What about tomorrow, next week? Where will they go? What will they eat?

In that brief instant, John experienced a myriad of emotions and thoughts. What kind of future do these children have? John realized they represent just two humans out of millions. Children not just in India, but Africa, China, Russia and many other nations. The image of those two young lives sitting alongside the curb, dirty, hot, probably hungry remained indelibly printed on his memory. The tears, matted hair and the look of empty desperation left a deep scar on John's mind.

John could not help but draw a contrast to his own children. At the time of the trip, John's small children slept safely in a warm home, cared for and loved. He struggled with the differences between his children and the ones seated on the dusty curb before him. Yet, it was commonplace not only in India but around the world. It didn't make sense and yet maybe one day he would understand.

John's memories of his trip to India suddenly and abruptly halted when Lenny stood in front of the Mendal team to cover the quality and compliance program for the site. Jeff, Sarah, Lee and finally Mary Ann followed to cover Northern Pine Technology operations. Granted, the memories of India were more riveting, but duty called.

After reviewing the standard presentation, a slight change was made. Normally, John would highlight the contract manufacturing business. The site was always looking for interesting projects which suited the technology and skill base, but today John chose not to focus on that specific aspect of operations.

The site provided components to Intellus, the largest chip processing company in the world and to Minnesota Minerals and Magnetics, a huge industrial conglomerate with operations all over the world. Minnesota Minerals started on the shores of Lake Superior and grew to be a successful, diversified business. These two customers, in particular, felt a little bit nervous about others seeing any aspect of their operations. The Twin Ports site, as their trusted partner, was obligated not to disclose anything which could comprise their customer's technology or products. It was not uncommon to avoid talking about contract operations, especially when dealing with potential competitors. However, whenever there was an opportunity to showcase the work accomplished at the site and potential for another sale, Northern Pines maintained confidentiality, but proudly displayed their best efforts for the contract manufacturing customers.

The morning ended with a floor tour. John walked the Mendal group around, and the technical staff did informal talks out on the production line, usually using a poster as a prop for additional information. The floor was always the most impressive aspect of the visit; to actually see things being made.

This tour also gave John time to interact with the operators on the production floor. John found if he sought out a few influencers on the floor, he could get an effective and mostly accurate message communicated. Sandy Severs worked as one of his influencers in assembly. John intentionally walked over to line four and informed her of the visit. The message, "Don't worry, Sandy. The site will be fine."

John noticed Doug Chambers in molding and relayed much the same message to him as he did to Sandy. A good chunk of the grapevine work would be taken care of by sharing the information. Both Sandy and Doug, if they had good intel from the boss, were highly likely to share with coworkers. The messages would be talked about in the break room as well as at shift change. John made certain he provided the linkage with the corporate announcement as well. His words were intentionally bland, leaving enough space to describe the partnership with a variety of interpretations.

Diane ordered in lunch. John was thankful Diane asked about dietary restrictions ahead of time. Often visitors prefer some foods to others, and this group was no different. Two of the four were vegetarians. The local Pizza Pit provided Day #1 lunch. They prepared two special veggie pies that were a hit with the visitors.

Everyone enjoyed cold soda and freshly baked chocolate chip cookies from 'The Pit' as it was affectionately known around town.

The staff and Mr. Anil Gupta's team spent the afternoon creating a plan for Wednesday and Thursday. It seemed as if a reasonable and positive working atmosphere developed, and John heard the team following the guidance set out the past Thursday. The local team offered help, but not too much help. John's team took his cues well and behaved much like one would in a formal audit. A few laughs emerged when misinterpretations occurred signally simpler terms needed to be employed.

Jeff arranged a few evening activities. Twin Ports' local college performed a three-act play on Tuesday night. The team agreed it sounded like a good time, so together they enjoyed a local talent production of "The Salesman" followed by coffee and dessert at the Java Joint. In the end, it was a good first day followed up by an enjoyable evening.

On Wednesday, the team picked up where work ended on Tuesday. Gupta's team came ready with questions, requests for information and was truly seeking to understand the operational aspects. Details were worked on through the balance of Wednesday and into Thursday.

The next planned offsite adventure occurred on Thursday afternoon. The team knocked off a little early and traveled 30 minutes east to demonstrate the fine art of ice fishing. John knew this would be a hit, even though he was not a fan and could not figure out the allure, he willingly agreed to serve as host.

Earlier, when Jeff suggested ice fishing, sitting for hours, inside a little house with heater, John shuddered at the idea of parking on a five-gallon bucket with a small pole dangling into a hole in the ice. The adventure was not John's idea of a good time. John quickly relented, however; it was not about him.

As always, the visitors got a big charge out of this activity, as Jeff predicted they would. The group brought their cameras and the idea of walking on frozen water unnerved them somewhat.

When the Engineering Manager, Mayank Puri – hooked a small perch, the group's reaction almost blew the roof off the tiny ice house. The North Dakotans might raise that kind of a raucous for a large Muskie, but not a six-inch perch. After a few hours; the mighty fishermen stopped by Mabel Milligan's on the way home and the carnivores ate steaks and the herbivores feasted on pasta primavera.

In hindsight, the week went better than John expected. At the debrief and wrap up meeting on Friday morning, the Gupta team showed their appreciation and communicated they had gained some additional insights into the products and how Northern Pines Technology Twin Ports is similar to ways they conduct their business.

Gupta's mission involved creating a plan to successfully transfer the operations, advance technology and improve costs. The team stated they remained confident costs could get down below $0.08, which would be an 11% improvement. John smiled while thinking, "Yes maybe you can. Maybe you can't, but you will never beat $0.07." Unlike the back and forth with suppliers, John enjoyed this cat and mouse game, especially because he knew the cards. When holding aces; not much will beat his hand.

Anil pulled John aside after the closing meeting and complimented him on a fine plant. "This was the cleanest and most energized facility I've had seen in a long time." John thanked him for his kind words. Anil continued, "The floors! I've never seen such clean floors in all my life."

After an intense week of interaction, John realized these are good people, doing exactly what their company asked of them. One aspect of business is creating the illusion of competitive advantage and effective posturing of the organization and its capability.

Nothing Beats an Afternoon of Ice Fishing

Diane accomplished her task of keeping the week running smoothly with food, accommodating the visitor's needs and making sure John could focus.

John and Diane debriefed quickly in John's office after the visitors left. "Set up two meetings next week with the staff for planning. Come up with your own code name and write them on the calendar, two afternoons for planning next week and a Friday morning weekly debrief."

John instructed, "Diane, take the afternoon off and go do something fun."

Diane mumbled, "Thank you. I'll knock off about 2:00."

John retorted, "1:30." Diane sheepishly smiled as she said, "1:30 it is," still smiling as she closed the office door.

Chapter 10: Friday afternoon and a Mental Rant

John is a book junkie. At work, business, quality, manufacturing and leadership books fill his bookshelf. The books which don't make it to work end up on a dedicated shelf at home. Or at least until recently when *Mike Mulligan and his Steam Shovel* and *The Cat in the Hat* commandeered the available shelf space. As a result, most of his business books migrated to work.

One overall theme permeated through all the books on the shelf. John coined it the 'silver bullet' syndrome. Every book dealt with tough issues as if they contain only one dimension. Fix the single issue and all the problems go away. His experiences proved otherwise; over and over again – the problems don't go away. The writers imply implementing new whiz-bang analysis A or salting in a little B and C on the really tough problems, converts to a solution for all current and future problems. John knew better, no 'silver bullet' exists. There never has been and never will be. Digging in, gathering and analyzing data, testing theories and finding the root cause is the key to truly solving each unique problem.

For example, one of John's experiences aligned more with solving a complex quality problem with threads of human resources issues. This problem manifested itself when the corporate incentive plan changed to emphasize quantity over quality. For years, Northern Pines Technology had an hourly incentive program based on production rates. It didn't take too long for workers to figure out more product out the door equaled more pay in the pocket. Sadly, the incentive program somewhat drove people to focus on quantity over quality.

John was on a team charged with gathering the information and analyzing the data. The team quickly discovered the root cause and the program modified to count only quality parts produced. If a defective part was made, missed and discovered by a subsequent shift, then the program added a punitive element, a quality escape.

John scanned the titles on his bookshelf. Crosby taught quality is free. Goldratt managed constraints. Deming was plan-do-check-act. Blanchard said Manage by Walking Around (MBWA), and in one minute, all was manageable. These books were all over the map. John wasn't exactly sure what he was looking for; his eyes continued to rove over the titles.

John decided he must be getting old as most of these titles were written in the 80's and early 90's. Now, it's the enlightened age of the 21st Century. Business and self-help gurus still pump out the books, as if assuming collective wisdom applies. In John's thinking, the world's problems far outweigh the ability to solve them, hence guaranteeing a steady stream of books.

His world was built around logic, facts and data. That is how John had been trained, to be a critical thinker, testing theories, and most of all, relying on data. As the old statistical mantra goes, "In God We Trust, all others bring data." The takeaway? The world is a complex, interconnected network. It is not one thing, but a collection of many influences on the system which create desired outcomes or cause deviation from a desired state. There is always a chance doing all the right things will not create the expected result.

Late in the afternoon, John walked back to one of his favorite spots in the plant. Over part of the manufacturing floor; at the back of the plant, a mezzanine lofts above the north-molding bay. Below twelve presses busily inject plastic pellets through complex equipment to be formed into diskette shells. John enjoys going up on the mezzanine and just watching these machines work. The visual imagery is stunning. It is easy for John to liken this sight to the elegance of a ballet or the preciseness of a conductor directing a symphony. The movement of these machines and technology all around directed to a common cause is quite magnificent. It is a reminder all around –

complex technology, with engineering precision and flawless execution is required to produce many seemingly simple products, like diskettes.

View from the Mezzanine, North Molding Bay

Johns' mind wandered back to the late 1980s when he was in graduate school. John graduated from Iowa State first in 1988; at the time, the economy was not very good. He graduated second in his class. The job market was tight and despite a few interviews, he decided graduate school was the best option. During graduate school, one of the topics John became more interested in was systems engineering. This is not a new concept as NASA, has been using it for years on major projects like the Apollo rocket series and the Space Shuttle. John's niche interest came from using some of the same systems engineering principles to solve manufacturing problems.

John's expertise and knowledge developed around concurrent engineering. The concept was to move as many design and development activities in parallel as possible, versus a serial approach. There was a heavy emphasis on modeling and managing risks. Johns' thesis provided a methodology to design the product, process and manufacturing systems on a parallel path. When the thesis was done, John was proud of the work. He learned a lot about writing simulation code, examining statistics and using an experimental design to develop an improved understanding of the variables which impact yield, output and flow in a manufacturing system.

In addition to the academic rigor, graduate school came with a life lesson as well. And it was this: a true and real appreciation for how everything is really a part of a larger system and subject to many of the influences, both internal and external observable in systems theory.

While the concept may seem academic, one really does not need to look much further than nature to see the parallels. During the twins homeschool studies, Kristin organized observations with ant colonies for the boys to follow. Since ant colonies are plentiful everywhere, it is an amazing to take a one-foot by one-foot square area and just observe. Ant colonies make great habitat to explore because they truly mirror a system of survival; transportation and habitation rivaling some of humankind's most complex systems.

Ant colonies may grow to contain half a billion ants. The colony that is built will generally be underground, dug by workers who will hold tiny bits of dirt in their mouths carry it to the exterior of the colony and deposit it outside. They then navigate back to where they were working through the maze and repeat this action, thousands and thousands of times. At the same moment, their work is not random. They are architecting a magnificent labyrinth of tunnels, rooms, food storage and nurseries. Interestingly, food is carried in much the same way and stored in the colony.

Ants are so advanced in their travel from point A to point B that very useful optimization algorithms have been developed based on their travel patterns. The ant colony optimization algorithm was developed as methodology for solving computational problems which can be analyzed by finding the best path or paths through complex geography.

John snapped back to reality when Press #59 alarmed. He did not know how much time had passed; but knew much was resting on his shoulders. He recognized what lie ahead for the site resembled a complex system engineering problem. His team needed to reduce the cost of production by more than 15% in less than 9 months, somehow influence a decision well beyond their control, all while keeping the plant running at peak performance with workers engaged, and avoid any leaks in the information John had given to his trusted staff.

The Campanile, Iowa State University

John did not know if ants worry about winters, predators, farmers plowing over their dwelling or things like pesticide. Maybe that is what made ants different from humans. The ants remained focused on the task, just charging ahead. John worried about all the things to be done and the number and size of pitfalls along the way. He easily counted a hundred ways for this to go south, and only one outcome likely to even create a possibility of saving the plant; not the best odds.

A second alarm, this time on Press #34, jarred John back to awareness. Honestly, he didn't know how long he had been standing there, maybe 30 minutes, and this was the second alarm in the area. John glanced at his watch. 5:17 PM – it was time to call it a day and a week.

It had been a very long week. The site survived Mendal Industries visitors; however, John knew next week, the team had to bear down hard on planning.

The long weeks were just starting.

Chapter 11: Planning

All projects need a code name; some clever alignment with a theme or topic – like rivers, colors or constellations. There were innumerable names: Project Orion, Project Missouri and Project Goldrush. John was a little more off-the-wall in that regard, so without a lot of thought; he dubbed this project: Blue Ox, maybe with just a nod and a wink to the great northwest and "Made in America."

John kicked off the first "Blue Ox" session with the entire staff by covering the agenda. In attendance around the rectangular table – to John's right, Mary Ann, Grant, Lennie and on the opposite side, Jeff, Lee and Sarah.

John prepared the outline in advance; he knew many topics merited additional discussion. Thus, he began the meeting by asking some open-ended questions. The questions came rapid fire out of John's mouth, "What is our biggest threat? Why does it take so long to get stuff done? Why do we seem to spend a good chunk of our time convincing our people to get on board, versus actually getting the work done?"

"Don't get me wrong," John said. "I think we have one of the best plants in the world, but that doesn't mean we do everything right or we don't have some significant things to work through when we manage change. This effort is going to require our absolute commitment, trust and willingness to consider everything; nothing can be off-limits."

John inherently knew one thing the site possessed; they are accustomed to change and highly adaptable. Those working in the business knew if the site stops improving, or slowed down the rate of improvement, the end comes quickly. It is then a question of timing;

it may have six months before the competition catches up and everything is irrelevant.

The site is nimble and relatively good at change, but John thinks at times it can be a bit numb, too. Which is also a risk – because so much is in flux at any given time. Maintaining balance concerns John as well. How and when to push rested squarely on John's shoulders as the site leader. He had to drive, but also had to monitor the pulse of change to avoid an overburdened and confused organization.

John learned along the way from a series of HR managers that change always is a process. Even good changes don't just happen without emotion, stress and the need to monitor implementation. In negative change, elements of shock, denial, rationalizing and eventually getting to a point of acceptance, accompany the process.

When trying to implement a positive change, the focus shifts to creation of a gap or need, a vision; followed by an explanation or plan of how to get there, which then results first in acclimation and then hopefully buy in, and ultimately a significant movement of the individual and organization. At least that is what the textbooks say. John thought the next few months the site will be a virtual laboratory of change.

John knew he had to make this concept of change real to his staff; create a lesson in how to manage change. He told a story, recalling one incident when he was a quality engineer at the plant.

"Many years ago, there were nine major changes going on simultaneously across the diskette product line. To manage all this change, of which I, as quality engineer was accountable. I sat down with Lenny Garst, who was my supervisor at the time."

John continued by explaining the situation and a proposed solution. Lenny took John through the A3 process, a problem-solving tool developed by Toyota. John held only a limited understanding of the problem, but with Lenny's insights and his mentoring, John mapped out the real problems, identified solutions and found additional countermeasures to help. The departments used visual management, creating a sizable, but useful matrix, which visually displayed the current situation. The tool aided planning and operations and allowed accurate information and access to what was qualified to run where and how best to balance the capacity across all the lines.

Lenny smiled as he recalled this time, now it was the student leading the teacher. Lenny just had to chime in, "Those early days, I am not sure you were every going to get it – but you turned out OK John."

John was eternally grateful to Lenny for both his time and influence on his career. He learned a lot from Lenny about work and life and now to be able to share some of those lessons was the true mark of a life investing in others. Lenny was one of a kind.

The discussion began halted and strained. John knew it would be tough; all understood the magnitude of the task. The team felt quite overwhelmed with both the gravity of the situation and the amount of work ahead. The future of the plant rested on the shoulders of these seven individuals. Their decisions determined the site's future.

Lenny spoke up first, "I think one of the issues we face is we often play catch up on quality. We do some of these changes, but don't have a good methodology to always predict what the consequences are going to be – creating scrap, rework and potential for quality escapes." Sarah and Lee both nodded. They had been through the school of hard knocks on that one, most recently Lee. Quality excursions proved painful; both on the cost and productivity side.

Jeff chimed in, "I am concerned about the people. One of the things we have learned in the past is we have to create a reason, a better future, for people to align with change." Several nodded, affirming he was right. This was going to be especially tough, because the employees knew the generic threat of competition coming from another company in Taiwan, China or Mexico. The site was keenly aware of the realities of global competition - competitive threats were part this business. Always, somewhere out there, the competition lurked and it had to be beat.

The difference this time is the threat had a name and faces – Mendal Enterprises. The challenge to Twin Ports livelihood is being architected and driven from the highest levels within the company.

The topic of training and workforce flexibility became the next area of discovery. Jeff shared an article he had been reading in the last issue of HR Monthly. It cited a study 82% of what is not put to use in the first two weeks after training is lost. He read the clip from his laptop, "Employees must use the ideas obtained in the training session immediately upon their return to work. Use it or lose it is a common saying in the training field. It is also a correct statement on us as humans. Employees must be expected to demonstrate the use of the training in a work environment that supports the use of the training."

Mary Ann chimed in, "That is actually good news, isn't it? If we can create an environment, where we are training people and they can put their thoughts, ideas, and skills to use right away; that works in our favor. Not only does the training stick, but there are results from training which can be shown immediately."

Lenny seemed to awaken a bit as he said, "Wow, this is easier than we thought then. All we have to do is stop making products and just go to training." Lee was there with him step for step, "I get it now, it is like a money-making machine, put $1,000 in one end of the training machine and get $5,000 out – all day long." A few eyes rolled, but most were used to sarcasm and appreciated the moment of jocularity.

From a site perspective, John was most concerned about the diskette area. The overall master plan was to shut everything down; however; he had a hunch and shared it with the team. His inclination was if the site could get costs down dramatically in the next six to nine months or maybe twelve on the outside, this group had a slight shot at saving everything. John had not seen the financial analysis – but he knew inherently how big a portion of cash the diskette business generated. His hunch was the effort on diskettes might be enough to swing the net present value calculation, at least for the site. He knew all cash saved in this effort would go right to the bottom line; making a decision to shutter his plant more difficult.

The staff was intrigued and wanted desperately to agree with John; after all, there really was not another path leading to success. The diskette departments equaled about 40% of the employees, but supported 68% of the overall infrastructure, based on the accounting allocation model. The allocations were not done by the site, but calculated annually by the corporate accounting group. It made logical sense, based on volume produced, cost of materials and shipping volume in and out that diskettes would carry a higher burden.

Other discussion ranged around workloads. Who is going to lead these efforts? What current agenda items was the leadership team going to stop doing? And how does the broader staff group get engaged? Each of the people sitting at the table had jobs which fully consumed their time and talents; how was the team going to be able to add more work on top of a full role and make forward progress? The question loomed in everyone's mind, including John.

Somehow, the team had to enlist additional help, he had six direct reports representing the senior leadership. Each had supervisors and/or managers who reported to them. It was the supervisors and managers who really ran the hour-by-hour, day-to-day details. They were the broader plant staff. John had two meetings per week with the various leadership groups. Monday staff meetings were at 9:00 AM. Senior staff, also called the plant leadership team, met on Thursday afternoon, usually from 1:00 PM – 4:00 PM.

The discussion lingered for 45 minutes, which was longer than John allocated on the agenda, but he let it go. The discussion was certainly not going backwards. Even if it was treading water, at this point that was better than sinking.

John jotted down some notes, but he wanted to see how the team would synthesize the discussion. He asked for thoughts and feedback, after a few seconds of silence, Sarah spoke up. "I think we have learned we are goal driven and usually, the bigger than challenge, the better we do." Lee built on the momentum, "When people see a big goal, it is usually something our people want to be a part of."

The surprise comment came from Grant, who until now had been quiet. He said, "Seven cents."

The words hung in the air for a moment, and no one said anything. All implicitly knew what the statement meant.

Seven cents represented a 20% cost reduction from the current unit cost of a single diskette. It was bold challenge. Seven cents represented a departure of $0.025 from where the plant was today. Mary Ann did the math quickly in her head. In total, seven cents represented $15 million dollars out of the operating expense. That was a huge chunk of money, but no one could argue it was probably about in the neighborhood of what was needed to save Twin Ports.

John felt both proud and reassured by his leadership team. His hope was to get them there, to the same place he ended up after his snowshoe trek, now two weeks in his rearview mirror. John believed with his whole being the only way to save Twin Ports was to achieve a goal so big, no one would believe it could be done.

Now his closest advisors and friends came to the same conclusion. The team talked about how the QICR process could be leveraged to take cash out of operations. The annual planning generated a good plan; but if this was going to work, the site needed to create a stretch plan the entire organization could rally around. QICR was a business process, now it had to be a lifesaver.

QICR developed in the division around the older tape products. It pre-dated John, but it was alive and well in Twin Ports. Back when the site was competing with Markwell, XJ8 and Infinitus on audio cartridges, the division assembled a task force to develop the outline of a program focused on two solid measurable deliverables, quality and cost. They balanced each other nicely as good quality certainly supports cost reduction in the form of less rework, waste and better yield.

The other side of the coin tipped when sometimes the business was forced to seek cheaper materials and methods of production to stay cost competitive. This could not be at the expense of quality, but tradeoffs had to be understood and managed. This also forced the entire site to take a hard look at quality, because in the end, quality is in the eye of the user and defines perceptions, trust and value.

The producer can try to understand, measure and monitor, but if the user sees the quality as adequate and the product reliable, it usually comes down to cost and/or brand preferences which drive purchasing decisions.

It is the managers' role to carefully calibrate appropriate expectations, because customer needs can be very subtle. If someone is buying a car, there is a basic quality expectation. This car is going to get them where they need to go in a reliable and safe manner. However, if they are putting down six figures and buying a Ferrari or Lamborghini, they have a very different expectation than if they are buying a Honda or Toyota. They still have the same functional expectation, but the performance is going to be vastly different and measured on a different scale.

John's knew this quality and cost tension from experience. In fact, his favorite QICR story is in metal stamping. The first ten years of the diskette, the site manufactured shutters out of stainless steel. The shutter is the metal door which is spring-loaded and closes to protect the media when the diskette is not being used. The shutter is: rigid, robust and engineered with a significant design margin. In the early days, diskettes were relatively expensive and protected critical data. People tended to treat them with care and the result was a reliable product. At the time, a steel shutter was $0.04 to produce, mostly in material costs.

About five years ago, the development team began exploring replacing steel with aluminum. In fact, Northern Pines was the first in the marketplace with the aluminum shutter. Timing could not have been worse as the release of aluminum shutters coincided with the growth in popularity of the early laptop models. The laptops used a diskette drive which was first half and later one quarter the size in height of a standard desktop drive. In moving from the full height to reduced height, much of the design margin was eliminated to allow the necessary functional parts to fit. There was not a lot of real estate inside the narrower drives and even less margin for variations in the diskette shutter to be accommodated.

Despite the awareness, Northern Pines forged ahead and released the aluminum shutters. Life was good for about two weeks; then technical service started hearing complaints. "My diskette is stuck in my laptop drive, and it won't come out." This created an instant crisis. Customers were reluctant to part with their laptop, so initially technical service sent a technical service person out to investigate.

Indeed, the diskette was stuck in the drive. Doing a bit of surgery generally extracted the diskette, but it took the field engineers awhile to figure out what was going on. They went back to the labs and tested while looking carefully at data. The diskettes coming from the factory seemed generally fine. Factory testing in the form of a product conformance audit remained stable. No signals indicated a change in performance.

A full effort now was on to find out why diskettes were getting stuck in laptop drives. The team worked day and night looking for a cause: packaging, shipping, environmental controls, material composition changes – no path provided any insight. It wasn't until Lenny had a hunch did the problem begin to unfold and true root cause understanding emerge.

Lenny asked two of the summer interns about how they used their diskettes. The summer interns disclosed it was quite common for them to carry diskettes either loose in their backpack, back pocket, or slid into a binder or book. On that tip, Lenny drove up to the university in Fargo and spent a morning observing students use diskettes coming and going from the computing lab. Sure enough, 73% of the students stored them in one of the three methods the interns claimed. A minority of students, about one in four, still used a storage case to carefully place their diskettes in when they were finished with it.

The takeaway was unmistakable. Nothing had changed from a quality perspective. The diskettes met all requirements; however, the use conditions had changed dramatically. The advent of the laptop and customer's general care and handling created a convergence where now incidental damage was causing shutters to deform and subsequently lodge in drives.

John learned an important lesson through this experience. It is always wise to stay close to the customer. Sometimes the market shifts dramatically, and if one does not have an ear to the rail, these gaps in knowledge do irreparable harm to the business. In the end, everyone learned the treatment of a $1.00 diskette is much different than a $0.15 diskette. The painful lesson is the hundreds of thousands of dollars spent replacing laptop drives due to a malformed disk being inserted into the reduced height drive.

Through the simple exercise and analysis, the problem needing to be solved was identified. The market had changed and there were newer use cases not being considered in the product development. How a product is used is not a static event, it changes with the times. The team brainstormed about what to do and came up with a three-point plan.

1) Educate people about proper care and use
2) Create a 'lip' on the plastic shell to give a little more design margin in the narrow drives
3) Make sure all the shutters are pointed inward (vs spread wider at the open end than at the bookend), to avoid catching and experiencing premature deformation.

The business struggled through a few difficult few months before the technical efforts generated positive results. The consolation prize was the accelerated learning curve and the ability in hindsight to watch competitors struggle with many of the same issues. Two of the competitors were in and out twice before they found the root cause. Northern Pines was the first in the market by nine months, resulting in material savings of $8 million dollars over three quarters. Some pain, but also tremendous gain.

Slowly the competitors followed and began to enjoy some of the material savings; however, Twin Ports didn't rest on its laurels. The engineers knew there had to be yet a better way. The initial development team had spec'd out anodized aluminum.

The evolution of aluminum shutters was just beginning. Another breakthrough came during one of the QICR brainstorming sessions. A team was finishing lunch and one of the operators made an offhanded comment, "I wonder where Coke gets their aluminum?" John looked at Grant and Grant looked at John. Interesting question on many levels – it was thin gauge, very high volume and came in roll-stock. Too many similarities to ignore. Immediately Grant knew his assignment.

It turns out a company in Colorado supplied all the major beverage producers. They made coiled aluminum from ingots by the train-car load and current costs averaged almost a penny cheaper than present sourced cost of anodized aluminum.

Coincidentally, the available aluminum measures within half a thousandth of an inch of the current material specification for shutter material, which through some simple tooling modifications allowed Twin Ports to adopt the Coke spec. The best result was a long-term supplier who understood ultra-high volume manufacturing. Few businesses measure their output in millions of units per day, and Coke is one of them.

A near Diet Coke addict, John never thought to consider aluminum can/aluminum shutter or its common ground. This discovery illustrated the unique and creative element of QICR in a very tangible way.

The company implemented the change to beverage can aluminum three years ago; and based on present volumes, the site saved an additional $18 million dollars based on one brilliant out of the box idea. The ultra-cool aspect of this is the idea didn't come from a degreed scientist or highly paid, newly minted MBA. One of Twin Ports' production operators saw unique perspective while eating lunch. "Hey! This is aluminum. They must use a lot of it, because there sure are a lot of cans of pop and beer consumed every year." It was too obvious.

John summarized the discussion, "So we need to set out the super aggressive target of $0.07 for diskettes. We somehow need to emphasize training and we are going to have to run our QICR process like we never have before." Heads nodded in agreement.

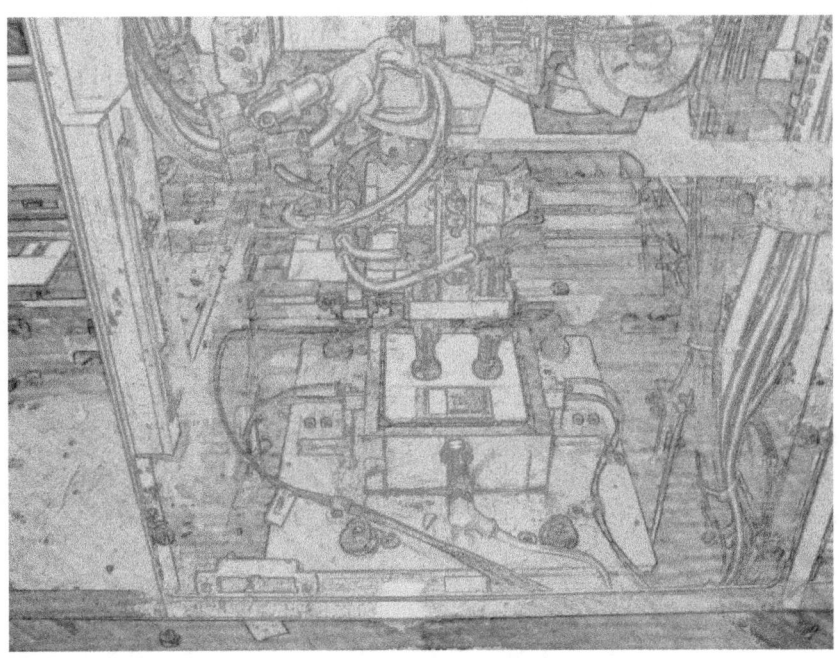

The Shutter Insertion Station

John thought carefully and chose his words to encourage this talented group, "This is good. Today we are not locking into anything. Decisions like this are huge and we all need to be 100% committed to the cause." John continued, "We'll keep working at this in our next meeting. Keep chipping away at the iceberg. The goal is two weeks from today; we must have a solid plan."

The meeting concluded and as the staff filed to the door, Jeff pulled John aside. Jeff attended a regional human resources roundtable meeting and shared with John that SunGrown, the new agriculture processing plant, was going to be opening sooner than planned. The area produced an abundance of wheat and other grains. Last year, the farmers merged to form a co-op and produce pasta and flours for the commercial restaurant industry. SunGrown hoped for an August 1st opening, but the winter construction season had been favorable and their equipment builds seemed to be ahead of schedule.

This was not necessarily bad news. One of the things in the back of John's mind, and other minds, too, was the reality the site required a sizable reduction in employees. The likelihood of downsizing 25 salaried positions and probably 75 to 100 non-exempt/hourly workers to make this reduced cost equation work loomed large. John hadn't done the exact numbers, but back of the napkin with current payroll at $30 million, John knew about $6-7 million overall had to come out of salary and wage expenses. This was not going to be without some job losses at the site.

After the SunGrown topic, John asked Jeff how he thought the session had gone. Jeff was generally optimistic, but in his 25 years here, this was the biggest challenge he had seen. John nodded in agreement.

John said, "Thanks so much for your insights and stability. This is going to be a rocky trail, and we are going to have to vent from time to time." Jeff asked, "Between us, what are the odds?" Jeff and John had known each other a long time; Jeff knew John could give him the straight story. John said, "I wish it were 50/50, but honestly, Jeff, I think it is more like 30/70. We just don't have a lot of time. This plant has generated results for nearly 30 years, but to create the results we need to, I am afraid we may be at the end of the runway and not yet off the ground."

Jeff smiled and nodded. Jeff's honest estimate was a little more pessimistic than John's 30/70, but on the flipside, he knew this plant was capable of some amazing results.

Chapter 12: Another Fork in the Road.

Kristin and John tried to get away from time to time. It was good for their sanity and marriage; although it probably didn't happen often enough. Both acknowledged the stress in each other's lives; each from different sources. The truth is both their jobs stressed them out. John was astute enough to realize there was no value in pretending who had more. Kristin stayed home all day with five kids; no question - she has more stress. Honestly, some days John did not know how she managed it all. At least, John interacted with adults every day and worked to save the world of diskette manufacturing from calamity. Kristin's day consisted of watching Barney, changing diapers, wiping runny noses, getting kids ready for activities, running to activities, getting supper ready and keeping a busy household running. John and Kristin worked as a team. She loved her job and John loved her.

Time alone with Kristin doing things not involving kids happened rarely; it took a deliberate effort to keep the marriage strong by investing time, energy and effort. Both John and Kristin realized in these days of simple, no fault, easy divorce, married people slowly migrate to roommates and love is lost. For them, growing apart is not an option. They stood before friends, family and God and committed to this gig of 'til death do us part. John and Kristin's parents celebrated long marriages. They were not perfect, but they definitely lived through the best of times and some tougher times as well. Their parents passed this heritage to them and hoped and prayed they would pass this legacy on to their own children.

John didn't know about other couples and their getaway practices, but for John and Kristin, there are a few givens. They try to get away ideally, at least, every two weeks, but more practical is monthly and sometimes it is even less frequently. Kate, their 16-year-old babysitter was available; so, this was somewhat of a last-minute thing.

Kate was awesome and the kids loved her. She came with a duffle bag full of new toys. Not that the Stanton kids were deprived of toys, but somehow when new ones show up – one would think it was Christmas. Shrieks of delight filled the house as Kate pulled out new dolls for Caroline; and for the boys, some kind of rock 'em sock 'em thing. John decided to make it easier on Kate and bring Mark along on the date. Believe it or not, one down from five is truly a break.

Date night often entailed a trip to Fargo. If they timed it right, Kristin could pick him up from work at 5:15 PM and head north right from the plant. They could eat dinner, have a few hours to shop and be home before it got too late. Kate had school tomorrow, so there was a promise to be back in town by 10:30.

There were several stops on the evening agenda. John's list included a stop at Home Depot for a few supplies. Kristin needed to run into Pier 1 Imports, and if possible, a stop at the bookstore. The final stop at the bookstore is always a relaxing way to cap off the evening, some quiet time for coffee and book browsing. John and Kristin made an agreement on the way on up a quick dinner was in order, so the first stop was at a deli on the west end of town.

The errands wrapped up, and the threesome arrived at Barnes & Noble at 8:30 pm. The hour afforded a little down time to look at books, grab a cup of coffee and still make the one-hour trip home by the appointed hour. John picked up some books on starting a small business and living off the grid, and Kristin selected gardening and a travel book on Russia for her looking. This time was always a highlight for both. Reading was a passion; however, with kids, work and life, reading became a pastime pushed down lower on the list of priorities. Both had a great time, a little conversation, some people watching and most importantly, a chance to be together. These times were rare, but both treasured the hour and it went by quickly.

John loaded Mark into his car seat. Tucked in his puffy warm snowsuit, he was big eyes now. A few miles in the quiet warm car would put him to sleep. The February air was cold and the night sky was clear. John maneuvered the car up onto the interstate ramp and toward the south into the snowy prairie. It must have been nearly a full moon, because once they left the lights of town, they could almost travel without the headlights on.

A few miles out of town, Kristin reminded John of a discussion they had in November. The conversation occurred in the same car traveling down to Iowa to visit family for Thanksgiving. It went something like this, she said, "Do you remember last winter, before Christmas when we donated some money to a charity called Reece's Rainbow?" John did. The boys got so excited and took some of their own savings to send to special needs kids they did not even know in the hopes for their adoption by a forever family. "Yes," John said. Kristin paused and said, "I have been thinking and praying, and John, I think we should consider adopting a special needs child from Eastern Europe."

John heard the words, but without fully comprehending the meaning. They already had five kids, one with special needs, and never talked about adopting. In fact, Mark was going to be the last Stanton child. John lacked any context for her words. In some sense, she might have been saying, "John, I think we should move to Mars."

Looking back, John recalls this was one of those surreal moments where he heard himself saying words without being fully conscious of what he was saying. His lips mouthed the words, "I agree. I think we should, too." There are at least a thousand good reasons why they should not do this. First and selfishly, there was the near crisis with Northern Pines. Second, they already had five kids. They had no training in raising a special needs child other than being parents of Caroline. Where was the money going to come from? Who would take care of their five during this time? How could John get away from work to manage an overseas adoption?

In the end, a decision was a decision and a commitment was a commitment. John had clarity and conviction to say, "I think we should, too." There was only one reason to say yes, and that was because John knew deep in his heart it was the right thing to do. Despite replaying the scene repeatedly in his mind, John could not rationalize it, but he would do the same thing again. To this day, the response transcends his understanding and strangely enough, he is at peace with the ambiguity.

It was a moment of clarity when even though this was a road far less traveled than many, John knew for him and for his family, somehow, they would receive the grace and strength to make this happen.

Tonight, on a crisp February night, driving from Fargo back to Twin Ports, the memory of a discussion from three months ago, was still fresh. It was one of those 'this is going to change our life' discussions.

For both John & Kristin, the intensity and desire to adopt grew, slowly at first and not without fear and anxiety. Over time, both became committed to helping these children, with added resolve to take the steps to save a child's life. To some it may sound overly dramatic, but it was true. These children were growing up with no hope, no future and a very miserable life with an equally short life expectancy. This was becoming a mission to save a precious, human life.

Even as they neared Twin Ports, John's thoughts came back to Caroline, his little princess. Right now, she was warm, safe and loved by all who knew her. John thought about the faces he had seen on the Reece's Rainbow website – including one photo of the child which hung on his family Christmas tree. Most of the children's faces were empty of emotion. The only feelings they knew were neglect, loneliness, and despair. Yet, these were just children, and behind the look in their eyes, John had to wonder. Is there a shred of hope? Do they have the capacity to still love and be loved?

No child should experience confusion, uncertainty, and disconnection from the love and security of a family. All these children find themselves in painfully difficult circumstances through no fault of their own. It was simply their diagnosis of Down syndrome or some other medical condition along with an unaccepting society which placed them in a cold sterile orphanage.

It gnawed at John his daughter-to-be was likely cold, scared and had never known the feeling of love. The only knowledge John had of her was a small photo and a name, Viktoria.

Perhaps the contrast and inequity are why the answer was what it was when Kristin asked the first question. Besides that, it was the right thing to do. John and his family had so much and these children had literally nothing today and even less to look forward to tomorrow.

John and Kristin claimed no expertise in raising a child with Down syndrome. In this short period of time John had been dad to Caroline, he had come to understand a few basic things. First, it is a bit cliché, but she is NOT disabled; she is differently abled. The distinction begins a new dialogue, rather than reinforces stereotypes. Caroline, John's precious daughter, absolutely lights up a room. She is full of life, joy, energy and every day, she finds new ways to make John a very happy father.

John would not change anything with Caroline. Even if he could turn back time, he would not wish away Down syndrome. John believes one of the primary reasons Caroline was placed in his life is a reminder for him to be sensitive to those whose are differently abled, to learn compassion and to slow down. John defines himself as an introverted techie, but those around him see aspects of a classic type A. The DNA fueling his body tells him to strive, achieve, push, accomplish.

Caroline showed him there is a different way to live. When John wants to be doing something all the time, Caroline quietly nudges him and teaches him daily that at times *being* is better than *doing*. When John has a tough day, that pig-tailed, gap-toothed, little wonder comes with a book. She just wants to be with him, and a forced change of pace makes some of the weightiest of life's problems melt away.

Caroline possesses tremendously astute insights and notices the most amazing things. John recalled recently, they were out on a walk and she pointed out the moon. Part of the nightly routine included reading *Good Night Moon*, and on her own, Caroline made the connection between the moon in the book and the moon she discovered. Her enthusiasm as she discovers her world becomes contagious. After seeing the moon, she wants to know everything about the moon. Who lives there? What do they eat? Do they have cartoons on the moon? When can we go to the moon for vacation?

John and Kristin never questioned Caroline's fate. From the moment of her birth, family and friends surrounded her with love that grows deeper by the day. Children born with special needs in Eastern Europe don't share the same outcome. In fact, almost all parents of children with mental or physical diagnoses are encouraged to leave their children at the hospital and go home; the state automatically becomes the caretaker.

The final few miles of 'date night' alternated between talking through all the next steps and some quiet time continuing to mull this major life decision. Initially, John and Kristin agreed to keep this decision to themselves until more of the details emerged. Dozens of hurdles needed clearing before this could be a reality. The news leaked to a few people. Most of the responses were positive, but some level of surprise and inquiry accompanied the news. John and Kristin were fine with that. These people knew them and knew their hearts. It would take some time for everyone to see the Stanton's were serious and intent on bringing an orphan from Ukraine into their family.

They arrived into the driveway at 10:21 PM. Kristin carried Mark into the house, and John stayed outside keeping the car warm. Kate came out a few minutes later and John drove down 7th Street, up to 15th Avenue and down a few blocks to where she lived with her family.

John loved living in a small town. Everything they needed (except Home Depot and Barnes and Noble) were available in the little community. John was close to the plant, so even at 10:30 PM; he could look up to the north and could see the steam coming off the stack from the boiler unit at the plant.

The factory was running the normal schedule. Twin Ports operated seven days per week, 24 hours per day and about 363 days per year. The plant was always down for Christmas and generally took 4th of July off for preventive maintenance activities on the plant utilities and systems. Typically, the site did not shut down for weather or many other circumstances. Northern Pines Technology ran their plants this way. It was too time consuming and costly to shut down and start up plants with coaters. In addition, with the high capital costs, it just made sense to install and run it 24/7 – maximum utilization.

John planned to run by the plant on the way home way to pick up his car, but with the deep discussion about adoption and Ukraine, both completely forgot Kristin had picked up John from work, so his car was at the plant.

John stopped the truck at the stop sign before turning onto 11th Street. At 10:30 on a Thursday night, the odds of another car coming up behind him were slim to none. John texted Grant quickly and asked if Grant could pick John up at 7:30 and give him a ride to work – his text came back, "SURE," so John turned the Suburban to the south and headed home.

Chapter 13: Harsh Realities

Fueled with a large strong regular coffee from Barnes & Nobles, he could not sleep. He debated if he should drive over to the plant and do a quick walk around. He did so about once a month, and people seemed to appreciate the fact he stopped by after hours to check on things and to visit from time to time.

John could not get the mental image of little boys and girls with Down syndrome sleeping in their beds a half a world away. What did they feel? Fear, sickness, despair, cold? How many would be sent to a mental institution before they could get to Ukraine? Was Vika even still alive? Why do we have so much and them so little?

John went to his study and pulled up news reports on the fate of children with disabilities around the world. The information was sobering. In many countries, especially those in which most families only plan for one child, if a child is delivered with a disability, it is abandoned. It is often the doctors who counsel the parents, and it is very common to hear the educated professionals say, "Go home, forget about this child, have another, lose your memories of this child – the state will take care of them."

Millions of abandon children around the world live as wards of the state. They move first to baby hospitals and then are transferred to orphanages until they reach five or six years old. A majority of the children remain confined to cribs, lacking any form of interaction, affection or anything beyond the most very basic of care. All are mistreated by neglect. For many, worse things happen. Commonly these children succumb to illness or just give up hope. They learn not to cry, because no one will come if they do. It is a hopeless existence.

After the children surpass the age limit of the orphanage, they transfer to state mental institutions, equally heinous places. Some continue in the same existence they experienced in the orphanages, the crib replaced by a bed. Many do not survive yielding to illness, neglect, abuse or hopelessness.

John and Kristin held the power to fix the problem, at least for one child, saving a child from enduring a tortured life. For them, it seemed the only humane thing to do.

Somewhere in the back of his mind, John remembered the two little children in India from years before. Now, he realized seeing those Indian children were much more than just coincidence. John believed he saw those children preparing him for a future moment of truth. He didn't believe in coincidences. That brief encounter in India marked a divine appointment, so that when the time came to be accountable, his heart was ready.

Ahead for both John and Kristin were all the steps and processes yet to unfold for this adoption to become a possibility. The first steps entailed registering with an agency and making the request for adoption. At the same time, they needed to complete a home study by an authorized agency. Then, it is a waiting game. The process sounded like lots of paperwork, formalities, and ultimately, lots of waiting; waiting for the officials in the country to issue a letter of invitation.

The paperwork and adoption process could take as much as a year or as little as six months. The adoption process for special needs kids in this part of the world is much different from a 'healthy' child. The legal aspects are all the same; but the waiting list is generally much shorter than for someone who wants a 'healthy, aka normal' child.

Sleep did not come easily this night, John last looked at the clock on his way upstairs and it showed 1:15 AM.

Halfway around the world – a new day was starting.

Chapter 14: Reaching Out for Help.

John knew his 'save the plant' endeavor needed additional help. One of the guiding elements from the framework or straw man being put together was improvements in training. John's team was well trained. In fact, 1% of the staffing budget was dedicated to training, developing new knowledge and skill improvement across the site. Throughout the years, the team learned quality circles, JIT, Theory of Constraints, Re-engineering, Six Sigma, Lean and just about every other variant of process improvement methodology known to man.

The site kept up-to-date with mandatory training: HAZ-MAT, confined space and lock out/tag out. The site was in the process of implementing ISO 14001, the international environmental standard to improve environmental performance. Each of the areas of operation underwent extensive studying and surveying, identifying potentially significant environmental impacts across the entire facility.

John knew workforce flexibility needed addressing as a primary issue for the site. Historically, the product lines enjoyed relatively stable production with staffing remaining consistent. When analyzing the trends for the month, quarter and yearly, he recognized a bit of seasonality. However, for the most part, the output required to support the demand was stable. The site never overcapitalized for capacity. Perhaps this philosophy was due to a conservative approach or the desire of not being labeled as money hungry. John and his predecessors always took a fiscally conservative approach, and now John was thinking the lean approach to capitalization was potentially a driver in site success.

At the end of the day, it always seemed as if there was enough capacity, albeit a bit tight. That natural tension caused the lines to be efficient, shrewd in the planning; and from time to time run with a bit more overtime than most people would like. It was always only temporary.

The workforce was well-trained around one line, or maybe best case, two. However, when two lines were down, the ability to move resources to another product line was somewhat limited. Even within the larger departments such as diskettes which contained multiple areas (metal stamping, molding, assembly and packout), there was not enough cross training between the departments.

Recently, Grant, along with the planners, were mentioning the compounding impact of demand changes. The site plans and runs to the business Sales and Operational Planning Process (S&OP). The sales staff estimates numbers and product mix, planners in operations recommends a supply plan based on inventory targets and other quantifiable factors. This is aggregated up to the executive team who reviews it. It is not a direct approval, but more of an oversight role. The site planners oversee supply decisions. Many of those with a pulse on the business could sense product demand shift. Signs of change were most visible in the oldest tape formats.

At Twin Ports, many of the legacy products used to run seven days a week, 24 hours a day. The volumes now were just a fraction of full volume and output. The impact of the slowdown meant running the line three to five days a month. This was a problem on the labor side more than anything else was. The equipment was old, paid for, fully depreciated and only handled a small percent of the overall plant burden. However, when the skilled labor expertise was needed to run the line and run it well, with high quality output, the site needed to have well-trained people. John couldn't get those folks off the street, so to speak. He needed a trained and flexible workforce.

A concept from Training Within Industry [TWI] intrigued John. He recently rediscovered an article in *Industry Week* highlighting how the "Old Was New Again." The article mentioned seeing resurgence across competitive industries. It was a recycled idea. Indeed, the concept had been around a while. John picked up the phone to dial

Steve's number, and at the same time searched Wikipedia. John found the condensed version of TWI.

> The Training Within Industry (TWI) service was created by the United States Department of War, running from 1940 to 1945 within the War Manpower Commission. The purpose was to provide consulting services to war-related industries whose personnel were being conscripted into the US Army at the same time the War Department was issuing orders for additional matériel. It was apparent that the shortage of trained and skilled personnel at precisely the time they were needed most would impose a hardship on those industries, and that only improved methods of job training would address the shortfall. By the end of World War II, over 1.6 million workers in over 16,500 plants had received a certification.

The specific aspect which piqued John's curiosity was the fact the Northern Pines site contained some of the same attributes required during the war – rapid skill enhancement, flexibility and a systematic way to accomplish this. After reading the article, John believed TWI was the best hope for solving at least a few of the training-related problems.

John reached out to the Dakota Manufacturing Partnership; Steve's friendly voice answered after three rings. John could hear from the ambient noise Steve was traveling in the car. John began, "Steve, John here from Twin Ports. How are you?" Steve responded, "Well, if you count my companions as a few hundred cattle and a few oil rigs – could not be better." John knew immediately Steve must be out in the western part of the state. A few manufacturers still existed out there, but most of the states' manufacturing base focused on the eastern border closer to transportation and workers up and down the Red River Valley. Cattle barons and oil speculators reserved the western part of the state – and those people desiring to live without neighbors within many miles.

After some small talk, John targeted the bull's-eye. "Steve, we need some consulting help and relatively fast." John briefly explained the last few weeks with the site launching a focused cost reduction initiative. At first, Steve listened patiently, and then peppered John with a dozen questions, which John had come to expect. John explained the plan, the rationale and the time constraints. They ended with a commitment by Steve to check his consultants' schedules once he had network access and get back to John. The bottom line: Expect someone to show up by middle of next week.

The discussion ended, and as John tried to sign off, Steve got pensive. John inquired to Steve about his sudden change in tone, and Steve reminded John TWI impacted the development and use of kaizen and standard work (a mainstay) at Toyota. Toyota and Job Instruction still teach the fundamental elements encapsulated within their work systems. The kaizen methodology is a direct descendant of Job Methods, and the United States has the Japanese plus Deming to thank for taking a good idea and advancing it further.

Steve was a true general in the war, fighting in the trenches for continued success and prosperity in American manufacturing. What John appreciated about Steve was he was not a protectionist; he was a realist who only asked for a level playing field. Steve understood very well the globalization forces at play.

Steve witnessed the battles firsthand and acted as a veteran of American manufacturing. When the playing field is level, it is a great competitive battle. However, when there is an unfair trade policy advantage, the United States consistently comes out on the losing end. In the big picture, Steve could see the short-term gain of saving a buck, but the gain was not a very good tradeoff with the loss of jobs and economic fortitude. Steve was pragmatic. The strongest would survive in a fair fight, based on a common baseline of costs. If someone wanted to cook the books and only look at labor costs or not consider subsidies or other factors companies or governments provided, the data could be bent to say almost anything.

As John hung up the phone, it was with a new respect for the work the Manufacturing Partnerships across the US to ensure industry remains highly competitive in the global economy.

The manufacturing partnerships are nonprofit organizations that exist across the US as willing partners in helping to create a strong and vibrant manufacturing sector. In some states, partnerships combine into regional organizations often coupled with economic development. Other states offer the services as an extension service, working out of universities. In general, the groups exist with moderate state and federal government funding as well as with some service revenues generated from the work done. John knew across the US they were an untapped resource for the type of assistance he needed.

Maybe he was biased, but in his experience, they had always done great work. John was just thankful to have as many allies as possible in his quest to save Twin Ports.

Chapter 15: Back in Class

John asked Lenny; aka Professor Garst to lead the QICR portion of Blue Ox. John could get away with ribbing Lenny, because at times he had a professorial aura to him. John also knew this was serious business and Lenny could get the job done.

He suggested the first session begin with an overview. It should outline the issues, create a sense of urgency and then solicit a strong commitment from each of the managers to drive cost reduction and quality improvements in their respective areas.

John normally did not do this, but he called a mandatory staff meeting on Saturday morning. The intent was to raise the sense of urgency. There probably had been less than ten emergency staff meetings in the 30-year plant history; John knew this would up the ante and let all know the plant faced a serious crisis.

John would never dare to call an emergency meeting during the summer months. But he felt he could pull this off in mid-winter. After all, what else is there to do in North Dakota mid-March? The plant runs 24/7 and so staff is used to being available every day, all hours.

John had an ulterior motive for calling a Saturday meeting. Twin Ports hired new members of the staff, and John wanted to see how well they were integrating within their new peer group. Moving up the ranks into a leadership position at Twin Ports marked one of the toughest transitions, especially among peers. John knew once the rest of the plant employees saw their leaders there on a Saturday morning, not only a few eyebrows would rise, but speculation would swirl as well. John decided a few trips throughout the plant during the morning to seed the cloud with salient information hopefully would continue to spread through the rest of the day shift and across the night shift to again tap into the informal plant communications network.

QICR is part of the DNA of Twin Ports. While the formal origins of QICR at Twin Ports remain a bit sketchy, John remembers the process was well established in the plant when he arrived. However, like many business processes, it evolved and was refined over time. The process and approach seemed to be a good match for the site's culture and resonated well with the people. For Twin Ports, it boiled down to an aggressive, but common sense approach in running a business. It also unleashed a common cause and a mechanism for people at all levels in the organization to turn good ideas into actions.

The natural cadence of the process began in the summer, starting with broad team-based events where open-ended brainstorming generates a list of new ideas. Some may be crazy, some impossible, but over the next few months, the department managers and engineers analyze ideas for impact, feasibility and resource needs. Through an analysis and vetting process, they would build the annual operating plan based on these commitments from the engineers and managers. To ensure timely completion, the projects also included the overall personal development process, which employees and their managers reviewed results quarterly and formulated plans for the next quarter of work.

John had to pull in the schedule for the annual QICR process, starting four to five months earlier than was typical; mostly because of the ticking clock. No time remained to wait for the routine cadence with the current crisis and threat.

This process was the fastest way John knew to jumpstart and deliver quick results. After today, no one could believe it was business as usual.

John kicked off the meeting by thanking everyone for spending the Saturday morning at the plant. As expected, he heard a few groans within the crowd, but the fresh cinnamon rolls and strong coffee took the edge off in a hurry.

John explained two things. Since this was the broader site staff; he had to be a bit more cautious in his choice of words. First, he said, "the site has become a little stagnant. Several areas hit a plateau in performance and it is going to be a problem for the site if action isn't taken." Everyone knew diskette cost had not moved for several months. Along with this fact, Twin Ports missing several commitments recently affected a few key cost reduction items needed in the next several months to drive cost even lower. Second, John reiterated the quickest way for Twin Ports to get the wrong kind of executive attention was to miss on the site's metrics: safety, quality and cost.

John turned it over to "the professor" to begin the lecture. It was not intended to be a lecture, but a training session for the entire staff on the QICR process, its use, and most importantly, how to set up the event, create the plan and drive results.

Lenny was well suited for the role of teacher. He was highly respected and passionate about quality. One of the more challenging aspects of this process is managing the message between quality improvement and cost reduction. Those two goals are not mutually exclusive. However, in a typical audience, some inevitably hear the quality message while others hear the cost message. A rare few can harmonize both quality with cost and seek solutions which accomplish both. Lenny articulated the importance of quality and could strike the appropriate balance better than anyone else.

Lenny explained the four tenets.

- Drive continuous improvement
- Identify cost and quality improvement efforts
- Identify individual program strategy to achieve business objectives in manufacturing cost and quality

- Provide focus on which project(s) to drive

Lenny stopped here to emphasize a point, of which John had not given much thought. QICR is not a set of tools; it is a process. Lenny explained where some methodologies break down. Companies rely on the tool and apply the tool whether it makes sense within a certain situation or not. QICR was about the <u>analysis</u> and <u>critical thinking</u> – the tools came later. John had probably heard this before; but in this context, it was more impactful.

Many engineers acquire a natural inclination to 'do' when sometimes it is best to 'think'. The skill to think does not happen overnight. But put a group of technical people together in a room, remove the constraints, free the critical thinking process, reduce or eliminate assumptions and paradigms, and it is amazing what creativity can be unleashed.

Lenny went on to explain much of the success came down to pre-work and having the right information available. The planning and preparation phases occurred simultaneously. Planning contained all the basic elements of finding the right location and time (daylong, offsite) and creating a theme. This became one of the most fun elements of the process. Lenny explained important of adding in some fun activities during the day, either sport related in playing kickball, volleyball and Frisbee golf or some other fun event.

The preparation phase arguably was the most critical. This provided the information and steering the team needed to quickly sort through ideas and work on ones that needed further refinement.

Lenny explained the processes in detail. It relied on data, data and more data.

Lenny was on a roll now, "Just because Dr. Sputnik discovered something 30 years ago in the lab doesn't mean it is still applicable (or even true) today! We hang onto some outdated ideas as if these ideas are carved in stone, this is not the case. Open your mind and think. Don't say no, say why not! Think critically."

This was one of the topics Lenny was passionate about and why he made such a good quality manager. He was pragmatic and an excellent critical thinker. He relied on data, thought systematically and generally biased toward the practical. Lenny rarely got lost in the proverbial forest.

Lenny outlined the four main areas then elaborated on each one.

1. Develop internal benchmark data of key historical performance
2. Develop external benchmark data
3. Develop information for cost understanding
4. Gather product and component samples

Step 1: Internal Benchmark Data

The site fortunately has a good history of internal data. Data exists for productivity, output, and labor spending for the last ten years. Supply chain analysts applied forecasting to these plots to show both the data trends and actual trends. Models also created and applied to determine reasonable objectives for the future, based on the past performance. Managers and engineers look at yield, cycle times, cost, productivity, maintenance costs, labor cost, and just about anything else measurable.

Step 2: External Benchmark Data

This was a favorite topic of John's, perhaps because years ago he was involved in the first global benchmark study. These sessions are one of the primary reasons why the site invested the time and money to benchmark global competitors. Not only are deep insights gained from the research, but also better knowledge is established to allow the engineers to construct competitors' unit cost models. Once the cost comparisons are established – it becomes much easier to see the entire landscape and leverage knowledge for competitive gain.

The local technical service engineer at the plant also bought product in the region and makes it available, so participants can tear apart competitors' samples, look for details in their molding, or marks on the plastic where it may be possible to get some insights into their approach to tooling and methods of manufacture. The comprehensive study looked at more than 50,000 diskettes from around the world to get a reasonable sample size for statistical significance.

Step 3: Derived Information for Cost Understanding

Lenny went on to explain some of the best ideas come from the factory floor. He relayed the story about the soda pop can innovation and how that changed the approach to thinking about ideas. Lenny said, "We now have the same aluminum adorning our diskettes that you have in front of you on your Coke can. Highlighting again the power and value of an idea; one that until we protected it – was available to all. That simple connecting of the dots and creation of an idea is worth millions of dollars and counting. This site would not be business today if it had stayed on steel shutters and we have a competitive advantage from everyone else in the world who wants to use this specific aluminum."

Lenny showed a slide detailing the other cost analysis techniques commonly used for QICR planning including: Benefits of incremental improvement (1% yield, runtime and productivity), Pareto breakdown of unit cost, allocation breakdown, volume/cost projections, raw material cost history/projections and status of existing programs as well as some not directly cost related but include organization structure and responsibilities.

Not all of these are always used during each session necessarily, but between the initial planning, brainstorming and analysis, the data set provides consistency and teams rely upon for baseline data.

The agenda called for a break at 10:00, and this allowed the staff to stand up and stretch a little bit. John asked Lenny how he thought it was going. Lenny replied, "I am really impressed with Tom, Katie and Kristi, our newest members of the staff. They really seem to be intent on seeing this for what it is." John saw the back of their heads mostly, so he took Lenny's observations as good news.

When the session resumed at 10:15, John ducked out to take a quick walk around the plant. He enjoyed being at the site after hours. It was a different place. The sounds and smells were unique to this facility. As John walked past metal stamping, he heard the gentle but rapid *thunk, thunk* of the tooling as it pressed out shutters at 150 cycles per minute. The molding presses sounded of a deeper rumble when the clamps forced the platen closed every 4.35 seconds, and packaging always sounded like one continuous air leak. Pneumatic actuators and air cylinder leaks made the area sounded like a bike tire with a persistent leak.

John sought out a few of his friends on D crew who happened to be working on this winter Saturday. Sandy was one of them in assembly. John went over to Line 4 and began a discussion. He asked, "How is the line doing today?" Sandy responded, "A little trouble with the spring bowls, the springs seem a little sticky today, we have had to wipe the bowls out twice already." Sandy went on to say, "other lines are having a similar problem, so must be a supplier issue; I have already filled out a corrective action request for supplier management to follow up on." Once the rapport had been established, John could segue into why the staff was huddled in the conference room. John jokingly told her, "They didn't get their work done during the week, so I called a special unpaid work session for Saturday morning, getting to spend time with their best friends." "What a deal!" Sandy chuckled.

Sandy knew the staff was working hard to keep the plant growing and strong. John made a trip to the north building as well. A few carefully crafted tidbits would also help the cause and keep the rumor mill from running amok with nonsense. For now, this was all about messaging, letting the entire plant team know things were critical for the Twin Ports site.

John may not be the sharpest knife in the drawer, but he had learned he could not possibly communicate to the entire plant about the meeting, but a few well-placed pieces of information to the right people would get most of the message across. Those who had good information were not shy about sharing what they knew and naming their source. The accuracy did not get much better than directly from the Plant Manager's mouth.

As John ambled back into the training room, Lenny finished up on the mechanics of the QICR session.

The list resembled something of a punch list with options to consider depending on how the session evolved.

- ✓ Session mechanics
    - o Select topics
    - o Break into teams
    - o Team brainstorming
- ✓ Groups rotate between topics and renew brainstorming
- ✓ Develop summary of ideas
- ✓ Estimate of cost savings developed
- ✓ Estimate of level of feasibility, risk, implementation cost
- ✓ Each group presents summary
- ✓ With prioritization (Big-easy / Small - hard) in Four quadrants
- ✓ Assign follow-up to appropriate teams
    - o Material related – sourcing
    - o Productivity – operations
    - o Product design – design & engineering
    - o Equipment – maintenance and engineering
    - o Organization – roles & responsibilities – management team

Lenny asked if there were any questions. Katie, the newest supervisor asked, "How many projects can be done if the list is longer than the people and time to complete them?" Lenny answered, "Great question, Katie. That is why the follow-up is so important. We must ensure not only do we figure out what ideas are the best, but if they can be implemented"

Lenny went on to relay a story which was an appropriate end for the day.

Lenny began, "Most people took for granted the little read/write latch in the upper right hand corner of the diskette. In fact, most people probably didn't even know what it was for. If in the closed position, it allowed the diskette to be READ ONLY, so no new data could be written until the latch was switched.

Lenny continued, "Our vendor in the Twin Cities, Progressive Plastics ran the molds to make this feature for the product. A long while ago, the sourcing manager had decided it just wasn't worth the hassle to run them internally. Over time, the cost of tooling maintenance, labor and overhead just continued to climb. We were paying about $0.0105 per latch. Again, 'diskette math' comes into play. It cost only a little over a penny each, but multiplied by 650 million per year does not take a math genius to figure out we were paying almost $7 million a year for read/write latches."

A QICR session several years ago challenged this idea and saw the opportunity where some only see a hassle. The story goes something like this: If Twin Ports really hired the best molders in the world, and in addition, contained a fully integrated tool shop in-house, there must be a better way.

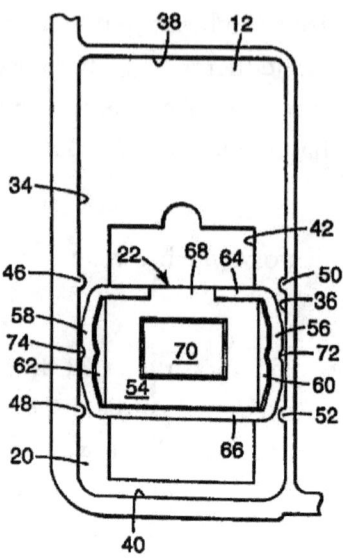

Filed under World Intellectual Property Organization WO 97/07508

However, this was not where the site wanted to hit a single, to use a baseball analogy. It would have been quite straightforward to take the traditional approach of just bringing the molds in house. Best guess, an engineer could develop a process and qualify in a quarter or two. Benefit, maybe a few percent savings on overhead and materials. Bottom line, the approach would not save a lot of money – remaining would be: material cost, equipment and maintenance cost, labor costs. Even 10% better, it still would be $700,000 a year savings and that was a stretch. In parallel, there also were issues in assembly as these small latches would bunch up, attract static and not go down the assembly feeder bowl very well.

To further the baseball analogy, several of the technical folks were looking for a home run, and not just a one-run home run, but a grand slam. They weren't looking for small potatoes. These engineers and technicians wanted to solve a cost problem, solve a run time problem, and maybe even make a quality improvement."

Lenny explained, "Our best engineering and tooling minds took on the challenge and came up with a way to create the feature as part of our current diskette shell molding process. Without going into too much technical detail, they prototyped taking the corner off mold and creating an insert. And since this was an open area, it meant there was solid steel underneath. So they created an alternate design in the space which allowed the read/write latch to be created while the shell was being molded.

Once the feature was designed into the shell, there was going to have to be a redesign on the assembly line to be able to shear off the small feature, turn it 90 degrees, place it and keep it in place for several stations before the other half of the shell could be mated to the shell and welded into place. All this had to happen at 100 parts per minute! No small task."

Lenny explained to Katie and the group this was a perfect example of QICR and planning. Twin Ports had the idea long ago to eliminate the read/write latch, but didn't have the right technical approach figured out. By continuing to identify the issue, look for alternatives and find an appropriate resource them, the team found a better way. A patent was applied for and granted, because it was such a novel idea. Patent number 5,748,419 records all the details and protects the idea.

"Again, the value of this single idea is huge. The capital was less than a million dollars, the material cost of the latch was very small; and if one just does simple math, approximately $7 million a year in savings. The patent was applied for in 1995. Up until the end of 2006; 11 years of savings at $7 million a year is a nice return on the investment."

Lenny ended, "The power of QICR is embedded in unleashing a common organizational cause fundamental to survival and following with a mechanism for people at all levels in the organization to turn ideas into actions."

Heady stuff for a Saturday. The group quickly disbanded and John remained with just a few of the staff, including Grant and Mary Ann. The consensus of the group was the day had been successful and to hang on. The ride was going to continue to be interesting and eventful.

John walked out into a snowy Saturday afternoon and was thankful for his life, his team and the opportunity to try and save Twin Ports. He did not bargain for this when he signed on for his dream job. However, during times of testing, leaders either sink or swim. He was determined to swim not for his sake, but because he believed in the people and the cause.

Chapter 16: A Day of Rest

Today was Sunday; chaos on Sunday was slightly different than the weekday chaos; Sunday was getting everyone up, dressed, fed and looking semi-presentable before 8:45 AM to leave for church.

John and Kristin chose to be in church on Sunday with their family. It was not a tradition or routine formed out of obligation, but one done by choice. Church allowed their family a chance to connect, to slow down from the hectic pace and to focus thoughts on spiritual things. In these times, church provided an anchor as well as a reminder all is temporary.

Both John and Kristin realize time and effort is needed to work through the big questions of life. Is there a God? Why am I here? What happens when I die? John had thought about these questions all his life.

In their searching for answer, they found a local community; a place where these questions could be explored, discussed with others who didn't pretend to know all the answers and who were asking many of the same questions. It was a place where questions were encouraged; it was just fine not to have all the answers and this suited John well.

The older John got, the more these questions both intrigued, and at the same time, bothered him. John realized these were personal questions everyone needed to answer on their own. People have been inquiring about these bigger issues of life since the beginning of time. Books written, philosophies derived and debated, new religions formed all by trying to answer a few simple, yet profound questions.

In his life, John studied and thought about these issues drew a few conclusions for him. First, John believed there is a God who created the universe and everything in it. How he did it? How long it took him? John concluded he likely would not know in this lifetime; and in the big picture, it doesn't matter.

Second, John believed in God's magnificent creation. God reached out to his most significant and complex masterpiece and made a way for us to restore our broken relationship with him.

Third, John also believed someone's religious beliefs are largely personal and the first step is to live what one believes.

He reached his conclusions and convictions by looking at the world around him. First, anything John knew to be man-made degrades with time. Every car, house, building, structure, the human body are all degrading, moving from a state of order to one of less order.

Yet, when John looked at the world around him, whether it was the dark skies above Isabella, MN, or the huge expanse of space, a spider spinning a web, or an ant making a maze of tunnels, birds instinctively knowing how and where to migrate, this level of design intent, precision, purpose and organization absolutely stunned his mind. Each thing obeys a natural set of unwritten principles humans continue to discover through science and mathematics.

In John's mind, when one looks at the evidence of precision, detail, order, structure, intent and so many other features which entertain the senses, the conclusion strongly suggests there is a designer, a mastermind, a creative talent behind all this.

Furthermore, the final product could have ended up boring, but it ended up magnificent and unique. Someone else may look at the same facts and reach a different conclusion; but for John, faith begins when he looks at those miracles and firmly believes they are the work of a creator, a master craftsman who used all the tools at his disposal to create a wonderful universe for humans to inhabit.

On this Sunday, the minister continued a study of what it really means to follow God. The sermon opened with a question drawn from Matthew 16:24, "And what do you benefit if you gain the whole world but lose your own soul? Is anything worth more than your soul?"

Even though this was off sermon topic; John's mind began to think back over the past two weeks and the questions he had been wrestling with work. Loyalty to company versus loyalty to the co-workers, greed of executive leadership versus good of shareholders, respecting the directions John had been given versus doing what he thought best for Twin Ports.

John struggled with both the weight and the consequences. John also had to search the own soul. What was his motivation? Was he on a quest for happiness? Is that why he was here? Was he here to make a good and easy life for his family? What is the real purpose? How does traveling halfway around the world to adopt another child fit in? How does the potential 'sellout' of Northern Pines Technology to Mendal Industries fit in? Why are so many people depending on him to figure this mess out?

John came to terms with the fact he was not going to get all these questions answered. At this point, there were too many unknowns. John knew this was his life, and he wanted to serve faithfully and well here on earth and wanted a life counting for eternity.

A quick check of John's watch indicated Pastor Mitchell would be ending his thoughts. Pastor Mitchell was prompt in his speaking. Perhaps someone at some time scolded him for a burned roast when he went too long. Also, John knew Pastor Mitchell was a huge Minnesota Wild fan, and with the faceoff at noon today, there was motivation to wrap it up. The pastor ended the message with a challenge, "Leaving here today, what you are going to do differently to ensure you don't lose your soul?"

During the closing prayer, Seth tugged at his hand. At the final "Amen," Seth broke free and was off. John walked through the crowd towards the lobby to begin the process of getting coats on. John saw Jeff Alberts and his family from across the room. Jeff was certainly one of, if not John's closest friend. John and Jeff had a lot in common and both knew, in their respective work roles, both would have to make some tough calls. Today was not about making the tough calls as it was about herding kids. John smiled and nodded as he chased his precocious child between the coat racks and the wave of people heading to the exit.

It was good to be in church. It was good to think about these things. Life was moving fast and if one does not stop to ponder some of the most basic questions; it can lead to an empty meaningless existence.

When Kristin and John moved to Twin Ports, they visited a few churches, but really found a fit at Red River Community Church. Over the past ten years, they had been involved in teaching, leadership and now were enjoying the benefits of a new church building. This congregation started out meeting in homes. The addition of a few families forced them to graduate to the law enforcement center. During the early years, they raised a little money and bought an old church across the river in Minnesota. For the next few years, the process and planning of building a new facility kept the small congregation busy.

John served as the church chairman during this time, so he ran between meetings to figure out financing, designs, affordability, contractors and how to best stretch dollars. It took numerous planning sessions and meetings to answer questions and keep the congregation informed on progress. Thankfully, this was during a time when he did not have the same work responsibilities; however, many nights John and the building committee stayed occupied with financial spreadsheets and phone calls; making sure this project could be done successfully.

The church broke ground in the spring three years ago and the building completed in nine months. Thanks to some awesome help and a very capable construction manager, the project came in on time, under budget and with a few unplanned enhancements. It was a great piece of teamwork and everyone hoped it would be a great place to worship and serve the community for many years to come.

John was grateful the project finished well, as his focus had to shift to other priorities.

This church is a part of who John is; as well as part of the rich and varied fabric of the community. Interestingly, John could count ten families, like the Alberts and Stantons, relied on Northern Pines Technology for their livelihood and attended the church. As John drove his family home, he realized between the two small cities called Twin Ports, this scene played out in a half dozen other churches.

Workers from Northern Pines Technology attending church and going about their normal Sunday activities without a clue people in positions of power were playing with their fates. John secretly wished the executive team at Northern Pines Technology could witness this scene and hear this message. It certainly seemed like the executive team's motive was only money, more money and more money, with little regard for the people, lifestyles and daily hard work which makes the company successful.

Chapter 17: Missing Pieces

Church ended, follow by a quick stop at the Chinese restaurant for takeout and the kids deciding how they were going to spend their afternoon. The twins and Seth settled into the family room to watch *The Incredibles*. The two little ones were down for their afternoon naps. John put on his winter gear and closed the front door quietly. He needed peace and quiet to think before the week started.

John's legs automatically took him on a trek rounding the corner of 7th Street and 5th Avenue and passing along the south side of his house. The painted, white fence boards paralleled the walk at least until he reached the alley. John kept walking straight. Their house was less than a half a mile from the Red River, which separated the North Dakota plains and prairie from the rolling farmland in western Minnesota. A park, one of several dotting either side of the river, sat right on the state line.

The city planners held an amazing sense of vision when they created this green space. The park was carved from a beautiful spot along the numerous bends of the Red River. A walking trail following the river for a few miles, which is about the distance John figured he needed to think through next steps.

John was only about two weeks into this new mode of operating, and it was draining and exhilarating at the same time. Two weeks ago tomorrow marked the now infamous trip down to the Northland Inn and hearing about Mendal Enterprises. John wasn't allowing himself to think about the consequences of failure right now; he was too focused on what the team had to do to pull this off.

John generally felt relatively good about the actions the team was taking. He intuitively knew the key to success was getting diskette cost below seven cents. Not only was the number a ridiculously low figure, it might also be just enough to disrupt the analysis and potentially cause a do-over in the close Twin Ports plan. If the site delivered seven cents, the financial analysis would not be favorable to a move in the short term, and the team had a shot at, by proxy, saving the rest of the facility. The staff in attendance at yesterday's QICR University could further analyze and hopefully complete the first steps of extreme cost reduction activities in a timely manner. The challenge now was going to be running three or four separate planning activities and then synthesizing the information, analyzing, putting plans together and executing all while running the factory at peak performance.

John engaged Dakota Manufacturing Partnership with the assistance of Steve to help shore up training. This came together quickly because the staff was already discussing how volumes and the business were changing. It was fortunate there had been significant pre-work as inherently, they knew the operations were reaching a point when the luxury of running everything at full capacity was ending. It was inevitable departments were going to have to figure out a way to train the workers to be much more flexible.

The area John was least sure about had to do with the people. The site met challenges before, John thought. He could use the word "resilient" to describe the people. Over the years, some of the stresses proved helpful, like the healthy tension aligned with growth and new product lines or the long hours by teams trying to figure out new processes. The optimist would say, the trajectory is positive and everyone knows the outcome needs to be successful. The pessimist would ask, is this the element to break the people and destroy the resiliency of the site?

This community had experienced significant stresses too. Just a few years ago, a good portion of the southeast part of Twin Ports flooded. In fact, the area John was now walking was under ten feet of muddy, icy water.

Flooding was a relatively common occurrence in this flat topography; however, the recent flood was especially severe. The spring runoff and rainwater swamped over forty plant employees' homes; some to the point of being uninhabitable. The plant banded together and despite the challenges from nature, worked to help those employees by filling sandbags, building dikes and providing housing and food for those displaced.

The plant also continued to run – not because leadership mandated it – but because the people wanted it to and knew it was important. Resilient is a good word to describe the population of Twin Ports.

The memories of the flood still linger fresh in peoples' minds, and John thinks the 'can-do spirit' represents just a small picture of what makes this community and manufacturing plant special. The plant is blessed with talented and dedicated people who are committed to doing the right thing. When the floods came, everyone stepped up and did what they could to support each other.

So much about this land and the heartiness of its people intertwines. John's walk took him by a set of ruts he can see across the river and continue into Minnesota. These ruts, now over 100 years old, are the tracks left by oxcarts – some of the first vehicles which traversed the prairie. They carried supplies, tools and accompanied people with dreams. It is from this stock of people from which the plant was forged some 30 years ago. That same rugged independence and determination gives John hope the plant will survive.

A light snow continued falling as John walked past the Ox Cart Trail. He wondered how many dozens, maybe hundreds of people crossed the river at this very spot and moved families onto the prairie to begin a life of farming, ranching and living off this fertile river valley.

John's mind wandered just like his feet were at this time. Somewhere on his bookshelf, at either work or home, John remembered a story, which just might parallel some of the adventures these early settlers experienced. Ernest Shackelton was an English explorer who at one time was involved in a race to be the first to the South Pole. He gave up comfort and security for adventure and to be a true explorer.

Shackelton, being the consummate adventurer and perhaps an early adrenaline junkie, recognized there were unexplored worlds to conquer. He took on the challenge of becoming the first to cross the continent of Antarctica from sea to sea via the pole.

John loved Shackelton's recruitment poster:

> "Men wanted for hazardous journey. Small wages. Bitter cold. Long months of complete darkness. Constant danger. Safe return doubtful. Honour and recognition in case of success. —Ernest Shackelton."

John remembered bits and pieces from the book and a recent public television show about Shackelton. From his sketchy memory, John recalled early in the trip Shackelton's ship *The Endurance* became trapped in an ice flow and crushed. Left without a ship and with limited supplies, he quickly adapted his mission from being one of conquest to one of survival. He was successful in his new mission, despite tremendous odds, none of his crew perished. Even though he felt a personal loss and until recently a lost history, his genius lie in he had the fortitude to lead his men in recognition of their situation, plan for survival, execute the plan and successfully reinvent their mission.

John reasoned somewhere in the story is a lesson for Twin Ports.

John thought, "Is that really what this comes down to? Is it a leadership question? If there isn't a vision, if there isn't a scout, if there isn't someone who is looking ahead, ships run aground, organizations fall apart, entropy destroys." The glue holding this together is not a single leader. The single leader is required to set the vision and chart the course. The success stems from the organization seeing the vision, agreeing with it and then doing their individual part to make it happen.

Perhaps this is the truest form of leadership. John loved the stories of visionaries like: William Wallace, Winston Churchill, Martin Luther King Jr. and other brave leaders who seemingly cared less about their own success and more about being known as someone who changed lives and subsequently changed history.

John continued walking without really paying attention to where he was going. He had turned south at the river and walked towards downtown. John started to be enthusiastic about Monday. He knew just before lunch – he faced his entire staff and needed to deliver a targeted, tactful and tough message.

John remained resolute and convinced not only can he make a difference, but the team of can-do people surrounding him needs to believe they also can make a difference.

He began to think about how to frame his words to set the tone for the staff meeting. He saw a path emerging that was going to make a dramatic difference in the life of the Northern Pines – Twin Ports.

John possessed a way of thinking which makes him draw in all types of facts, facets and angles. With enough time, he can generally synthesize the data into a complete picture. Perhaps it was his analytical mind; he intuitively knew when something was missing from the picture. Maybe it is illogical, maybe it is the systems engineering background, and maybe it is fear. Whatever "it" was, it was very real. John needed to see the three legs of the proverbial stool before he would sit down.

His time today walking in the snow thinking about early pioneers, reminding himself of the lessons from history, all were parts of the process and helped fill in a few of the blanks. After thinking and walking, he was feeling much more at peace.

He was truly beginning to craft his message; perhaps the most important one he would ever give to his key employees tomorrow. It went like this:

> **Step One:** The site needs to drive QICR to get costs down
>
> +
>
> **Step Two:** The site needs to train to achieve flexibility, which will allow the plant to absorb the ups and downs of the business better.
>
> +
>
> **Step Three:** The site leadership needs to create a shared vision and help people understand **they** are the leaders and are going to make this happen.
>
> =
>
> **Desired result:** Be disruptive enough to change the financial analysis from favorable to unfavorable. Twin Ports needs to win!

As John walked along downtown, he could practically see early pioneers walking along boardwalk sidewalks, coming into the dry goods store or the feed store to get supplies for their farm. Oddly, John felt good knowing nothing new was really invented; he was just tapping into the same sensibilities the settlers of this land had brought 150 years ago.

As he arrived home, took off his coat and boots and walked into the family room, the movie was just at the part where *The Incredible's* were set to do battle with Syndrome.

Kind of ironic, it didn't matter if it was arctic explorers 100 years ago, a town fighting a flood a few years ago, a plant battling for its survival or a children's movie, the struggle and challenges are always present. What changes? Maybe it is just the scale, the stage and the players.

Chapter 18: Approaching the Staff

Staff meetings were commonly a routine event. The structure was set, beginning with: safety results, quality, human resources/staffing and supply chain updates. To close, one of the production managers presented a topic on unique projects or work in their area.

Diane gave Sarah Bergstrom a heads-up John was trumping her allocated time at staff meeting to discuss a special topic at the end of the meeting.

John intentionally compressed the front end of the meeting a bit. No safety incidents occurred in the past week; and since it was late in the month, most of the production numbers rolled up reasonable and as expected. The departments landed in the 90% range of commitments for all products, so the review breezed over these numbers. Normally, if an area was behind, John would insure a recovery plan was in place as well as a communique drafted from the planning team to the business unit informing of the shortage or delay.

To begin the talk, John flashed a picture on the screen of a grizzled, arctic explorer. It could have been an image of Grizzly Adams, someone's long lost grandpa or perhaps any settler of the Dakotas from the 1800s. John asked, "Anyone know who this is?"

Silence.

John thought Lenny might have muttered "the abominable snowman" under his breath, but it was not loud enough for many to hear. John continued, "If this guy gave you the following pitch – would you go with him? 'Men (or women) wanted for hazardous journey. Small wages. Bitter cold. Long months of complete darkness. Constant danger. Safe return doubtful. Honour and recognition in case of success.'"

Still no hands.

John went on to explain, "This rugged man is going to be our guide for the next few months because he did something remarkable – a feat until recently, history had forgotten. In fact, partial credit is due to the PBS show *Nova* for reviving the truly heroic tale of the *Voyage of the Endurance*." John continued, "Ernest Shackelton was a fearless adventurer and an inspiring leader. He led because he had a passion and vision for exploration; however, he was also smart enough to realize when the first goal became impossible; he had another role to play – also of leader, but with a twist; a very important twist."

John purposely did not say too much. He knew during the next few months –the staff would explore and learn how Shackelton led his men in their new endeavor; and, how the journey paralleled what Northern Pines needed to do. There was not an arctic adventure for Northern Pines, but there was an important pivot to a new goal; the new goal being nothing less than survival.

John reminded his team of the mission of Twin Ports. He said, "This statement embodied what we strive for. It is our guiding star:"

> *To deliver the highest Customer and Corporate value, through exceptional people in manufacturing, product development and new business commercialization.*

The same mission guided the plant for as long as John had been a member of the team, which dated back to the early 90s. John said, "The site has endured a lot of challenges in the past 30 years. Some of you remember the early days of diskettes, when getting 100 diskettes per hour was a challenge. Today, lines push out 100 diskettes per minute! And remember, more recently, when the task was scaling up Glacier. All of the late nights we endured trying to get the molds to run in concert with the automation so spools could be installed on the hubs without damage?" A few staff knowingly nodded around the room. This example was fresh in people's minds.

Many in the room had contributed to the Glacier ramp during the past year.

John stopped, cleared his throat and with as much conviction as he could muster, he bluntly said, "Our site has a new threat. One not easily perceived." John continued with his pitch. "In the late 1970s, there were more than a dozen companies making televisions in the US; many of them in the Indiana and Ohio region, both states a part of the great manufacturing belt at one time. We can still recall the names: RCA, Emerson, Zenith, Sylvania, Admiral and Tackett, to name a few. That same area is now known as the rust belt, because industry is gone. The high-tech jobs disappeared, the factories shuttered, the towns decimated. Less than ten years later, the television companies mentioned earlier were all gone and replaced with names like: Sharp, Sony, Vizio, Funai, LG, Samsung. Many factors caused this, but some of the most common were lack of investment in new technology, lack of attention to quality, government policy, labor costs and changing market dynamics."

"As your leader; one of my roles is to watch out for similar competitive threats, and steer our organization away from danger and threats. Just like Shackelton was responsible for charting a course, so are we. I use the Shackelton example, because it has a good ending and I use the examples from the television industry, because it had a poor ending for those impacted."

John went on, "We need to be thinking not about just executing our plan, but looking ahead and thinking, what are our threats? I know it may sound a little contrarian, but threats are not bad things. If you analyze carefully, a threat can be a good thing because it can focus energy."

"Remember when Twin Ports had historic flooding a few years ago? We had people walking the town, inspecting the dikes day and night. What were they doing? They were looking for threats. They were looking for those weak spots; and once those were identified, we could call in whatever resources necessary to strengthen the area and then move to the next. Once they found a threat, did they let off the gas and say, 'Great, we found it. Now I get to go home to the recliner?' Nope, they started looking again, for the next one."

John knew this wasn't a perfect example; but since so many of the plant folks lived those days, he thought the example might resonate with most.

John continued his monologue, "I wish I could be more specific with you, but as the leader of this organization at this point in time, I believe it is my duty to make us ready to face these types of threats."

John pondered how far he was going to go with the staff in spelling out the threats and what he learned in the last two weeks. He decided he needed them to see the possibility, to create the burning platform and spell out in the strongest terms a rationale for radical change.

A new slide appeared on the screen and John talked through three imperatives to help the site identify these threats and begin shore up the organization over the next few months.

John embellished this slide graphics with his own thoughts, "First, as a site we are going to resolve to go after the seven-cent diskette. This is not a new idea, but today we are committing the site to go "All-In." I am making a calculated, but risky gamble the future viability of the site rests on our success in this product. In doing this, I want to prove definitively Twin Ports can not only compete, but win, on a global scale. If the site delivers a seven-cent diskette, there will be no one who can argue we are not the world's leader in low cost production."

"Second emphasis or initiative, if you will," John continued, "is we are going to introduce a cross-training program. We have talked about this at staff meetings before, but our business is changing. We are seeing now, today. We are not going to be able to always run

Glacier, Keystone, 5476, diskettes and optical lines at capacity all the time." John added, "I see a day very soon when we are going to have to take operators, maintenance and technicians from 5476 and have them seamlessly go over to optical and run different equipment. Likewise, maybe diskette operators who are cross-trained in Keystone or Glacier run the lines."

John paused for emphasis, "I know we have had the luxury of being able to have dedicated and highly trained operators for our key production lines, and we still will. We are just going to have to enhance their skills, training and knowledge so they know two or more lines very well, rather than just one."

Lastly, John said, "I am going to use our new mutual friend, Mr. Shackelton, as an example of the type of leaders we aspire to be. We will train the entire plant in lessons learned from his leadership principles. These challenges are too great not to give everyone the opportunity to contribute. To succeed, we need to see the vision, agree with it and then each one do our individual part to make it happen. That how I define true leadership and it starts with me, however I can't do it alone, I need each one of you committed to join and do whatever it takes to get the job done."

It was just a few minutes before lunch, but John gave the staff a chance to ask any questions they might have. Tim Bloom, one of the new supervisors asked, "I hope everyone does see the opportunities and gets it, so to speak, but what about those that don't, what happens to them?"

John paused, thinking for a moment. "Tim that is a very insightful question. It is also my hope we can bring everyone along on this journey, but I am going to go back to our friend Mr. Shackelton for a minute. What do you think would happen if one of the crew decided he was going to chart his own course, maybe sneak extra food rations to maintain their strength?" Tim said quietly, "That isn't fair to those who abide by the plan, is it?" John responded,

"No, it really isn't, so I would imagine that person would have a chance to remedy his behavior. But if he isn't committed to the greater good, ultimately the group is better without him, right?" Tom nodded, acknowledging the gravity of the situation. John paused and added, "This is a level of threat we have not seen before, and I am ready to make those tough decisions, not because I like to, but because I have to. I cannot overstate, our survival is at stake."

John ended the meeting with a final slide including a rough timeline. It was standard operating procedure to have all employee quarterly update meetings, which were already scheduled for the following week. Without having to further interrupt production, John would be speaking to all four crews during the next three or four days. John gave unambiguous guidance he was going to go over this information with the entire plant.

People would soon realize, if they had not already, the next few months would not be business as usual. The cross training or Training Within Industry (TWI) activities were going to begin very soon. John turned the TWI portion over to Jeff and the general production supervisors. They were much closer to the action and he had strong confidence they could assess the situation, create the appropriate analysis and figure out how best to diversify the labor talent across multiple product lines.

The meeting ended and people left in hushed voices. There was definitely conversation about the last hour, but it was done with a somber tone.

The afternoon was a series of meetings, report generation and a few phone calls. John popped into Jeff's office and asked him for a summary meeting on Friday to brief the leadership team on the groundwork completed that week, so the overall plant leadership team was aware of all the upcoming changes. He agreed and said he would have Diane schedule something for Friday afternoon.

John arrived home at 5:45, only to learn the hot water heater quit. Hot water turned lukewarm in the late afternoon; and by the time supper preparation was in full swing, it was nonexistent. Having five kids and no hot water for dishwashing and baths was a not a viable solution for more than a day. John hopped in the truck and headed down to the hardware store. He was hoping to get there before six, as he knew they were closing in a few minutes.

John opened the door, heard the familiar bell ring and quickly found Harold, his best buddy, standing at the cash register. This was an old-fashioned hardware store and had been there every step of the way for John to learn plumbing, basic wiring, and all the other things which come with being a first-time homeowner and aspiring handyman.

The store was not the lowest price always, but they were convenient and had everything. When John wanted one washer or one hose clamp, he could get it there. Try doing that at a big box home improvement store.

Anyway, at this hour, the topic at hand was electric hot water heaters, preferably large capacity. Harold directed John to the far wall; they had three electric water heaters. He sold John a set of fittings, two hoses and the latest 60-gallon water heater. He promised with 60 gallons, even a house of seven would not run out of hot water. John pulled out the credit card and the rewards card and Harold scanned it just as the clock hit six.

As John wheeled the beast outside, Harold told him to keep the dolly and bring it back tomorrow. They had a spare to get them by at the store.

The evening entertainment consisted of the twins coming down to the basement from time to time to see if anything cool was going on. There wasn't. Kristin descended the stairs to remind John to turn off the electricity to ensure he didn't electrocute himself, which John had already done. John reminded Kristin he had just upped his life insurance policy, which resulted in a balled-up t-shirt being thrown at him from the stairs.

It was 11 pm before John turned on the water again. Fortunately, there were no leaks and he could hear the tank filling. John waited 15 minutes or so and turned on the water heater; no sparks and in the quietness of the basement, John could hear a small hum coming from the heater. John looked down at the thermostat and set it right in the middle, hoping that was a good place to start.

With success at hand, John realized he hadn't eaten supper. In the rush to get to the store and wrangle the water heater down to the basement, he had just forgotten to get anything to eat.   After one last check in the basement, John threw his tools into the toolbox and headed upstairs. When passing through the kitchen, John turned on a delayed start for the dishwasher and hoped for the best.   He grabbed a cheese stick and a handful of peanuts, sat down on the couch for a few minutes of *Late Night with David Letterman* and drifted off to sleep.

Sometime after two, John stumbled up the stairs and fell into bed in a heap, only vaguely aware his decisive moment would be in the morning when he turned on the shower. The twist of a knob would determine how successful the plumbing escapade had been.

Worst case, the kids could use the basement as an in-ground swimming pool if his plumbing were an utter failure.

Chapter 19: Steering the Ship

John awoke early on Tuesday. His efforts on the water heater from the previous night appeared to have been successful. At least the outcome was good: a hot shower, no leaks and clean dishes.

The night crew was wrapping up their shift when John opened the front door of the plant. John graciously held the door for the stampede out. Hard to blame them for the mass exodus; John knew it had been a long night. While he had been home enjoying the evening, or at least replacing a water heater, this crew had been hard at work during the last twelve hours. One more shift for them and their 'weekend' would start. Staffing around the clock is a complex task. Years ago, the site settled on a four-crew rotating schedule. Those who did it seemed to like it the best. People had every other weekend off, alternated days and nights and either worked two or three days in a row, depending on shifts.

The Twin Ports human resources team realized early on it is impossible to make everyone happy; but for those actually working this schedule, it seemed to meet many of the needs of working families. The scheduled contained an added benefit. When a husband and wife both worked, they sometimes opted for alternate shifts. Then someone was always home and they shared weekends and days off. It worked for many, but all acknowledged nothing is perfect. A few joined the ranks of the four-crew rotating shift schedule and the circadian clocks just never could get aligned to the changes in schedule. They generally sought employment elsewhere after an adjustment period.

John walked through the administrative area to his office in the corner and witnessed the first hints of a rose-colored sun coming up from the east. John sat down at his desk, paused for a few moments and began to jot notes for the rest of the week. As his laptop was firing up, John poured coffee from the Thermos and watched the steam rise and then swirl slowly over the mug.

This was going to be an interesting week. John was still working on a detailed framework for the improvement effort. With crew meetings and staff all queued up, it was 'go' time. A quick glance at the site visitor calendar also highlighted a visitor from Japan, Mr. Akio Yoshimura. Yoshimura-san had been coming to the plant for at 15 least years. He held the position of engineering manager in the Tokyo office; however, more recently he had morphed into a quasi-sourcing, quasi-business role.

The plant performed significant OEM work for some of the large diskette brands in Japan, and it worked well to have him serve as the business interface. In fact, in the last three years through Yoshimura-san's effort, the site acquired the OEM business of the top three diskette brands in Japan. These manufacturers began to see an overall decline in unit volume of diskettes and decided it was time to begin their exit strategy.

Unit volume drop in Japan indicated where new technology was emerging to take the place of diskettes. Japan is known as a leading-edge market, so many of the indications seen in Japan begin to ripple through the rest of the world in time. Products like removable flash, USB drives, network-attached storage, and even to some extent, the significant rise of optical media were all drivers which ultimately would render the diskette obsolete.

The interesting dynamic was not that it would be obsolete quickly. The intrigue was in the rate and which regions would be rapid adopters of new technology and which ones would hold on to the older technology.

If one manages the business correctly, good money can still be made in the mature phases of product lifecycle. Leadership must be very prudent and careful with cost management, inventory management and drive towards a very simple and flexible product offering. For most portfolios, simplicity is translated to a dramatic reduction in SKU count. This creates a few product offerings to fill a variety of market needs, but offers efficient transportation and delivery and point of sale merchandising.

The Japan producer's loss was Twin Ports gain; and at over half a billion diskettes per year produced, the site was clearly still the largest producer in the world. Yoshimura-san did not come for quantity, however. He came for quality. This man was the toughest quality critic on the planet. Early on in their interactions, John took a bit of offense to his 'coaching,' but over time, John learned to take the valuable insights and implement much of Yoshimura's collective wisdom. His challenges consistently made the site more focused on quality, which was good.

During his time as a quality engineer, John hosted a plant tour for Yoshimura-san. That was many years ago, and it might have even been his first visit. John learned a very important lesson during the visit. It was not wise to leave him alone on the production floor. Inevitably, Yoshimura-san would inadvertently trip a light curtain or lean up against a machine and hit the E-Stop. The operators took it in stride, but they also let John know it was *John's* responsibility to make sure his visitors didn't stop the line.

Before any Yoshimuri-san visit, the site prepared by cleaning the machines, the floor, the area nearly hospital clean. Yoshimuri-san always looked for things in the most obscure places. Sure enough, true to form, Yoshimuri-san peered behind a machine and found a small spring, probably 3/4" long, used in the assembly area of diskettes to provide the force to close the shutter.

He asked, "Where is the diskette this spring belongs to?" Of course, John didn't have a ready answer. He could only assume it was in a box and was sent to pack out and was long gone. Yoshimuri-san said, "Until you are perfect, John, I keep coming," and gave a hearty laugh. The plant would never be perfect. Yoshimuri-san and John knew that, but the lesson stuck. Perfection is the ultimate goal.

John jotted notes quickly for the QICR leaders. John appointed Lenny Garst, the quality manager, and Mary Ann Tackett, Engineering & Technology Manager, to help organize and facilitate the QICR sessions. Lenny had been with the plant longer than almost anyone had. He was a North Dakota native having been born in Twin Ports and left only briefly to attend college in Grand Forks. He was a chemical engineering graduate and a strong supporter of the University of North Dakota. Lenny was well liked, and John appreciated his approach and the results he delivered. John and Lenny shared a special relationship with Lenny, because Lenny was John's first boss at Northern Pines Technology – Twin Ports. Lenny recognized something in John and hired him. For that, John was thankful. Mary Ann would add a little spice to Lenny's ultra-methodical approach. Between the two of them, John thought they would make balanced team leaders for this project.

John wanted to be able to give the teams some guidance on how to approach QICR. Plentiful examples of programs existed where team's fully leveraged vertical integration, conducted first principles research, and developed and implemented improved processes. John knew the site could identify several of these types of programs. His fear remained the results would not come within the time needed. Diskettes needed a faster implementation cycle and more immediate results. It was common for a project of major significance and impact to go back to the lab for significant product testing, but there wasn't time for iterative learning.

One of the most practical things about the QICR process was its scalability. It worked equally as well for the large development programs as it did for the smaller programs. The process was the same – identify opportunities, categorize and analyze (impact/effort), put together plans and execute.

John knew from his experience, several areas which had not been fully tapped for improvement, first on the list - process yield. The site was not alone in this. Across many industries, yield loss is a symptom of poor processes, poor quality and is too often accepted as a cost of doing business.

Yield is one of the best sources for improvement because there is a triple benefit; extra capacity (machines aren't making waste), cost benefit (product isn't being thrown away) and quality, some of the yield loss inevitably leaves as a quality escape. The diskette departments maintain good yields, but even a percent or two somewhere could make a huge difference. For the diskette department, one percent yield equals at least half a million dollars of cash savings and some intangibles as well. The effort was well worth the pursuit.

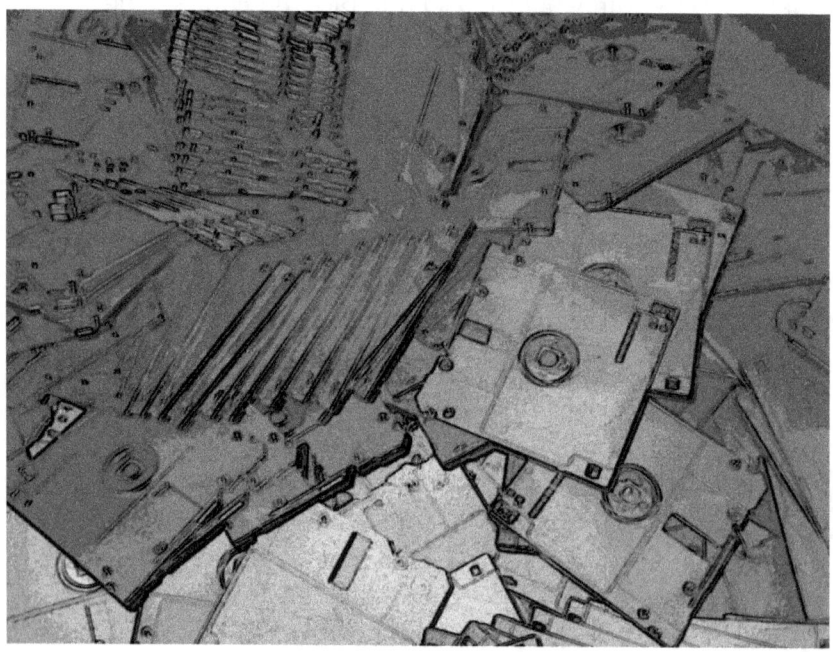

More Waste than Can Be Afforded

Another area typically ripe for harvest were sourced material costs. The process of changing resin or aluminum was lengthy, costly and risky; however, the sourcing department found ways of getting lower unit costs by consolidated buys. Two years ago, the site pioneered the formation of a plastic buying consortium with a few companies in Fargo. Fargo retained a significant number of window manufacturers using PVC and a large PVC pipe manufacturer. Twin Ports used polystyrene, but if there was a way to cooperatively leverage the buying power (resin, colorant, silicone, other additives) and maybe save some on transportation, a few cents off per pound would definitely be worth the effort.

In addition, careful engineering and financial review of raw material purchases through the entire value stream can be a productive source of savings. Shelly Haberman, a finance intern, discovered the site was selling scrap shells for regrind at $0.10 on the dollar. That discovery started exploring regrinding the reject shells in house and introducing a 10-15% regrind blend back into the processes. The site dabbled with this for a few years, and with increasing resin costs, it was time to dust this work off again and see if it made financial sense to try the approach again. Shelly was the daughter of one of the production operators, Bill Haberman. She was the first in their family to go to college and Bill was very proud of his daughter and her internship work at Northern Pines. The analysis was ready for a refresh and perhaps a nice cost savings for the plant.

Categorically, the engineers tended to think of cost reduction opportunities in different buckets: product design, material cost, quality and yield, labor (direct and indirect), equipment and usually a miscellaneous category. The team usually brainstormed good ideas about labor optimization, but there was something in the equipment area John was trying to remember as he sat with pen and paper in hand writing notes.

As John added to his ever-growing list of thoughts and ideas, he tried to go through the QICR process in his head; and somewhere back in the cobwebs, he recalled an electric motor on one section of the assembly line which seemed to cause periodic trouble. It was last fall when a series of failures caused some unplanned downtime.

John reached for the phone and dialed 77, the paging system. "Greg Fellwitz, call 1161, Greg Fellwitz, 1161." Greg worked as the maintenance manager. He was a small soft-spoken man, but Greg knew equipment, runtime and site maintenance. Trained by the Navy as a mechanic, Greg understood preventive maintenance and he created an awesome team of trained mechanics who could fix just about anything, anytime, anywhere. Greg buzzed back and reminded John the motor in question was a custom Hitachi drive motor. Greg rattled off the specifications faster than John could write them down.

At the end of the page, John looked at the list and proclaimed it a good start for Lenny and Mary Ann. Normally John would not have been so active in these sessions; however, things were different this time. This was not the annual QICR cycle. – the site has about two months to start showing dramatic results, and the unit cost numbers need to begin a rapid decline to have any chance of saving this operation.

John turned to the computer and started working on slides for the employee meetings. John began with the last quarter presentation and pulled in the updated slides off the network share folders. This was the easy part.

Next, John attempted to craft a compelling reason for change. He knew people listen to these words and he wanted them to be impactful, but, without issuance of a threat. Once the reason for change was clear; he then needed to articulate a plausible strategy which made sense to everyone.

John thanked his computer, because if he had been scribbling notes by hand, he would have produced a floor full of wadded up papers.

Instead he had a blank screen. John was getting nowhere.

Chapter 20: A Small Idea....with Possibilities.

John went home for lunch Tuesday feeling more than a bit dejected. Crew meetings started in nine hours, and he lacked a way to communicate the most significant threat the plant ever faced without scaring the pants off the employees and the community. In the back of his mind, the risk losing his job due to a violation of the non-disclosure agreement was also a distinct possibility. He was stuck.

Over lunch, John tried his best to explain the dilemma to Kristin. The kids ran around and John watched Mark sitting in his high chair, grabbing Cheerios with his chubby little fist. He was changing so fast. Every day brought a new skill, a new insight, a better knowledge of his little world.

Both John and Kristin thought for a minute, but neither could come up with anything. Thoughts around change, the world changes, the universe is ever changing. It doesn't ever seem to stop. Neither one spoke, but an idea hit Kristin about the same time neurons fired for John. Is there anything that doesn't change?

John drove back to work continuously thinking about this theme. What drives change? Sometimes it is a threat, sometimes it is improvement, sometimes it is natural system degradation and probably many other reasons, but this was a start for now. John started to get more excited about this embryonic idea. Finally, maybe something to go on.

John thought to himself, "What is the best kind of change most people can think of, short of winning the lottery?" The best John could come up with was something an individual had control over, included a benefit and perhaps benefitted others, too. This idea lands squarely in the elusive category of a 'win-win' arrangement. John concluded, "That is the best type of change one could envision; after all - what more could be asked?"

Back at work, John wove these ideas into two slides. In fact, they were some of the simplest slides John had made. The first said simply, "Everything changes – Agree or Disagree?" and second "The Best Changes are _____." John hoped to warm up his audience a little by doing discovery. John took a risk, but had to see if his thoughts aligned and resonated with the rest of the workforce.

After a quick trip home for supper and helping begin the nighttime home routine, John returned to the plant promptly at 8:30 PM. He wanted to make sure the coffee was fresh and treats arrived. Everything was in order, so John took a few quiet moments to gather his thoughts. John leaned against the podium and looked out at the 100 or so chairs set up in the room. In just a few minutes, employees would begin to filter in, each representing a family with responsibilities and other people relying on this site for a paycheck, benefits and some assurance this would continue.

Their jobs met needs. For most, the job provided income, but it also provided value, worth and a sense of purpose, a part of their identity. It was deeply a part of John's identity, too, even though he wasn't a 'lifer' in Twin Ports. He took pride in the fact he managed a world-class manufacturing operation and provided not only employment, but technical challenges and opportunities to the entire workforce.

John's mind also roamed over 6,000 miles to Ukraine. He could not help thinking about Vika. As his today was ending in North Dakota, her tomorrow was just beginning. An eight-hour time difference separated them, so it was early on Wednesday morning in Ukraine. It was winter in Ukraine as well. What was the orphanage like? Inside and outside? Was it warm? Did they have adequate clothing? Did they ever go outside in the winter? Was she healthy or sick? If she was sick, did she have medical care and medicine available? When would they get word from the officials in Ukraine an appointment had been granted and the family could travel? Was it days, weeks, months away?

John thought a lot about how he would juggle and manage the work back here. There were a couple of potential scenarios. One option was make one trip and stay until the adoption was finalized. Another scenario, especially if there were delays was to make two trips. Go for the initial visit and court appearance and then return after the waiting period was over. There was not yet enough available information to make the decision, but at least there were options. Neither was going to be easy, but there was not much easy about his life right now.

Workers began to filter in bringing John back to the here and now. John began the presentation with site metrics, safety, quality, cost, and ended with human resources, training hours, presenteeism and highlighted the new hires from the last quarter. At this point, the site only hired to replace attrition, but it was still good to highlight the stability in the workforce, and the addition of three or four people each quarter was viewed positively.

The presentation shifted to the topic of change. Despite best efforts, the first question: everything changes, agree or disagree? fell flat. There were many blank stares and just a few brief comments. The crew opened up and talked about the second question: the best changes are _____?, John heard some really insightful and meaningful input. John wasn't sure if there would be much audience participation, but the site has a lot of good change going on. John learned about the purchase of a new truck, a new grandchild and a vacation planned to Cancun starting next week. It was easy to affirm change as being positive and he hoped momentum would carry over to his next points.

John mapped out the facts to the workforce in as clear language as he could. He then shared with them the three things he was going to be working with the entire plant to change.

"It is imperative the factory changes. We can count on one thing; the site must anticipate the threats and take appropriate countermeasures.

A countermeasure in this case is using what capability exists at Twin Ports to enhance our value to the business and make us irreplaceable." John then explained the three countermeasures.

"First, cost reduction – across the site. We are striving to reach the goal of a seven-cent diskette by year-end; and at the same time, other areas must be worked on as well. This was a change to strengthen the site's position and value within the company. The data clearly shows Twin Ports diskettes are the lowest manufacturing cost so if the efforts accelerate, an even larger delta is created between the site and all our competition.

Second, training – the days of being able to run all lines at capacity were ending. The site needed a more flexible workforce where people could move to where the needs were and thus respond to ever-changing customer demand. John reminded them this change would build capability and flexibility. It was one of those 'good' changes; it was going to require effort, but it would put the site in a better position to respond to rapid customer changes."

Lastly – John introduced an arctic explorer whom history had largely forgotten, but he did the impossible. "He is a leader for the ages and he is going to be our reminder nothing is impossible."

John gave a quick biography, "Ernest Shackelton lived as an explorer in the early 1900s. He possessed all the drive of a vintage explorer, cut from the same cloth as Columbus, Admiral Byrd, and Neil Armstrong. His goal was to complete the first crossing of the Antarctic continent. He set out to accomplish this by coordinating the British Imperial Trans-Antarctic Expedition. At the time, this was considered to be the last great polar journey."

John went on to explain things do not always go per plan, "After being shipwrecked in Antarctica in 1915, he had charge of 27 men." His mission no longer was to be the first to cross the continent, but a more foundational and ultimately more important mission. His job was to keep his crew alive and return them safely to their families.

John concluded, "Tonight, I am not going to tell you how this worked out. We'll discover these truths together. It is a great story – filled with lots of twists and turns."

As the meeting ended, employees shuffled back to the floor to their machines. Their night was just starting.

John was thankful his was ending.

Chapter 21: A Home Study

One of the primary tasks to be crossed off the adoption list is the home study. The basic objective, as John understood it, meant someone validating them as capable parents. The study involved securing a licensed agency to provide a survey, ask references about the prospective parents' character, come into the home and evaluate their ability to parent a child successfully. In the back of his mind, John defined this as a non-value added activity, based on the obvious. However, he resigned himself to the fact the home study existed to protect the children as well. Unfortunately, not all intents are noble. An outsider looking in could see John and Kristin were already juggling a full life with five kids and had been doing it with reasonable success for almost ten years. It seemed a bit silly paying someone to complete a few hours of observation and paperwork, providing the authorities enough evidence to make a valid assessment.

Kristin scheduled the home study for Wednesday afternoon, so John stayed home after lunch. It was supposed to take about two hours, and thankfully, the assessor discerned John and Kristin were serious, capable people and was mercifully short on the overall inquest.

Most of the session involved getting to know John and Kristin and understand their motivation for adoption. After seeing the family in action and their plans for the future; the caseworker/assessor said the follow-up report would be available in seven to ten days; this was critical because the entire report had to be translated into Russian and approved; prior to sending off the paperwork to Kiev.

Other collateral material included passport photos and applications at the local post office. John used the balance of the afternoon to take the twins down to the post office, sit for photos and file the necessary paperwork to apply for passports. Previous adoptive parents warned the passport process took up to 60 days, a byproduct of a post 9-11 world, so it was desirable to start early and avoid passports being on the critical path. John's passport was current from his travels to India a few years ago.

Planning for this trip generated numerous challenges. Three remaining children needed a place to stay and care for up to four weeks. After much thinking, talking and scheming, a plan emerged. All along, the twins planned to accompany John and Kristin on the journey. At almost eleven years old, both Kristin and John thought a trip to Ukraine would be both a good adventure and an eye-opening experience. It would also be good for them to see where their sister came from to better understand her background. The boys were going to play an important role in her integration to the family.

Everyone loved Caroline, but one family from their church, especially loved her. When the first discussions began about adopting and the associated travel, they offered to take her for the entire time. She loved them and there was no question where she would go during the adoption trip.

It was decided Seth and Mark would stick together and spend a few weeks with Kristin's sisters and split the balance of time at John's parents. Many more logistics ensued, but a basic plan started to fall into place.

Elements of the final planning depended on time of the year of the trip, too. If the trip occurred in summer, John only needed to find someone to mow the yard and come in from time to keep the plants alive. If travel happened during the winter, additional plans would have to be put in place to ensure someone came in daily to check the heat and keep up with shoveling outside.

The details in planning a trip such as this are enormous; John cleared his head and reminded himself he couldn't think too much about every detail at one time. Each day had enough trouble of its own.

Since the home study ended early and they were finished with the passport application at the post office, John took the twins through the drive through at McDonalds for ice cream. Even though it was February, ice cream tasted good anytime of the year.

Caroline

Wednesday night meant Adventure Club at church. Adventure Club is a crazy time of the week when 100 kids invade the church for a Bible lesson, games, snacks and encouragement. John did not know where all the kids came from. Probably 20% of the kids have parents who attend church, but somewhere word got out the church was a safe and fun place to be on Wednesday night, so the church has extra helpers on hand and do their best. John helped for a few years and he generally looked forward to it. Seth and the twins were regular attendees. The theme tonight was camo-night, so they dug up all the Mossy Oak and blaze orange available and made a night of it.

The kids had a great time playing tug of war and relay races. The lesson was on the Good Samaritan, a timeless story of the unexpected person going out of the way to help. In a sense, the person who helped was camouflaged, because it wasn't the one everyone was expecting; it was the one least expected to help who stopped and took care of the person who had been robbed.

The twins begged to stay afterwards for a little while and play basketball in the gym. The boys liked the time to run around and burn off some excess energy. John gave them fifteen minutes to run off steam. The crowd was down to just a handful when it was time to wrap up. The kids went through all the classrooms, turned off the lights. John turned down the heat and made all sure the doors were locked.

As they headed out into the star filled night to the truck, it struck John by how embedded he and his family were in this community. This was home to him. Roots grow slowly, but once they reach a point of firmness, it really doesn't matter how deep they go. Kristin and John arrived in Twin Ports as newlyweds and now; this community was their home. It was all their children had ever known.

The thoughts of all the turmoil created by what was going on at work made John think about all the other families and what was pending for not just his family; but all families. Church was halfway between work and home, so the truck barely got warm by the time they pulled into the driveway.

The night ended with bowls of cereal and kids getting to bed by 9:15. John retreated to the desk to tackle the pile of bills and mail stacked up over the past week. He also glanced at his monitor to scan work emails. It looked like 72 had come in since he left at noon. He hoped Diane would have called for anything urgent; the rest could wait until tomorrow. The pile of bills reminded John he had to find the time to do the taxes. April would come quickly.

Chapter 22: A Flexible Workforce

Jeff contacted Steve's recommended Dakota Manufacturing Partnership [DMP] consultants and agreed to an offsite meeting with the leadership team and production supervisors of Northern Pines on Thursday. The Partnership provided expertise in solving manufacturing problems, including training, and John also served on the board of directors, so it was a good fit. Diane booked a room at the local college, North Dakota College of Technology. Northern Pines and the school shared a great relationship, a mutually beneficial partnership. The site supported the school with donations, internships and technology, and they reciprocated their support with highly skilled workers.

Steve sent out Daniel Christensen, one of their TWI instructors. John saw Dan in action at the annual DMP conferences. He was a straight shooter, acknowledged as an expert and involved in TWI initiatives across several diverse industries. John was glad to see Dan could help, because he really understood the benefits of TWI and how it could best be tailored to fit the current flexibility dilemma at Twin Ports.

John prepared slides on the projected volumes of the five major product lines to better illustrate the driving force of additional flexibility. Overall, the diskette product was the most stable and the only foreseeable change was staffing may have to drop down a few lines during the summer, which for the past few years had been common. Historically, the third quarter was strong, driven by a retailer push on back to school items, but since the advent of the USB stick, optical media and now more recently network storage, demand was softer during late Q2 and into Q3.

The other product lines formed a different picture. In fact, John hadn't fully appreciated the variability the departments were being asked to absorb until he displayed the volumes visually, on a graph.

Not only was there an impact from the strategic decision to run with lower inventory targets to help with corporate days of supply (DOS) metric, there was an overall downward trend in sales volumes. The inventory drop did make sense as technology ages, there is less appetite to have stock out in the field that isn't active or rotating. At least getting Twin Ports to pace itself with customer demand made sense analytically.

When one studied the numbers, the site not only had to get ready for significant drop in 5476 during summer, but figure out how to maximize production in Keystone and then fulfill the ramp required in Glacier by year end. The good news in this mix was Glacier beginning to replace the volumes from 5476. With higher margin and higher ASP, John readily agreed to take the challenge on; and with the growth year on year in Keystone, a nice upside resulted for the plant.

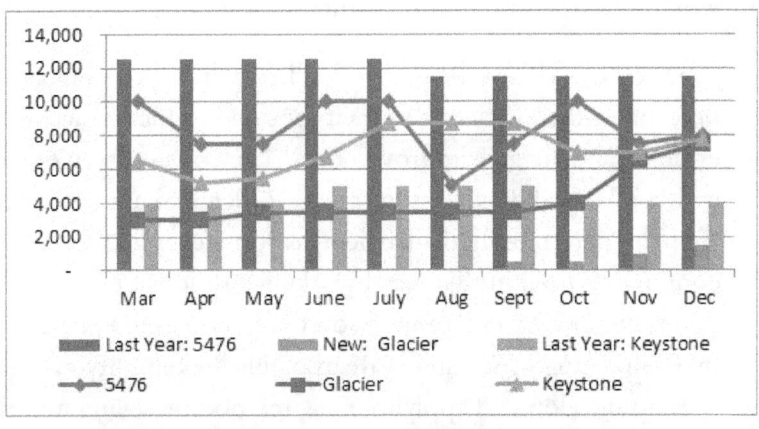

Projected Volumes —Northern Pines Technology Tape Production

As the meeting started, the staff took a few minutes to digest the information and its implications. They knew structurally problems persisted trying to ramp both Glacier and sustain a higher level of Keystone volume during the same period. The other dynamic remaining was a significant user base in 5476 and the demand. While falling off somewhat, it is still relatively strong.

Dan explained the four modules within TWI. His viewpoint rested in the solid understanding and application of two provided the site with the best value. He used the slides directly from the training and explained the differences between the Job Instruction (JI) and Job Methods (JM).

> Job Instruction (JI) - the course teaches trainers (supervisors and experienced workers) to train inexperienced workers and get them "up to speed" faster. The instructors were taught to break down jobs into closely defined steps, showing the procedures while explaining the Key Points and the reasons for the Key Points, then watching the student attempt under close coaching, and finally to gradually wean the student from the coaching. The course emphasized the credo, "If the worker hasn't learned, the instructor hasn't taught."

> Job Methods (JM) - the course teaches workers to evaluate objectively the efficiency of their jobs and to methodically evaluate and suggest improvements. The course also worked with a job breakdown, but teaching students to analyze each step and determining if sufficient reasons remained to continue to do it in that way by asking a series of pointed questions. If they determined some step could be done better by Eliminating, Combining, Rearranging, or Simplifying, they were to develop and apply the new method by selling it to the "boss" and co-workers; obtaining approval based on Safety, Quality, Quantity, and Cost, standardizing the new method, and giving "credit where credit is due."

The discussion quickly evolved to standard work or job methods. The site training process created well-defined procedures for the 'how to' do a variety of manufacturing tasks. Compliance drove this as well as the desire to reduce variation in processes. If everyone does

176

a job the same way, there is likely better ability to control the process and produce a high-quality product with consistency.

The other aspect to generate discussion was the inherent challenges with automated equipment. The variability does not come from the 'worker' but the ability of a worker to know the equipment, understand what all the settings are and ensure adjustments occur within knowledge of the process. The supervisors agreed the biggest challenge in TWI is defining these steps, so someone coming into the area and equipment not familiar can very quickly learn the subtle aspects of operation and avoid the temptation to make an adjustment when not needed.

The term coined for this was process tampering. John did not know if this is common in other industries, but the site learned with the host of automated processes and equipment to primarily trust the process control and not think humans can make it just a little better with a tweak here and a tweak there. Inevitably, something goes awry. Unfortunately, the plant learned the hard way, repeatedly. Very simply, trusting the process controls and only acting on solid, verifiable data equaled the best approach.

John departed for an Economic Development Council [EDC] meeting, so he left the team to continue discussing the challenges and formulating a plan.

Before leaving, John circled back with Jeff and let him know they were on at 7:30 AM Friday for an update. John thanked him and Dan for the help and was on his way to the next never-ending series of meetings which punctuated a typical day in the life of a plant manager.

The EDC meeting fortunately was also at the North Dakota College of Technology, so John took the opportunity to swing by Dennis Cooper's office. Dennis managed the Outreach & Customized Training efforts on behalf of the college. Dennis happened to be out, but John left a note with him to the effect the site needed some customized leadership training based on the life & times of Ernest Shackelton. Originally, John hoped he could develop and give this himself; but as he looked realistically at the time he had and the long list of things needing to be done, it was something he reluctantly had to delegate to Dennis.

John was bummed because studying leadership and teaching on leadership topics are both things he enjoys and helps him grow and stay connected. John often wondered what his life would have been like if had he stayed in school to get a PhD. His end goal would have been a math professor or perhaps teach physics at the college level. In that world, he envisioned himself walking down a tree-lined street; pipe in hand with a tweed jacket, patches on the elbow without a care in the world. He doubted it would really be like that, but it was always fun to dream what might have been.

John walked down the hallway of the administrative building to the Sioux Conference Room where the EDC meeting was about to begin. The meeting agenda was routine except for the update on SunGrown, the new food processing plant located west of town. The recent EDC meetings provided a good forum for John to keep up to date on the building progress. The utilities in the building were going to be operational later in March and equipment was arriving around the same time. They hired a scale up team, which included a skeleton crew to be present for the equipment installation, debug and ramp up process. A series of job fairs would occur in the next few weeks to provide career information and screen candidates.

John stopped over at the construction site last fall and met Rick Gettle. Rick was in his 50's, salt and pepper crew cut and had spent most of his career in the food industry. He worked at the ND Mill in Grand Forks when recruited by SunGrown to manage the construction, start-up and operation of the pasta and flour plant. Rick admitted he thought he was going to retire as the mill manager in Grand Forks. However, the SunGrown opportunity came along.

His kids lived in the Twin Cities, and a move almost two hours closer to his grandkids tipped the scale toward SunGrown.

Rick indicated in his presentation the initial staff would consist of an HR manager, Production Manager, several engineering positions, both equipment and process and up to ten maintenance technicians. More positions to be added in the late spring or early summer as they prepared for full-scale production, which meant converting most of the grain in the local area into flour and pasta. The summer harvest would go just up the road to SunGrown versus being loaded onto railcars and end up in Minneapolis or on a freighter in Duluth threading through the Great Lakes.

Even though Rick and John had not discussed operational strategy much, John knew inherently Rick's effort was going to be successful. He could see the planning and logic behind his thought processes; Rick's proactive approach and his strong ownership for the organization will create a strong culture. Rick performed the scale up just as John would have, loading up on technical talent early for advantage of training from the equipment manufacturers as well as overseeing the installation and then the scale up process.

John knew the consequence of potentially losing some talented people. It was good news SunGrown selected Twin Ports and established it as its home base. A vibrant and diversified manufacturing community is a great complement to the existing agricultural base.

As the meeting continued, John discretely checked the messages on his phone. He missed a call from Yoshimura-san during the meeting. John quickly listened and learned Yoshimura-san was not going to be able to make it up to Twin Ports this trip and would see them during his next visit likely in the summer.

The clock on the Sioux Conference Room wall read 5:25. It was time to head home for dinner and whatever form of chaos was presently holding court at the yellow house on the corner.

The North Dakota College of Technology was just a few blocks north of Stanton's church and home. From the time John started his truck to pulling into his driveway, literally a minute passed.

Chapter 23: A Trip West

Thursday night's events turned out a little differently than planned, mostly because there was no plan. After supper, John received a call from Dave Adams, a friend and former neighbor. Dave and John moved to Twin Ports about the same time, were similar in age, and ended up attending the same church. Dave worked for Northern Pines Technology for a little while and then took a job as the engineering manager for StockPrime, a local cabinet fabrication shop. They operated a variety of technologies including taking MDF and adhering a foil/laminate on top using a vacuum draw process. They sold cabinets and millwork to Menards, Home Depot and Lowes. Dave managed a completely different type of complexity in a different industry, so it was always interesting to compare notes and talk shop when they were together.

Dave had been looking for a four-wheeler for his farm. He and his family moved out of town a couple of years ago to some land and woods by the Red River. He needed a four-wheeler to get around, pull a trailer and as a workhorse for all the improvements, he had envisioned. He located one in the green pages and wanted company along with him to look.

Dave drove his truck out past the small town of Mooreton and along State Highway 13 halfway between Gwinner and Mooreton. The selling party indicated they were right off the highway, just past County Road 56. The night was cold and still with the moon hanging over the prairie like a giant balloon floating in space. Dave was a North Dakota native; a lifer, apart from a stint in the military. John lived exactly one-third of his life in North Dakota, so much less time to appreciate the state.

One of the aspects of life in North Dakota growing in intensity for John was the stark beauty of the prairie. When John first arrived, it seemed so flat, barren and open, just a big uniform spot on the earth where the wind blows strong and cattle outnumber people. Over time, John began to enjoy the changing of the seasons and its impact on the grasslands and fields. Winter brings a white continuity. Summer shows green grass and yellow grains waving in the hot winds. Spring and fall each bring their own unique personalities. There are few sights more beautiful than the sun descending over a field of ripe grain during midsummer; it is simply stunning.

Dave and John arrived at the farm, a quick scoping revealed a large grain operation and maybe they ran a small herd of cattle too. A large, stocky mustached man came out and introduced himself as Red. As they walked across the yard to the machine shed, Red talked about being a 4th generation farmer. His great, great grandfather worked on the bonanza farm located near his section.

Bonanza farms were unique to this area. They were large-scale operations, some encompassing tens of thousands of acres and operated much like a corporate farm of today. They took advantage of the newest technology, which at the time was steam equipment, and used cheap labor. Thanks to James J. Hill, the railroad facilitated the easy transfer of crops from these Midwest farms to the Twin Cities for milling into flour or directly to the east coast. Bonanza farms hired up to 1,000 workers and were like a small city. A great example of a historical site is the Bagg Bonanza Farm located just west of Twin Ports.

The four-wheeler was stored in shed, covered in dust with more than a few pigeon shots covering the seat. It was a bust; the machine had been driven hard and not well maintained. Dave and John each looked at it and reached the same conclusion. The price was right, but knowing it needed new tires and new brakes to make it safe broke the deal. Both men thanked Red, a new farmer friend, and headed back to Dave's truck.

Dave and John shared many common things. They both had five kids and both of their respective last children were infants and not exactly planned. The Stanton's had Mark about six months ago, and Dave's little girl, Taylor, born just four months ago. Both knew they were getting too old to have kids with the shared experience of being the oldest people in the delivery room when the last children were born. Often Dave and John talked about the highs and lows of each of their families, lives and careers. Tonight, the drive back was quiet.

As the men drove east towards town, the lights and steam coming off the chillers and heat transfer units at both Northern Pines Technology and StockPrime were visible from a long distance. Due to the topography of this region, one could probably see Twin Ports from 15 miles out from the west.

In the quietness of the drive, John's mind wandered to the time spent in Twin Ports. He was thankful for his experiences, the people he worked with and the many opportunities along the way. John is a driven person; the drive comes from inside him and can be the best friend and the worst enemy all at the same time.

John came to this community as a 28-year-old, fresh out of graduate school, and with two years of Northern Pines Technology's management training program. He was ready to tackle the world, complete with a list of all he wanted to accomplish. It was comprehensive to the point it included where he wanted to be and what he wanted to do. When thinking about the list, it hit John, he had accomplished most of the things. John wanted to buy a house, pay off the house in less than ten years, have a family, grow in the career and become the site manager. On that count, John was batting 1000.

Not all was rosy however, plenty of disappointments transpired over time. John's first experience as a supervisor resulted in a terrible experience. He recovered, but with each assignment came new challenges.

In fact, John distinctly recalled a quality disaster one year in December. He was running low on vacation, so he opted to work the week between Christmas and New Year's. Traditionally, this is a quiet week to be at the factory. Production is humming to meet year-end orders and revenue targets. Much of the staff are off and things generally just run which makes for good routine and quiet production days for managers and engineers trying to get end of year tasks done.

This particular week, however, proved anything but quiet and routine. The day after Christmas, John prepared for the morning production meeting when the phone rang. It was Mike Sunberg, John's counterpart at the facility in Arizona. His few choice words began the conversation, but his message was clear. Apparently, Twin Ports tape operations recently sent them 5476 blank cartridges for them to wind into finished data cartridges, but they failed in their automated testers. Mike's quick triage developed the working theory Twin Ports mistakenly placed the wrong ID Block on the cartridges, incorrectly identifying them as cleaning cartridges. John quickly looked up on ProdMaster, the inventory control system, and greeted with the news four pallets of 2,750 each were in route, probably bad as well, with another four pallets still at the plant. A major quality screw up.

John paged Jill, the shift cell coordinator, and asked her to meet him in Aisle M in the warehouse as fast as she could get there. Their worst fears were quickly confirmed. The first pallet was bad, and the last pallet bad as well, so John could be sure everything in the middle was also bad. John quickly got the details and quantities and headed to the morning production meeting ready to drop a bomb no one knew was coming. The bad news was enough to disrupt the normal flow, and everyone knew the site had both a quality issue and a service issue needing immediate attention and required all hands-on deck.

John remembered engaging Lenny and had him work with the quality engineer and technicians to identify a disposition and rework plan.

The only thing that would have been worse was if they were all scrap. Without tape, they cost about $15.25 each, resulting in a scrap bill just north of $500,000. By the time he was done with rework, John thought maybe the scrap would have been the lesser of the evils, but at year end, it was never a realistic option.

The rework plan seemed easy enough. The ID blocks would pull out if carefully removed by grabbing the top of the block with pliers. A direct pull would pop the block out and the correct block then reinserted by using a small part of the line. The cartridges then placed in a destacker and pulled off after ID block insertion.

Since other areas of the plant were running at full output coupled with the holiday week, the site was short on labor and imperative to keep the line running. John, the production supervisor and Renee, the materials control scheduler, set up a makeshift rework station. For the next 18 long hours, the team pulled ID blocks off. The effort required two trips to the hardware store for gloves and new pliers and finally at 2:30 the next morning, the rework operation completed the last layer of affected parts. Renee palletized the last parts and placed them in the warehouse under MRB. Due to the lack of available press time, the general molding area needed to mold some new ID blocks and run them after the first of the year. John personally had touched over 4,000 parts, one part every twenty seconds, for nearly 18 hours straight. His hands, shoulders, back and legs felt every tug.

To close out root cause, the maintenance staff quickly added a small, discrete camera after the ID block insertion to ensure the machine 'recipe' matched the color of the ID block. This would never happen again. John could not believe this was missed on the FMEA, as normally this process successfully finds and mitigates failure mechanisms.

Adding to the insult, this cartridge ran for four years, and to John's knowledge, this mistake never occurred before this. John felt disappointed with himself, because the departments and people were better than this. John speculated forces of chaos reign, even in well-engineered designs and processes.

This incident resulted in a painful lesson seared deeply into John's quality philosophy. He vowed to be a champion for prevention by spending the extra few dollars at the onset to avoid these types of costly and painful outcomes.

The incident marks one of the low points in John's career. John remained positive the site manager at the time never knew what happened. For the next two months, John readied himself for a call to the corner office and a well-deserved field dressing; but fortunately, it never happened. If the site manager knew, he never mentioned it; maybe he just chalked it up to the accountability. Who knows?

While in John's little thought vacation, Dave drove through town and sat in front of John's house. John thanked him for the night's entertainment. A ride in the country was about as crazy as it got for two middle-aged men from North Dakota. John was okay with that.

Chapter 24: Three Boxes of Doughnuts

John needed two things at the top of his agenda crossed off the list this week. First, an update and assessment from Jeff on how the TWI session ended; and second, he needed to get in touch with Dennis Cooper to figure out the plan and structure for the upcoming lessons in leadership sessions.

Jeff and John scheduled a 7:30 AM appointment. On this Friday, Jeff beat John to the office. The discussion among friends started by sharing briefly the boondoggle out past Mooreton last night, and Jeff gave a knowing smile.

As the discussion transitioned to work, Jeff remarked Dan asked numerous questions; and by the end of the session, they both agreed there was a good fit for a focused training effort.   Dan clarified the two modules making the most sense for Twin Ports: Job Instruction (JI) and Job Methods (JM). He asked many questions to understand standard work and training structure at the site.

During the discussion, Jeff shared the site did not have dedicated trainers, but relied on skilled workers to do the training. Some excelled and took to the role very studiously, and others viewed it as a distraction.   At one time, the site supported the training department and dedicated trainers; however, with a relatively stable workforce and cost pressures, they became a halftime role and finally absorbed back into operations as a productivity enhancement.   A somewhat expected evolution for mature product lines.

To begin the session with Dan, the production supervisors compiled a complete value stream map. It covered inputs, process steps, buffering and testing.   This was certainly helpful for Dan to get a sense of the overall work content and flow of the vast operation.

Then the team spent time mapped out the biggest challenges. Using the production forecast for the upcoming year, the group agreed the best opportunity to begin cross-training labor was in the 5476 and Keystone product lines. 5476 was dropping 20-30% in overall volume and Keystone was doubling. The technology and lines to make the two products were vastly different. The 5476 product line was one main assembly line, but three feeder lines. The 5476 product had a metal baseplate with the process flow capturing assembly steps, a hub/spool feeder and a door subassembly machine. It took 14 people to run this line. This line also included the ID Block insertion station, the source of John's holiday dismay from a few years ago.

The Keystone product is a much simpler design. There are two main components, the single reel hub/flange inside the cartridge and the cover with the door assembly. The line was only about a quarter of the footprint of the 5476 equipment and used only four operators to maintain the designed line speed.

The tradeoff was going to be very favorable. However, based on the team's recommendation, Jeff needed Sarah to provide direction and ultimately a decision on some other balancing questions.

Jeff pulled out his laptop and opened the summary slides:

1. Standardization of e-stops, message boards and line operation. The equipment was originally designed using two different PLCs, but there was now an emulator. By adding a translator to the older equipment, it could mimic the new equipment. This would cut down on the learning curve as much of the instruction could be programmed to look like what the operators were familiar with already.
2. Videotape and study the different operations which were not routine and make an E-learning module which covered some of these less frequent occurrences on the line.
3. Basic product knowledge – so the operators knew and understood product use, what happened to the cartridges after they left Twin Ports and access to the Customer

Database (CDB) to get information on tech service and complaint handling.

4. Raise the skill level of the operators. This idea came from the maintenance staff, but there were a few key maintenance adjustments which could safely be done by operators. Twin Ports had a long-standing unwritten rule operators don't use tools. If an adjustment required a tool, the decision was to call maintenance, but there were several items the maintenance team deemed could be done safely and effectively by a trained operator.

After thinking about the contents of the presentation for a minute, John quizzed Jeff about the last point. This had been a point of contention with Jeff and the previous site manager. Some of the production managers argued unsuccessfully the operators should have tools. The production managers believed this was essential to survival. Departments are squeezed every year on costs; and yet when the line is down the operator must wait, page an available maintenance person, wait for them to come, make an adjustment and then start the line back up. The analysis pointed out this systematic gap was potentially (on a constrained line) a 1-2% utilization impact.

Over the past few months, John's confidence had grown to the point where he believed a subset of operators were technically capable and ready for the next level of responsibility.

Earlier, Jeff fought the staff from an HR perspective. Jeff reasoned he had to deal with the fallout. Jeff argued, "very soon after implementation, I will have newly empowered employees knocking on my door saying, "Hey, we are adjusting machines, turning wrenches, fixing issues, and we are making $12.54/hour. We know maintenance is making a lot more. We want some of the action."" He had a point; the last time John checked, the maintenance personnel wages were in the $19-$22/hour range. Unfortunately, it was one of those Solomon-type questions – there really isn't a good answer to make everyone happy.

John had tremendous respect for Jeff; but disagreed with Jeff rather strongly in this area. Jeff came from an equity and human resource professional point of view, and John was coming from a business survival point of view, there was little common ground on the topic

John asked pointedly, "Jeff where are you on this issue of operators and empowering them to make significant machine adjustments?" Without hesitation, Jeff said, "Based on what you have told us the past two weeks, I think we really have to think outside normal operating parameters. Knowing this place could disappear in twelve months is going to take all of us outside our comfort zone, and this is something I must own and manage. Call this my contribution." John appreciated he was now ready to take on this challenge.

Human Resources had to be the enforcer in so many ways, so John did not take Jeff's commitment lightly. John knew Jeff was stepping up to the plate on this one. Once an operator has worn down the supervisor on an issue like pay, the next step is always, "I'm going to take this to HR." Jeff had a listening ear, but when he had heard enough, he was confident enough to say, "Maybe this isn't the place for you. I can call Scott over at Goodsons. I know they are looking for the graveyard shift, and I hear they pay about 70% of what we do. Interested?" Usually the astute person gets the message and gives up the cause.

The conversation morphed from operator duties into a structural reorganization, which John had not thought much about. At Northern Pines Technology, it seemed every 18 months there was a required reorganization of duties, whether it is needed or not. The switch flips from regional organization and autonomy to centralized or a headquarters-based organization and a few permutations in the middle. John was not a fan of reorganizing for reorganization's sake. Often the very act of reorganizing creates posturing, politics; and in the end, most of the relationships and work connections morph back into the established old networks and way things used to be anyway.

The best-executed reorganizations are those where the management team wants to send a signal to the organization things need to change and change dramatically.

The last major restructuring at the plant occurred in 2000 when the businesses organized around Personal Storage, Small and Medium Business and Enterprise. The site aligned the focused factories with the same thinking. It made sense and it allowed the teams a direct line of sight into the businesses they supported. In fact, the site even had seats on the business council so the production managers heard firsthand what was happening in the business. It was a strong alignment and they maintained it even after the business had morphed into a new strategy based on customers. These never worked for Twin Ports, because the site serviced and supplied customers with product from three focused factories. Twin Ports maintained the focused factories and dealt with the ensuing matrix.

Jeff said he was open to meeting with a few of the department heads and thinking through some options for a new organization. John encouraged him to look at it from all angles. John said, "I realize for everything we fix, we probably break something else. So, let's just make sure the destination is better than where we are today." Jeff agreed adding, "Slow and steady."

Diane rounded up Dennis for a 10:00 AM call. Jeff and John wrapped up, and John went down the hall back to the tool shop to see Steve Kroft. Steve is the tooling services manager, and today he was helping John with a 'government' project. At the cabin, a five-sided bolt turned the water on and off, the master key. The shop said they would make a custom wrench so John could turn this thing. Before shutting down the cabin for the winter, John snapped a few pictures and took a few measurements. Steve finished it, and so John now had few minutes to wander back to pick it up.

The fabrication shop does amazing things. Early on, John knew very little about this area of the site. His specific training and background was not in molding and tooling, but John acclimated to the fact within his site, this was one of the hidden gems of Northern Pines. John showed it off with passion and conviction, because it really was a premier example of a world class tool shop. The craftsmen could fabricate anything. For example, just last month the shop hosted engineers from a startup company trying to use a 24-inch glass array for into for some type antibody capture work they were doing for a top secret biomedical application. Across the array of glass, they required a surface profile varying less than one millionth of an inch. It took the shop two weeks to fabricate the unit and complete the job. By all indications, the company deemed the resulting prototype successful. They searched all over the world for a shop which could do this, and only found a few. Since this was for a sensitive application, they found some comfort in finding a stateside shop which could fabricate to the critical tolerances required.

John thanked Steve for the work and jokingly asked, "How much do I owe?" He responded back, "Boxes of doughnuts every Friday would do just fine." John compromised and said, "How about three dozen next week on Friday to keep the shop happy?" They shook; fair price for a job well done.

John called Dennis a few minutes after 10. Dennis was somewhat excited. A company by the name of Colby Training has taken information and already done the 'translation' into business-speak. Apparently, others also thought Shackelton's adventures would translate well into leadership training. Dennis directed John to their website and talked through what might make sense.

Scanning through their material, John checked the areas he thought were most applicable for the site, given the present situation.
- What is leadership and how to develop leadership skills
- Getting the best from each person
- Overcoming obstacles by picking the right team
- Leading in a crisis

There was a lot of good stuff here, but John thought narrowing this to five main points was going to be about all the organization could digest and use in the next few months.

John had two objectives, which he went on to explain to Dennis. "First, for the entire plant population, I want to create an awareness and expectation everyone on the site understands and follows these principles. Also, I think it would be extraordinarily helpful if we had common language of being able to recognize when we are in a crisis and when we need to 'pick a team' we are not selecting favorites."

John further explained, "When we have attempted things like this in the past, we have had hard feelings, as to why they were not chosen to be a lead person or to be part of a pilot project. I need everyone on this to understand, we are selecting based on skills, abilities and putting a collection together of the best people to achieve a very difficult goal."

John ended, "When we are successful in the pilot project, we will expand to more people, but at the beginning, we absolutely have to have a strong focus on a smaller set of people. I am hoping when people see the Shackelton story – they will make the same connection. The goal for the entire team is survival and everyone has a part to play."

Dennis responded affirmatively, saying, "I understand, we have the same type of response sometimes at the college, we have to make tough decisions and sometimes that creates tension."

Regarding the staff and leadership team, John wanted to go deeper. He wanted to offer assessments on their leading ability and identify what they do well and where they need to improve. He then wanted the ability to provide some level of coaching to help build their capability in the area of leadership.

Dennis asked questions about the number of staff currently and how best to work within the confines of the four-crew schedule. He had a good idea of the needs, but wanted to run it by a few of his facilitators before getting back to John with a plan in a few weeks. John challenged him, "We don't have a few weeks." Dennis committed to returning in a week with his thoughts and a plan.

Dennis asked, "How well do you know the story?" John had read Shackelton's Incredible Journey by Alfred Lansing, which if memory served him correctly, was written back in the 1950s. Together they marveled at how such a great story, mothballed for almost a hundred years, then dusted off to provide so many great leadership lessons for today.

John did not know this, but in researching the book, Lansing spoke with ten of the surviving crew members for a firsthand account. There is no better account of a story like this than from the men who lived it. It truly is a story of heroism for the ages.

John smiled. He knew the plant was going to enjoy learning about a fiercely, independent explorer who fought all the odds to reach his goal.

This reminded him of a plant that was fighting the odds to survive.

Good stuff.

Chapter 25: A Trip to the Head Shed

Doug Walker, John's boss, typically brought the site managers (his direct reports) into town the second week of the month. By then, the sites had analyzed unit cost numbers, production attainment, service commitments and could report on results and deviations. This was the last month in the quarter, so there would be additional pressure to show good numbers to support a strong close.

Twin Ports' numbers would be predictably acceptable. John sensed a different focus to the meetings, especially after the experience with Doug last month and now knowing there was a plan. If the grand plan came to fruition, Mendal Enterprises would take over these operations. John expected periodic updates and assessments from the folks at Mendal. John was also curious to hear how the site visits had gone at the coating facilities.

The time in town also should shed some light onto the coating analysis as site managers were supposed to get an update on the consolidation of coaters. It was framed as a 'status update' from the technical team who was tasked with figuring out the most capable coater and the costs associated with an international move.

Doug began the meeting promptly at 8:00 AM. All of Doug's direct reports were in Aquarius, a standard issue medium-sized conference room and scattered around the shiny walnut table. The meeting consisted of the division's four plant managers, the finance manager, R&D Director and supply chain manager. Doug's executive assistant joined the group, taking notes and following up on items and information the senior managers and directors needed throughout the day.

A painstakingly slow, line-by-line review of plant spending, sales and service metrics consumed the morning; with absolutely no new or interesting news. The sales trajectory of the division seemed to be holding into the new fiscal year as well. Northern Pines traded off-market share with the competition and pricing was reduced to a street fight. The one with the lowest price could steal business; but if they took it below cost; everyone knew it wasn't sustainable. The fighters traded back and forth on customers and segments. All agreed it is not a real satisfying way to run a business, but it is hard to break the cycle. The only way to get ahead was rapid and sustained cost reduction.

In the afternoon, the agenda transitioned into the plant reviews. Each site had about 45 minutes to go over the standard slides. Since John conducted the local employee meetings last week at the site, he only had to update a few things in preparation for this week. John did add one slide. He was interested in the reception of the information; it was a teaser.

Ray Mullins from the Arizona facility went first. He began with the agenda; but somehow early on, his presentation took a turn and morphed into a general discussion about the Mendal visits to the sites. Ray went on to explain he was not sure the folks from Mendal had seen a magnetic media coating operation before, a good number of their questions centered on the ovens and web handling and very little on the coating head and die. Everyone knows this is the most critical for the application, caliper and overall coating consistency.

Mendal asked questions about compounding as well. John thought, after hearing the discussion, they were under the impression the slurry is purchased when in reality the mixing, milling and processing of the slurry is at least as important as the coating operation. It also seemed from the discussion Mendal were quick studies. Some of the questions at the Arizona facility served as future probing for the next visits to California and Oregon.

As the discussion wound down, John shared Mendal was quite familiar and conversant with the hard goods industry. The visitors seemed to both appreciate and understand the work done at the site in tooling development, machine building and running the assembly operations. John continued, "They seemed a little less comfortable with the concept of vertical integration; however, clearly they understood the benefit after their time at Twin Ports."

The phone vibrated and John looked down. It was a text from Diane informing him Doc called. This was interesting. Dale Shaffer, better known as Doc, was the first manager of the Twin Ports plant. Diane's text message was as follows:

```
John, just had call from Doc; he is in town,
congratulates you on promotion and wants to
have coffee.   Set up for later in week?   - D
```

John thought it was a little curious Doc wanted to see him; but reasoned Doc probably just wanted to get caught up on plant news.

John's turn came at 4:34 PM. The previous reviews ran a bit long. John knew everyone was tired, so he spared them the 45-minute version of Twin Ports February performance. He had done enough of these types of presentations; he mentally prepared the short and the long version. Long version was used if the tone of the meeting demanded detailed answers. John read people were tired, not wanting to hear another view, and most people had checked out. John did share one slide at the end, which started another round of discussion. John called it Continuous Improvement with 3 points.

John knew several questions would arise, and rehearsed the comeback, trying to strike the balance between not being a jerk but not pushover. He was still trying to find his ground with a new group of influential peers. Even though he was officially the rookie, John wanted them to know, he hadn't planned on being a freshman very long.

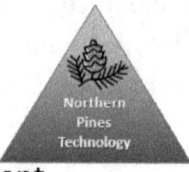

Continuous Improvement
Twin Ports

1. QICR

2. TWI

3. Leadership Development

It was Charlie Wilson from the Oregon operation that asked the question, or maybe better lobbed the softball, "John, you heard the same thing we did two or three weeks ago. Why are you talking about these types of activities for Twin Ports and taking on new initiatives? Doesn't it seem obvious from the meeting at the Northland our operations are moving offshore?"

John simply said, "I think the role of our collective sites is to bring the maximum value to the overall organization. And whether we are making products or someone is making them for us, we have an obligation to provide them the best and healthiest possible scenario. With a product like diskettes, as you know, if we slip a quarter or two behind on QICR, we are going to give up margins we have worked so hard for and we'll begin to lose business in retail. They clearly now want the lowest price. We just have the benefit of giving them six-sigma quality at the lowest price. If we lose business, they are going to have to learn that lesson the hard way."

John went on, "TWI is something we have talked about as a division." John recalled, "As my team dug in and started doing more research; as we transfer operations, having standard work, job methods and a structure to lean on is going to be advantageous and help Mendal."

Tough to argue with logic, at least that was John's thought as pondered carefully his words, both what was said and what was left unsaid.

John knew it would not surprise anyone his passion for leadership and leadership development. "If I am going to turn 450 people loose into this lousy job market, the least I can do is help them understand they can be leaders and have a huge influence and impact from where they are. The best leaders are not always those that hold the title."

John delivered his message; trying to tow the company line. It was a fine tightrope to talk; but in retrospect, John was reasonable pleased with his speaking performance.

Discussion wrapped up about 5:10, and the plan was to meet at six and head out to Cattle Company for red meat. Normally, John enjoyed the crew, as most of the time John did like their company and it was always good to socialize a little. It helped build relationships, but Doug gave John dispensation last week to miss the first evening 'team building' event.

Kristin was aware of a couple in the Twin Cities who recently returned from Ukraine with their adopted child. She learned of their trip through Reece's Rainbow, so she set up a meeting with the Green's for John during his time in the Twin Cities.

Steve and Kelsey Green had been to Ukraine between Thanksgiving and Christmas and had adopted a special needs child named Sergei. He was now home with them in Brooklyn Center, and John wanted to meet them, see their family and get a first-hand account of what to expect when their time comes to make a very similar trip.

Chapter 26: Meeting a Miracle

John called the Greens on his cell phone as he navigated the rush hour traffic. He told them best estimate to be there was about 30 minutes. Steve Green said supper would be ready. John had not ever met Steve and Kelsey, only read bits and pieces Kristin shared as she followed their adoption blog.

It was disconcerting for John to be walking into a home and family he never met to talk through some very personal topics. Everything about this adoption was stretching him. He never envisioned even a year ago that he would be on the cusp of a trip to Ukraine to pick up a little girl he had never met and was slowly beginning to think of her as his daughter. He used the driving time to both decompress and think of good avenues for conversation and questions. He hoped the hosts would be open to his questions to find out what it was really like to go through this entire adoption process.

John knew the Greens traveled to the Crimean Peninsula and specifically to Sevastopol. From watching the movie K-19 starring Harrison Ford, John knew Sevastopol was much like Richmond, Virginia, home the former USSR naval operations. In fact, since the fall of the Soviet Union, the remaining Russian Navy carried a lease arrangement with Ukraine. The area remains highly strategic and is home to the USSR Black Sea fleet. Beyond those few facts, John would have to learn as much as he could from their firsthand experience.

John arrived at 5:50 PM and parked on the street. The area had as much snow on the ground as Twin Ports. John looked for the driveway to avoid climbing over the mound of snow covering the boulevard. He walked up the driveway to their modest home in a well-established neighborhood. Brooklyn Center was once a thriving center for agriculture, but as North Minneapolis spread out, it became enveloped and its role changed to near city suburb. Still it was a good place to buy a starter home and begin a family.

The Greens lived just to the south of 694, west of the Earl Brown Center on Ross Drive. Earl Brown was an early resident who established one of the larger farming operations in the area. He was a man of many talents and was instrumental in setting up the Minnesota State Patrol. The city preserved his farm and it sits just south of the interstate. The road to the Greens ran adjacent to the Brown farm.

John rang the doorbell, immediately triggering a dog bark. Steve answered the door, firmly pushed and verbally shushed the dog back out of the entryway. Steve said, "Watson, back. The dog is harmless. This is a case where the bark is worse than the bite. She'll settle down in a minute."

Sure enough, as John came in and took his coat off, Watson calmed down and was much more curious about the new smells instead of warding off the intruder. Steve and John shook hands and Steve offered to take his coat.

John glanced over to the sofa in the living room and saw a small fine-featured boy, sitting on the floor rocking gently back and forth. Steve approached Sergei and looked intently at him. Sergei rocked for a few more cycles and then stopped. A calm look replaced the blank stare, and the boy reached up his arms quietly mouthing a word sounding like 'up.' Steve picked him up and introduced John to his son, Sergei. Sergei seemed very petite; in fact, his arms and legs seemed not much bigger than John's fingers. John reached out to shake his hand, and he withdrew. John noticed the characteristics of trisomy 21 in his eyes and facial features. Steve just held him tight as he retreated into his daddy's sweatshirt.

A petite and pretty thirty-something woman emerged from the kitchen and John introduced himself to Kelsey. She and Kristin talked a few times on the phone, so John presumed they knew more about him than he knew about them. John thanked them in advance for having him.

John remembered Kristin gave him a present to give to Sergei. Buried in his pocket, John fished out a small package wrapped in bright blue paper. John asked if it was okay to give Sergei something and Kelsey said, "That would be fine; he loves gifts." Caroline and John visited the drug store on Saturday, and Caroline picked out a little car for Sergei. John asked Caroline to pick out something from the toy aisle. He needed to contain a minor fit when Caroline chose an Ariel doll. John told her Sergei might not appreciate a mermaid and maybe a gift for boy might be more appropriate. Together they found a small Jeep and trailer – which Caroline finally agreed would be good fun for Sergei.

Sergei – Adopted by Steve & Kelsey Green

John offered the small package to Sergei. He grabbed it instinctively, but it was apparent he did not know exactly what to do with it. Steve

202

reminded him it was like Christmas and then he smiled, remembered and started to open the package with his small hands. He grinned from ear to ear when he saw it and wanted down on the floor. He seemed to know what it was and was especially pleased when it had a removable trailer. He quickly realized the trailer was the perfect size for a Hot Wheels car. Soon the jeep, trailer and Hot Wheels car scooted around the floor in a circle surrounding Sergei. He was lost in his own world in a good sort of way.

Kelsey invited John and Steve to the kitchen for dinner. John smelled meatloaf as he walked through the kitchen to the dining area. He loved meatloaf; he always had. Steve prayed thanking God for the food, life here on planet earth and for protection and comfort for the orphans without a home, including Vika. John was touched by the reference to his yet unseen daughter. Sergei sat in a booster seat and looked out of the corner of the eye, one hand on the car and the other covering his eye, trying to pray maybe.

John asked if questions during mealtime were okay, and they assured him they expected it; so, John began to pepper them with questions immediately. "What was the motivation for traveling halfway around the world to adopt a special needs child?" Kelsey explained she worked as a personal care assistant in college. She cared for a little girl named Olivia who had Down syndrome and fell in love with this little girl. Olivia taught Kelsey so much about life and living, how to be content, using one's God-given potential, and never to label or think less of someone because of his or her disability. Now in her teens, Olivia sends Kelsey an email almost every week. Olivia reads types and communicates very well despite her disability. Kelsey said, "It is funny, I have known Olivia almost all her life and the least interesting thing about her is the fact that she has a disability. She is so vibrant, full of life, ideas and thoughts on how the world works – that I don't even think about it anymore." Kelsey and Olivia don't see each other often, but are still very much in each other's life.

The idea of adoption intrigued the Greens and seemed like a reasonable approach. They did not have biological children yet and with so many children without a home around the world, adoption was something Kelsey and Steve could do, a very small step to change the world, for at least one child.

They started in the US adoption system and realized that it was a multi-year process. Through research, they became aware of special needs kids around the world, particularly in Eastern Europe. This started the process in earnest to bring Sergei home. In fact, they decided on this course of action on Valentine's Day of last year, and Sergei was home by Christmas. "About 10 months then," John calculated. "That's fast."

The Greens' process confirmed the Stanton's process: home study, submit dossier, wait. The steps sounded familiar.

Steve began retelling their story beginning with travels to Ukraine. They left in the middle of November, traveling first to Kiev for a meeting with the Centre of Adoption at the Ministry of Ukraine for Family, Youth and Sports. During this meeting, officials presented them with children available for adoption.

The Greens looked at only one picture. The image of the first little boy shown to them won their heart. They traveled to Sevastopol via train the next day. It was a long train-ride, and they arrived late at night. Their facilitator, Alexandra, met them at the station and they hopped into her Lata. Ten minutes later, they climbed the dark steps of their new home away from home.

Excited, scared, and jetlagged, Steve and Kelsey had no idea what the next few weeks held, but they were ready.

Steve continued, "We waited one day to get permission from the orphanage to visit. Alexandra reassured them this was standard and not to worry. Our first day consisted of finding the local market, stocking up on bread, cheese, meat, and muesli. Alexandra pointed out a dumpling-like dish called varenyky. We strolled around the streets adjacent to our apartment, but frankly we were afraid to venture much further. Even though every block was different, there was sameness and a lack of language that made navigating by landmarks a little challenging."

Steve admitted, "Even in a relatively small area, we could see ourselves getting lost. So many areas were deceptively similar. I envisioned us walking down a street and suddenly having no idea where we were." Kelsey chimed in, "Our boldness grew over time."

Steve continued, "Meeting Sergei for the first time and the process of bonding along with some of the curiosities of life in a Ukrainian orphanage was an experience I will never forget. Sergei was four; however, he looked more like two. Just a few oddities, toys were scattered the floors of the orphanage, but I never observed any of the children playing with them. Workers were clinical in their approach, not showing a lot of emotion. The orphanage was warm, food was available, yet all the children seemed small and their eyes somewhat hollow. When we walked by the babies lying in their cribs, we heard whimpering, but very little crying."

Kelsey picked up the story, "Sergei was assigned to a group of seven other children, both boys and girls. The assigned "grupa" was their family for all practical purposes. They ate together, watched soap operas with the workers together and slept in a common room together. When one was sick, they were all restricted to their beds. The grupa was their whole world, and we never saw any affection between workers or between the children." Kelsey surmised, "The children didn't know how. The workers never modeled affection."

After dinner, Steve, Kelsey, and John retreated to the living room where Sergei resumed his synchronous rocking back and forth. Kelsey learned almost all the kids in the orphanage develop some form of self-soothing behavior. Kelsey elaborated, "Some children sucked their thumbs or their tongue; some rocked. Some behaviors escalated to self-injury, such as banging their head. I have read mixed opinions and theories exist on the "why's" of this behavior, but many equate it to the children's own form of self-nurturing, or a way of coping in a very stressful environment."

Steve reiterated, "most of the recent literature defined the self-soothing behaviors because of Distress Tolerance. This acts as one of four alternatives that help one cope with overwhelming negative emotions or intolerable situations. Several recent studies point to creating shared emotions as strong as soldiers who experience Post Traumatic Stress Disorder. Pretty heavy stuff for a four-year-old with Down syndrome to process." John nodded, it was sobering to hear firsthand some of the challenges his family had yet to face.

Steve continued, "When you think about it, it makes sense. These children never learned about love or security. The only needs that were met were the minimum required for their survival; food and medical care if they had a disease or were injured. Even these needs were not always consistently met, so between the uncertainty and the lack of affection, behaviors to compensate are learned." Steve mused, "Just think about the internal stress that would cause; a permanent state of flux, not knowing who was going to take care of you, when you would be taken care of and if care would come at all. The body and brain react to that as stress; and the response? The children develop their own internal coping mechanisms."

Sergei and Kelsey disappeared down the hall a few minutes before 8:00, and John assumed it was bedtime. Even though it was quiet tonight, Steve admitted bedtime was a challenge. Steve said, "Sergei does not nap and is up early and once up, is up for all day. Sleeping doesn't come naturally to him. He fights it, acts as if he is scared."

Steve and Kelsey wrestle with why. Does he miss his grupa? Steve said, "We have tried everything we can think of, turning on music and lights. Making it noisy, quiet, well lit, dark – and every combination in between. The only thing workable now is rocking.

Early on, Sergei disliked physical touch, but one of the most reinforcing behaviors is now Sergei seeks us out for hugs." Steve said, "that is absolutely the best. He now hugs us much more frequently and also seems to know they mean affection."

John asked about the process, the courts, the paperwork and challenges with navigating the Ukrainian legal system. Steve reassured John, their facilitator, Alexandra, worked miracles, and it was only through her skills and abilities they navigated the system successfully. Coincidentally, the Stanton's chose the same agency. It reassured John to know a level of competency accompanied the agency. Who knows? Maybe the possibility existed for Alexandra to facilitate their adoption, especially if Vika lived in an orphanage near or in the Crimean Peninsula.

John knew the hour was getting late, but he could not get a quick peek at his watch without making it obvious. This information was invaluable. He needed to take good mental notes because Kristin would fire questions at him when he returned home.

John finally managed to glance down at his watch. It was 10:30. John apologized for the lateness of the hour, but thanked both Kelsey and Steve for the meatloaf, their time and wished them well in the new adventure of parenting. They promised to stay in touch and exchanged phone numbers and email addresses.

John encouraged the Greens to follow Kristin's blog and join their journey. John walked into the starry, dark, Minnesota night. Again, his thoughts travelled halfway around the world to a little girl named Vika, who remained unaware of a father and a family waiting just for her.

What a truly amazing night! John's mind raced as he drove back to St. Paul. John stirred during the night as between awake, dreams and sleep he recalled the answers to his questions. Some things the Greens stated comforted John; but frankly, some terrified him.

Chapter 27: A 30-Year-Old Promise.

Doc was in town. Diane set up a meeting with Dale Shaffer, better known as Doc, on Thursday after John returned from the meetings in the Twin Cities.

Doc worked as the first manager of the Twin Ports plant. John always knew him as Doc and never figured out why or how he earned his nickname. He oversaw the design, construction and scale up of the first operations dating back to the early 1970s. Many interesting stories and legends exist about the opening of the plant and early plant operations.

John's first meeting with Doc occurred on John's second day of employment at Twin Ports. John was working through the list of 'people to meet' that Lenny prepared, and Doc appeared on the list. Doc was the quality manager when John started 15-plus years ago. He served as a mentor to John for the first few years. John held a healthy respect (and a small amount of fear) but John trusted Doc inherently.

Doc was old school, and that was okay. He ran a tight operation. He would come in late evenings and look things over. He had the expectation the job was being done exactly the same way, irrespective of who was watching or time of day. People always stood up a little straighter with Doc in the house. John thought highly of him, and Doc certainly gave John excellent insights into quality, life and career John still carried throughout his tenure as plant manager.

Post retirement, Doc was living the good life. Summers were spent in North Dakota and winters consumed by his newest passion of golf. He did not start to play golf until he was retired and prided himself in his +4 handicap. He must have been in his mid-70s now, but Doc could keep up with the younger guys just fine.

Diane explained Doc likes to stay in touch with the plant when he is in town. Since John became plant manager in October and Doc left for AZ in November, they had not connected yet. This was one of John's unwritten job duties, but one that was enjoyable and promised to be interesting.

Prior to meeting Doc, Diane clued John in that Doc was famously frugal, so this was John's treat. Diane knew Doc well. She worked as his administrative assistant for part of his time at the Twin Ports plant. John knew the information gained from Doc would be more valuable than a $3.00 pot of coffee.

A funeral brought Doc to town. One of his golfing buddies and a former city council member from Twin Ports passed away, so Doc traveled back for the week. Doc ran the plant back in a time when the plant and city were almost one. In the early 70s, rural areas clamored for jobs and industry. Northern Pines Technology or MN Consolidated Industries, as it was known back then, was a prime catch. MN Consolidated located in communities with good transportation access, a technical college, a small city with enough infrastructures to support a plant. Twin Ports fit MN Consolidated's search for a new location well.

John and Doc met at The Fryin' Pan, a local family restaurant. On any given morning, all sorts of groups met. The farmers, retired businessmen, the construction crew working on the SunGrown plant and others called this place home for their morning routines.

Doc looked good, the Arizona sun produced a bronze shade to his skin. Those who lived in the north and did not see much of the sun until the weekend exhibited a decidedly different complexion, basically like pasty white bread. Doc golfed, walked, and in general, enjoyed the spoils of frugality and retired life.

Doc asked John how things were going at the plant, an expected and typical lead off question. John knew he could not share everything, but did suggest the competitive pressures were always great and seemingly, someone was always lurking in weeds ready to take away the business. John explained that most of Northern Pines' competition came from low labor cost countries like China, Taiwan, India and the Philippines.

He explained to Doc the new dynamic in the past few years. Times had changed since Doc managed the plant. The notion of outsourcing a product to those areas would have been unthinkable when the plant opened. His reign over the plan took place at a day and time when US manufacturing was dominant and seemingly unshakable. John thought, how quickly the world changes. First textiles, then televisions and electronics, and today it is almost every industry faces the intense pressure of global competition.

Technology connected individuals and encouraged them to have the latest and fastest. Big box retail drove the desire for cheap goods. Corporate leaders looked at labor and overhead costs as a primary variable to drive sourcing decisions. John recognized he might be oversimplifying, but many days, it seemed it could be reduced to an easy, yet flawed equation.

Doc began talking about the early days of the plant. John heard bits and pieces of this story, but he was absolutely fascinated to hear it firsthand. Doc began his story in 1973. He said, "I was working in the engineering department for the magnetic recording division. At the time, this involved several products: IBM 3420 tape used on the Model 3 5 and 7 IBM mainframes. This also included some products in the consumer and professional audio and video markets. Two different markets, but built from the same technology."

The next part of the story proved especially interesting. Doc continued, "The decision to build the plant occurred in late 1973. The groundbreaking commenced in April of 1974. Construction continued into the fall to enclose the building. Exterior construction turned out relatively simple utilizing concrete tip up panels fabricated

90 miles away in Alexandria. The workers dedicated the late fall and early winter to finishing off the interior infrastructure. You know, a significant amount of air, water and vacuum lines were needed for the early molding and assembly equipment."

Doc continued, "The odd part of the story was even though the building as up - the plant operations did not start up for almost another two years. The economy was doing poorly, inflation running high, the oil embargo in full force, gas prices doubled; and on the political scene, Watergate remained very fresh in peoples' minds. It was a time of tremendous turmoil. I remember the executives struggling with how to bring a new plant on-line during all this chaos. MN Consolidated Industries' conservative leadership persisted in their unwillingness to procure the final investments for full operation until the economic picture improved."

John asked Doc, "What did you do for those two years?" Doc smiled and said, "Well, I went to a lot of meetings at city hall, got to know the mayor and the council very well. The members were just beside themselves. It was like the kids' Christmas morning that never came. They were counting on these new jobs and increased tax base, and opened a new area in the northwest part of town. They added roads, city utilities. The spec houses built were empty and no one was interested in buying or building."

Doc went on to say he spent a lot of time doing research on molding, assembly, material handling; because when the signal was given to go, he wanted to be ready.

Doc said, "These were tough times, John. I was the new guy in town. Other than being from North Dakota, I did not know the local politics. I was in a bit of a pressure cooker here, because all the focus was on me." Doc continued, "In a small town, I was the face of the company. I think the city was having a hard time figuring out, as was I, what kind of business MN Consolidated ran?" Doc asked John,

"Did you ever hear about the near bankruptcy of Twin Ports?" John had not, and asked Doc to tell him the story.

Doc lowered his voice a little, "In 1975, things got so bad. It was a horrible year for crops as well. The hot, dry summer withered up a good chunk of the corn, soybean and sugar beet crop. In fact, yields were down in the 60% range when compared to an average year. The plant was built, but the little tax revenue and the local economy struggled the same as the national economy. Anyway, when the tax revenues were collected, the budget was slashed. There was not enough money to keep the basic services going: water, sewer and police protection. So, the town prepared to go to the state and basically say they were bankrupt."

By now," Doc went on, "I was more savvy about the local politics and knew this really might happen."

Doc also knew this put MN Consolidated in a horrible position. They were one of the contributors to the financial mess. Twin Ports expected and budgeted tax revenue based on the projected plant start up.

Doc served as mediator and connected the mayor of Twin Ports with the Chief Legal Counsel at MN Consolidated, a gentleman named Harris Thronson. He continued his story, "They traveled to the cities, and the mayor and Harris hit it off pretty well. Harris apparently was from the eastern part of South Dakota, so between a shared love of pheasant hunting and small town life, the pair established common ground.

They continued with a series of follow-up meetings, and when it was done, MN Consolidated and the city of Twin Ports agreed to three things."

Doc quietly stated three points:

1. MN Consolidated originally was given land for the site at no cost. Harris agreed to pay fair market for the land, which would provide the city some much-needed operating funds.
2. They jointly developed a formula in which MN Consolidated would receive a reduced tax rate for the following 30 years, but taxation would start immediately, based on projected operations. This would help alleviate the short-term cash flow issues of the city and bridge the gap between now and when the plant did indeed start up and tax revenue would begin to flow. MN Consolidated received the benefit of a lower rate for the future by agreeing to this tax structure.
3. Lastly, MN Consolidated would notify Twin Ports City Council and give them at least three-year notice of any planned plant closure as a future hedge against this happening in the future.

Doc raised his voice a little, as if the secret was over, "When it was all said and done, each party gave something and each party gained something. It was a very reasonable compromise allowing both entities to move past the unpleasant situation. The city was grateful Harris understood the impact of a large business or operation in a small town, and MN Consolidated wanted to be a good corporate citizen."

John sat stunned for just a minute. John did not know if Doc noticed it or not, but John asked him to repeat the last part and then subtly tried to ask about the current state of this agreement. John's mind raced: Was it written down? Who knew about it? And most importantly, was it still in force?

Doc continued explaining the plant did open in January of 1976. MN Consolidated started adding to the city coffers per the agreement several months earlier. The plant hiring started in November, and by March, the first products began assembly in a state of the art manufacturing plant. The central coating plant, located in St. Paul at the time, produced reels of audio tape, and the team in Twin Ports molded reels, cases, covers, components and all types of other plastic parts to be assembled into cartridges holding the hits from the music of the day including: Elton John, The Doobie Brothers, The Eagles and Glen Campbell.

Due to rapid changes in technology in the recording and information storage industries, the plant continued its path of success. A series of prudent expansions as new product lines were introduced creating solid growth. The plant and the town, in some senses, grew up together.

Doc and John both reminisced. Twin Ports remained a great plant with awesome talent, good people and a long record of being a rock-solid business partner. Doc said, "At the time, we did not have quite the legacy of the mining or auto industry. During my time, an employee's child could graduate from high school in May, begin working for MN Consolidated in June; and if they were dependable and hardworking, they could make a good living and a long career. The plant has now been a fixture in the Twin Towns for over 25 years. You know what – many did just that; there were more than a few multigenerational families at Twin Ports."

For as many years as John could remember, Twin Ports heralded as the premier manufacturing employer in the region, because of their good wages, solid benefits and opportunity for advancement. The site held a subtle advantage over other manufacturers. Due to the products and process requirements, the site was air conditioned in the summer, a luxury not available at any other facility in town.

Doc sipped on his coffee and looked wistfully out on Main Street. He said, "The site manager job was the best job I ever had. It had its pressures, but knowing the talent that existed in the plant and the drive and desire to get things done, most days were very rewarding." John nodded in agreement. Even though John was the rookie, he could see the same perspective and John looked forward to having the years of confidence of a man of Doc's tenure. Realistically, John was more worried about making it through the next quarter, let alone years to come.

The last thing John needed to discreetly extract from Doc was information about this mystery agreement forged over thirty years ago. John asked somewhat casually, "Doc, this history is really interesting to me. Some of those documents that you talked about, do they still exist?" Doc recalled the last time he saw them, they were in a safety deposit box at the bank. John remembered an envelope in his desk drawer with a key that said, "Twin Ports – Safety Deposit Box: Plains Bank and Trust." John made a note to take the key to the bank at the earliest opportunity and see what was in the box.

John was quite certain few, if any, others knew this information, and he was also confident none of the people calling the shots in the Mendal Enterprises deal were aware of this. If the documents still existed and it was some type of legal document construed as a contract, an interesting and new wrinkle factored into the equation. Twin Ports might be on the hook to notify the city three years in advance of a plant closure, especially if Northern Pines used the reduced tax structure benefit as well.

John thanked Doc for the visit, and said he would look forward to seeing him in a few months when he returned to Twin Ports for the summer. They shook hands and Doc left John at the cash register to fork over $4.27 to pay the bill. John smiled.

He asked Doc to leave a tip and noticed he left $5. Maybe his ways are changing.

Chapter 28: A Long Week.

Lenny and Mary Ann busied themselves working directly with the production teams at the plant.   It was grinding, tough work. The desire was to involve all crews as well as staff in the brainstorming through four different sessions. John wanted these done as soon as possible, so a Saturday session for D crew was scheduled.

John committed to Lenny and Mary Ann he would attend a session, and this was the only one which fit into his work and travel schedule. He sat in the back, originally intending to be an observer; but soon, Zach Adams invited John up to a table. Zach Adams happened to be Dave Adams' nephew and a member of the maintenance staff. John quietly eased into the seat and began looking over cost information.

Lenny and Mary Ann did a good job explaining and answering the question, "Why are we here?" John recognized often it is easy to focus on the output and no one takes the time to explain why the group is gathered. At a high level, everyone understood the competitive pressures. They knew the site was global cost and quality leader, but also knew this was not a position that allowed the site to rest on its laurels. Others trailed right behind, and a slip-on performance meant someone else would rapidly win the business.

The first session centered on the Fishbone diagram; a quality tool commonly used to help create a focused cause-effect discussion. The facilitators used a variety of tools to try to attack the problem from different angles. Each group received one major aspect of the fishbone to brainstorm. John's table happened to be methods or procedures. At the right-hand side of the chart, the problem was defined: We have a business requirement to attain a $0.07 unit cost in diskettes in less than one year. The teams' job for the next 45 minutes was to think of all the things from a procedural standpoint which were barriers to getting to the goal.

The sessions started by using silent brainstorming. The facilitators prepared data in the form of unit cost statements, policies and procedures, past QICR plans, component information, quality data and a blank pad of 3x5" Post-It notes. The job of the sub-teams was to think of as many ideas as possible.

As the exercise began, John was a bit more removed from the operations than at first, he realized. Five years ago, John was sure he could have rattled off 20 ideas; but right now, his mind was in a bit of a fog. John sat silent, hoping others' thoughts were more plentiful and richer.

Despite the lack of productive ideas on John's part, this was still a great reminder of the power of collaborative thinking. The views on the operational side were generally limited to reporting metrics and ensuring operations had operational improvement plans in place. John hoped Zach was thinking about preventive maintenance procedures and asking some tough questions about timing, effectiveness, and efficiency. He silently hoped Nancy across the table was thinking about quality checks. Were they efficient and effective? Or was some of it waste? Likewise, he hoped Paul, who was a cell coordinator, was thinking about the paperwork he had to fill out and asking himself if a better way existed, one that would provide the information ERP system required, but not require as many steps? Tapping into that wealth of knowledge is the true power of collaboration; critical thinking focused on true value and elimination of waste or non-value adding steps.

It was going to be up to Mary Ann and Lenny to sit down with the diskette general supervisor, engineering manager and others to sort out these ideas. Sometimes the day allowed a simple effort/impact matrix to provide some guidance to the analysis teams. This seemed to help focus because ideally it was desirable to put the initial efforts in the area where the impact was greatest, but the effort was least.

When it came time to share within the subteam, some good ideas emerged. Michelle, a cell lead was nominated to lead the group, and after about 20 minutes of silent work, she called the group of five together and asked the members to go around one at a time. Michelle explained sometimes something said triggers another thought. This systematic, round robin approach was what she thought best to share initial ideas.

Michelle started with John. He quickly scanned the five Post-Its of ideas that he has mustered and picked what he thought was the best. John read, "Implement a web-based system for our Red/Green hourly production charting." Those at the table needed no explanation. Operators still relied on paper to track a green hour (meeting of the production goal) and a red hour (with causation identified. Putting it on the network would allow more rapid follow-up when problems occurred and helped with tracking and trending information over time.

Zach followed up with a point about operator training. Zach was a skilled maintenance operator, and it was obvious he had thought a lot about this. He went on, choosing his words carefully, "There are a few key maintenance adjustments that could be done by operators." He mentioned a spring adjustment station, changing out drives in the diskette auto format machine and adjustments to the portion of the line called the D machine, where adhesive was applied to the hub to create a bond between media and the hub.

Paul and Nancy also shared their ideas and the group continued in this manner until the ideas slowed to a trickle. This process of sharing proved interesting. Building and thinking about issues, just with respect to procedures and methods, had taken over an hour. The group brainstormed probably 30 solid ideas to consider. Not all would be ideas to pursue, but a good roster of potential ideas for future analysis.

John also noted he had trouble filling up five or six. He was only really pleased with the first one on Red/Green charting. He needed more connection with operations. He realized his current role made him too high level with not enough details.

In addition to methods, this sub-team tackled machines, which included maintenance and overhead spending. This was completed before lunch.

The organizers ordered barbeque for lunch, which gave everyone a chance to socialize and relax.

No QICR session would be complete without some type of teambuilding activity. These ranged from serious to silly, depending on the facilitator.

The team building exercise on this day was one John had a part in developing. In Cub Scouts, the boys do the rain gutter regatta. The scouts build a small wooden boat from a kit, attach the sail, and race the boat using boy generated wind power aka blowing. John recently did this with the Cub Scout troop and thought it might be fun as a team building exercise as well.

John supplied a parallel set of rain gutters capped at the ends and filled with water; teams built a boat utilizing a kit. The final challenge was to find a windy few from the team to blow their boat to victory. It also fit in loosely with the Shackelton theme.

After lunch, Lenny and Mary Ann allocated 20 minutes for teams to build their boat, using the best engineering techniques in the timeframe allotted. Once designed, teams secured the parts using quick set glue.

The decisive moment came with the announcement of the race pairings. Everyone participated in the double elimination, round robin tournament. Most races were close; however, there were a few blowouts due to some design flaws in the boat. The final race paired Team Breeze vs. Pirates of the Caribbean.

In the end, the Pirates took an early lead and the Breezers just did not have enough wind to catch up. The Pirates won ribbons, but more importantly, they secured the bragging rights for another year.

All Work and No Play Makes QICR Dull

In the afternoon, the groups stayed together and tackled materials and new business opportunities. It was customary to include things outside the plant in the brainstorming as well. A few successes paid good dividends by driving actions and behaviors outside of the plant.

One of the most favorable examples involved moving to a menu choice for packaging options. A constant struggle exists in most plants between the sales and marketing teams and manufacturing. Most of the designs added complexity because of its uniqueness, which meant new set ups, new debugs on the lines, and lessons learned not incorporated into new designs. The engineering and maintenance teams dreaded the new packaging promotions, because every new one was at least a two-week headache until teams could debug and get the line back to running at rate.

The breakthrough idea involved creating a menu or choice board. With this, the plant could easily communicate manufacturing friendly options. For example, a design could pick up to three inserts or size and shape based on what capability existed on the production lines. The last idea incorporated labeling placed on the outside of the package. Once standardized and communicated, the site could commit to a reduced lead-time.

If the above items held true, the maintenance team had high confidence the equipment could run at rate during the first 24 hours. Without these items factored in, anything outside would be both an upcharge and a longer schedule.

Afternoon sessions seemed a little tougher as people got mentally tired. Plenty of caffeine, snacks and breaks helped people stay focused through the end of the day.

Each group wrapped up the day by rating their top three ideas in terms of impact/effort. Which ideas did the team think have the most promise? John enjoyed the wrap up. It was good for him to listen as the individual groups shared. His takeaway from this included the idea there were still a lot of great ideas to be considered. Some larger and more complex, some relatively small and simple, but all represented a better way of doing something in the operation. Maybe it was MacGyver who said, "You are in trouble when you are out of options."

The Chinese have a famous and profound statement: The longest journey begins with a single step. Each of these ideas represented a single step and offered a start on creating a path to meeting the seven-cent challenge.

Each group shared their ideas. The thoughts started with the Pirates of the Caribbean focusing on machine and equipment improvements. Each team followed:

1. Black lights on the D-machine so operators can see glue on the table
2. Start/Stop station on the backside of A-Machine – avoiding having to walk around the machine to start.
3. Spring draw Cam evaluation - find an easier set-up or fewer rejects

Breezers:

1. Create an employee Training board (Recognition of who is trained where with a star.)
2. Balance pack out output to Assembly capacity
3. Use Oracle "Flow" manufacturing and have work-order-less completions. Schedule floor via Kanban.

Diskette Dudes

1. Balance out the Vactra 4 (oil) usage - Metal press 2 uses 1/2 of what press 1 does - 1/2 gal. / shift less x 2 x 360 days/yr.
2. Keep shell inventory but pull system between assembly and packout (minimal inventory of disks between assembly and molding that can be kept on floor) - eliminate warehouse handling
3. Use braided oil hoses to reduce the opportunity for pinhole leaks; which create significant downtime and a big mess.

Michelle's Monsters

1. Operators trained to do simple maintenance tasks.
2. Make minimum order qty for private label on 20' or 40' container and ship direct to customer from factory
3. Employ our own driver to do the loads to and from the Twin Cities - can we piggy back with other companies in the area

Lenny prearranged for John to add a few closing comments. John spoke from the heart.

John paused, cleared his throat and said, "What we are doing here today is probably the most important activity we do all year. First, it involves all of us. This is not just something cooked up by the management team, it is a team effort. Second, now more than ever, we have competitive threats. Some we can see, and some we cannot. The ones we cannot see keep me up at night." John concluded, "What we are doing here is unique. You will find other companies that plan, but I believe in this process, this is THE key success factor in keeping us competitive year on year."

"I remember previous general managers coming and saying that diskettes would peak in 1996, and then it was 1999 – just before Y2K and then it was 2004. The truth is, no one knows. Technology is fickle. There are good and competing technologies and the lowly diskette won't last forever, but we have had a great ride and I believe that if we continue to drive costs, we will not only be the last one manufacturing, we will maintain a good business, with good jobs and good margins."

John ended, "Thank you everyone for being here today focusing on your drive to get better and your commitment. Now, go home and enjoy your evening." No one on the crew needed reminding they were scheduled to be back tomorrow morning at 7:00 AM.

The group cleared out and John moved up front to talk to Lenny and Mary Ann. They were encouraged by today saying it was one of the best sessions. The previous session with A crew turned a little bitter mostly due to a few who had strong opinions and couldn't stay focused on the task. John thanked them for their work and asked about follow-up.

Lenny, Mary Ann and team blocked two days the following week to sift through the ideas, make follow-up assignments and hopefully have a rough idea of the potential impact. John hoped he could take part in some of the analysis as well, both to show his commitment, and because he was very interested in the outcome.

John walked by his office to pick up his coat and headed to the parking lot. By now, a light snow was falling and as he turned his car south towards home. The snow crunched audibly under the wheels as he began his short commute.

Chapter 29: Thirty Years of Gathering Dust.

Things were coming together, at least from the standpoint of having improvement plans in place to boost site competitiveness. Ideally, John should have a program manager coordinating activities and schedules and making sure things weren't dropped, but he really didn't have the staffing to pull someone off their current tasks. Running without was a risk that John was going to have to accept.

The first person John saw on Monday was Steve Kroft. Just one look and he remembered a forgotten promise. He had not supplied Friday doughnuts, as promised. John began to apologize when Steve said, "Covered for you. We knew you were busy, so we had lunch brought in and charged it to ADMIN." Touché – not much John could do. John thanked him for covering and hoped they enjoyed their lunch.

John's first task was to find the key to the safety deposit box and visit the bank. John had a break between 9:00 AM and 10:00 AM. He told Diane he had to run an errand downtown.

John parked on the street walked around the corner to the Plains Bank and Trust. Kristin and John's personal accounts resided in this bank as well. John looked for Laura, guessing she would be at one of the tellers' windows. Sure enough, she was helping another customer. John took a spot in the queue out of earshot of her and the other customer.

She greeted him with "Don't see you here too often on Monday morning." John stepped up to the counter with the key for the safety deposit box. Laura called to Mark Holmquist. Mark was the vice president of the bank and near neighbors to John and Kristin. He asked, "What can I do for my favorite neighbor?" John informed Mark of his need to check out the contents of the plant safety deposit box.

Mark and John meandered down a long hallway in the center of the bank and turned into the vault area. The safety deposit boxes lined an entryway before the actual vault behind a door that didn't look like it was going to be compromised anytime soon.

John looked on the key, AA17. Scanning the wall, Mark picked out the box. It looked like about 6" x 12" x 12", and as John slid the key into the lock it turned hard. John guessed in the last 30 years the box had not been accessed too many times. He opened the box and inside was a stack of papers not yet fully yellowed, but John could tell they were old. The first looked like some real estate papers, titles and deed information. Under those document, a few clippings from the newspaper, and under it all, an envelope.

With no glue remaining to close the envelope, John removed the contents and scanned the letter. No question this is what he was looking for. It was a letter between Harris Thronson addressed to Bud Smits, mayor of Twin Ports. John skimmed the contents and John read the three agreements Doc mentioned. John's eyes caught something at the bottom of the letter. It said, "MN Consolidated will notify Twin Ports City Council and provide at least three years notice of any planned plant closure. In lieu of advanced notification, MN Consolidated may at its discretion pay a sum of 20% of the previous year sales value of production to the city of Twin Ports. This agreement is null and void after a period of 40 (forty) years from the date of this letter." John snapped a photo of the letter with his phone, folded it up and slipped it back in the envelope.

Back in 1975, 20% of the SVOP may not have been a huge number; but today, Northern Pines Technology was a $1.5B company. This touched about half the value of the product Northern Pines Technology sold. Twenty percent of 750 million dollars is a lot of money. John knew for certain no one in the company knew there was this type of liability associated with a shutdown. That figured out to be in the ballpark of $150 million dollars. John did not need the financial calculator to figure out with a negative $150 million on the side of the equation, there would never be a positive ROI to the Mendal deal.

Now what? Options flooded John's thoughts. He could bring this to the legal team at Northern Pines Technology. Or, he could pass this information along to Doug. Or, John could sit on it for a little while. John decided that since this information had been locked in a box for 30 years, waiting a few days would not change much. Maybe a few days would help clear John's mind and give him some other options.

John closed the box and locked up this little nugget of information safely at Plains Bank & Trust. John thanked Mark.

The minute John stepped in his office, he hopped on the Internet and started researching legal information related to contracts, agreements and binding. The basic question looming in John's mind was whether this letter, unknown to all, was legally binding. That was the million-dollar question.

His first click linked him to a primer on contracts. Per the Legal Information Institute of Cornell University Law School, a contract is:

> "An agreement creating obligations enforceable by law. The basic elements of a contract are mutual assent, consideration, capacity, and legality. In some states, the element of consideration can be satisfied by a valid substitute."

Now, what did mutual assent, consideration, capacity and legality all mean?

Mutual assent meant: "An agreement by both parties to a contract. Mutual assent must be proven objectively, and is often established by showing an offer and acceptance (e.g., an offer to do X in exchange for Y, followed by an acceptance of that offer)."

Consideration: "Something bargained for and received by a promisor from a promisee. Common types of consideration include real or personal property, a return promise, some act, or a forbearance. Consideration or a valid substitute is required to have a contract."

In contract law, a person's ability to satisfy the elements is required for someone to enter binding contracts. For example, capacity rules often require a person to have reached a minimum age and to have soundness of mind.

Lawfulness. In contract law, legality of purpose is required of every enforceable contract. A contract to have someone murdered cannot be enforced in court.

John was not a lawyer, but as he read the information, it seemed both parties signing it created the mutual assay and there certainly was consideration. Harris Thronson was likely dead and gone, but if he was the chief legal counsel at MN Consolidated in 1975, it would be difficult to argue he was not of sound mind and body. As far as John could tell, there did not seem to be anything unlawful about it.

The other angle for John to check out was whether Northern Pines had been the beneficiary of reduced tax rate all these years. John made two quick phone calls to other managers of facilities in the city. Both said their city tax rate was 2.4%. John knew that the local tax rate on Northern Pines was 1.9%, which matched the 0.5% rate reduction offered in section two of the agreement from 1975.

Every angle John thought about brought him to the same conclusion. It is possible that he wanted this wrinkle to pan out, as it would certainly throw a curve into the overall Mendal deal. He tried to maintain his objectivity, but every thought seemed to bring him to the same conclusion.

John possessed a valid, legally binding contract either requiring Northern Pines Technology to give a three-year notice of closure, or, pay an insane amount of money or wait ten more years to close the plant when the agreement expired.

This information left John both excited and filled with a level of anxiety. It was good news for the plant, but somehow in his mind, John didn't think it would be that easy.

Diane knocked on the door startling John. She reminded him he had to be at a 10:00 AM meeting in the north building. John quickly shut his laptop, picked up his coat and safety glasses and began the trek through the plant.

Chapter 30: A Change of Seasons

Admittedly, the past 45 days left John in a bit of a blur. Between juggling work, adoption and family life, John hardly noticed the North Dakota winter slowly giving way to spring. South facing tulips pushed through remaining crusts of snow finding their way up to the warming spring sunshine. Easter quickly approached and the farmers began readying their equipment for early fieldwork once the frost left the ground.

Fortunately for the region, a moderate amount of snow left no indications of significant flooding. Cities up and down the Red River collectively breathed a sigh of relief as winter's grip was slowly being released. The spring warm up pattern generally predicts the flood equation. A quick warm up with nights and days above freezing is the worst recipe. A gradual warm up with days above freezing and nights below freezing was the best equation for a gradual thaw and lowered risk of flooding.

The site hosted a follow-up visit from two Mendal employees, Mayank Puri, engineering manager and Agarwal Rajesh, chief engineer. They returned for a week to acquire some additional information and validate their assumptions on moving equipment. At the meetings, the planning and purchasing teams also provided updated volumes and new material cost targets to share.

The plant was a whirl of visible activity. Many of the plans identified just a few weeks ago were now coming to life. People were engaged, excited and the sense of accomplishment grew with every change.

TWI sessions commenced, and crews made progress on cross training. The previous month, the site completed a pilot with two opposite crews: A crew and C crew, after going through the TWI work, documenting standard work, making some of the programming changes to make the lines more similar, each crew ran a weekend shift where quality and yields were at parity. The downside, utilization lagged on the crews with new trainees by 5.6% which was not too bad. John expected perhaps a 10% impact.

Future trial runs start in a few weeks. Quality had been at predicted levels and only a few other minor bugs identified which were not currently on the issues resolution list.

The Shackelton leadership series was going better than John expected. The plant was divided into several waves of training, so not all employees received the training at the same time. When PBS reran their series on Shackelton, John encouraged the employees to watch it. John knew the adventurous spirit of Shackelton was a good fit for the plant culture. The site contained some of the same rugged determination as Shackelton and his Irish crew showed during their adventure in the South Pole.

 John remembered his Easter commitment at the last possible moment. He was due to play the Easter bunny for the site in less than a week. John asked Diane where the suit was stored. Diane directed him to the mezzanine storage shelf and to a large opaque bag. The site built a new engineering office in 1993, shortly before John arrived at the plant. The old engineering office resorted to somewhat of a boneyard for old and infrequently used stuff.

John located the head and the suit covered by plastic garbage bags. John rescued it from the wrapping, and his first reaction was less than enthusiastic. John thought to himself, this is ugly and a bit scary. John hoped the kids would not have nightmares because of the image of the large bunny with the extra-large bow tie. Maybe the candy and treats will compensate.

The QICR plans and actions initiated over the last month were now in full swing. Lenny and Mary Ann worked diligently and mapped out a program for reaching the goal of seven cents in just a little over twelve months. John pushed hard for acceleration, but with the data and facts, there wasn't much left to create a logical argument for acceleration.

Now, only wishful thinking by a site manager would allow for a faster timeline. There was always optimistic thinking, but being a believer in data, facts and logic, John inherently knew Lenny and Mary Ann were probably close in their forecasting.

The plan came together nicely. If everything hit, diskettes would beat the $0.0700 target by $0.0002. Not a lot of margin, but a remarkable accomplishment given no one on the planet thought a $0.07 diskette even possible.

	A	B	AQ		AS	AT	A
28			Q1		Seven Cent		
29	Item / Department	Description	Average Unit Cost		Programs	Cost Down Impact	
30	4200B027822	2MB OEM MEDIA	$0.01335		Format Yield & Media @ Fcst	($0.00307)	
31	11F01816625	LIQUID A RING	$0.00020		D machine yield	($0.00085)	
32	1120000K508	OVOH LINER MATERIAL (new)	$0.00038				
33	78801W98169	SPRING TORSION	$0.00098				
34	78809621M01	3.5" HUB	$0.00358				
35	788077R7200	SHUTTER OEM	$0.00614		Reverse image - less ink	($0.00006)	
36	78811R22256	2MB BLACK RESIN SHELL MOLDED	$0.03016		Shell Optimization - molding	($0.00581)	
37	1675 LBR	MN TECH TwinPort 5432-1 3 HALF INCH	$0.00956		Productivity - line speed	($0.00096)	
38	3171	MN TECH TwinPort 5432-1 ADMIN	$0.00349		Volume OH Redux	($0.00100)	
39	3571	MN TECH TwinPort 5432-1 ENGINEERING	$0.00132				
40	3272	MN TECH TwinPort 5432-1 INVENTORY MGMT	$0.00065		Kanban - one dept scheduler	$0.00019	
41	3271	MN TECH TwinPort 5432-1 RM SF REC AND W	$0.00199				
42	1675 VOH	MN TECH TwinPort 5432-1 3 HALF INCH	$0.01182		Drive savings & lapping film	($0.00225)	
43		Unit Cost $	0.0836			$ (0.0138)	
44		Units	53,473,890				

John was extremely proud of the team. This was a stunning piece of engineering work. It represented cost reduction at its absolute finest. To think that less than ten years ago, the unit cost of a diskette was in the $0.50 range, and fifteen years ago, it was north of $0.75. The net result here was a sustained reduction in cost on a per unit basis that was unheard of in most industries.

Using the computer memory cost reduction curve, a very interesting calculation emerges. In 1975, the year the plant opened, a single MB of memory cost $420,888 to produce. In 2005, that same memory cost $0.092 to produce. A reduction factor in cost of over 4.5 million.

In the technology space, the skill of rapid cost down is a requirement for survival. The question is not will the costs go down, but how rapidly will they go down? Technology drives the slope of the line. This part of the business intrigued John, but terrified him at the same time. It is as if one is on the downward side of a rollercoaster all the time with the bottom always just a little further ahead.

The week ended with John donning a very thick pink bunny suit with a massive head which did not breathe well. John chose to be a silent bunny so all his gestures had to be over-animated; thinking this was less scary for all the children. John waved, hopped, and performed all the things he thought bunnies were supposed to do. The kids loved it. The parents were happy, and John felt rewarded for being the silent bunny that created many smiles on children's faces.

Down deep, he wondered if next year he would have another child to bring to Bunny Day. Would Vika understand? Would she be afraid?

Bunny Day with a Cooperative Soul

The three older boys knew it was their dad and took great joy in pulling his tail, and generally trying to knock John (aka dad) off his game. Caroline and Mark were terrified and refused to sit even for a quick photo. Thankfully, they were the most terrified of all the kids, so John could take comfort in the fact that he hadn't terrorized anyone worse than his own children.

The kids enjoyed playing with the tiny bunnies Steve Kroft and his family brought. The kids also enjoyed running through a cardboard maze set up in the conference room and ate cookies to their heart's content.

The day ended with John exiting the prison of a suit and taking a trip to Pizza Ranch. After dinner, it was home, baths and bed for the kids.

Kristin entered the living room after the kids were down and snuggled up to John on the couch. She had something on her mind, John could tell. She said she had been thinking about the adoption and she thought they should be open to bringing home two kids instead of one. She looked on the adoption website and Reece's Rainbow and saw a little boy who tugged at her heart. His name was Sergey. Ironically the same name as Green's little boy, but spelled slightly differently.

Oddly, John resisted when he first heard this. Whether it was the stress of work or something else, John was not at a point where he could commit to another child right now on the spot. In fact, his first internal reaction was, "Aren't we already doing a lot by bringing one into our family?"

John asked her why she was drawn to Sergey. Kristin said, "His face looks like what you imaged Caroline's would be, if she were a boy." John had to agree; his fine features looked as if he could be one of theirs.

John was torn. In his heart, he knew that if the Stanton's could be a forever family for one child, perhaps they could do it for two. Yet his brain and logic fought back. This doesn't make sense. Where will the money come from? Where will they sleep? How can we feed seven kids? No one has seven kids anymore.

Kristin and John talked about Vika and wondered when 'the call' would come. John reminded his wife the Greens traveled nine months after they initiated their adoption plans. They counted back. They were on about month six or seven, so it literally could be anytime. As of now, they did not have the luxury of knowing where their dossier had landed. It could be on a desk somewhere, a mailroom or lost. It could be anywhere.

They agreed to have faith it will get to the right desk for consideration by the right person at the right time.

The issue of another child remained unresolved that night. John knew it would take some thinking on his part to process and figure out if this was possible.

John turned off the lights in the living room and headed upstairs for the night. As another day ended, another was soon beginning at a small orphanage outside of Kharkov Ukraine. One orphan there certainly had no clue that soon her world was going to change. Plans made, papers studied and a place prepared for Vika to come to a new home in America with a future and a hope.

Likewise, John and Kristin knew little how their world was going to change.

Chapter 31: Finding Our Stride

Routines change when spring arrives on the northern plains. Neighbors emerge from their homes and conversations begin again over the fence. People ride motorcycles and walk their dogs. Kids swap ice skates for rollerblades. One of the wonderful things about a location with four distinct seasons is the activities change with the time of year. In the fall, John looked forward to the winter coming. The family read more, played games, watched movies. It felt cozy and a warm time to be alive in a cold climate.

Inevitably, the winter does get long, and spring is a welcomed change. John enjoyed all the reasons to be outside again, taking care of the lawn, doing spring chores, cleaning up and getting the bikes down from the rafters. John anticipated an occasional commute via bicycle in the spring and summer. He hopped on a trail three blocks from the house and could ride directly into the plant parking lot.

Another thing spring brings is one of his more time consuming but favorite pastimes. The Stanton's own an original, minimally restored 1934 Ford Victoria; handed down from a great uncle. The "Vicky" is a unique car because it was the first year of production for the Ford V8. This car has been in the family for the past 70 plus years, going to ball games, picnics and vacations. It is a beast, with solid steel frame and exterior and everything is original; even down to the factory installed spark plug wires, installed by hand over 70 years ago. They are just ends of wire bent in a U to grab the spark plug.

A direct connection with history is perhaps one reason John respects the genius of Henry Ford. His vision was to design and manufacture a car for the masses, and in doing so, created a great American industry. John is proud to own a unique piece of Americana as well. The car is not perfect, but has aged very gracefully.

Spring brings out the Ford Victoria from its winter resting place in a friend's barn. Early in the spring, Dave Adams and John charge up the ancient 6V battery and usually end up pull starting it behind Dave's pickup truck. The kids have lots of fun riding in "fancy car" down to the ice cream shop, especially because of all the looks received on the way and maybe a little side benefit there are no seatbelts.

The Victoria – First Production V8 1934: Ford Motor Company

Based some in fact and some in legend, but here is a famous story about this car model as well. The story goes the gangsters of the day were enamored with the V8 because of the speed and power. The police at the time did not have the same horsepower in their cruisers, so the gangsters and robbers could usually get a sustained jump on the police. Once out on the open road, it became very difficult to match the V8 for speed. The legend has it that Clyde Barrows of Bonnie and Clyde fame, penned a letter, spelling mistakes included, to Mr. Ford that read:

```
Tulsa, Okla
10th April
Mr. Henry Ford
Detroit Mich.

Dear Sir: --
    While I still have got breath in my lungs I
will tell you what a dandy car you make. I have
drove Fords exclusively when I could get away with
one. For sustained speed and freedom from trouble
the Ford has got ever other car skinned and even if
my business hasen't been strickly legal it don't
hurt anything to tell you what a fine car you got
in the V8 --

Yours truly
Clyde Champion Barrow
```

Spring brings work with the fun; fixing what winter has either degraded or broken. While John was puttering around in the backyard, taking out hoses and rakes, getting ready for yard work, his mind was elsewhere. He was starting to draft a plan for his upcoming absence. When the site manager job was offered to him last year, a condition of him accepting the position involved arranging a schedule for the real possibility of adoption.

He crafted an agreement where he would take his computer, plan to be on-line and engaged in work half days. John reasoned he could effectively work four hours a day. With manager approval, the family could double their time away if needed. John hoped the trip could be completed in either two separate, two- week segments or one four- week segment, but that was a decision could not be made now.

John had total confidence in the staff to manage the operations when he was gone. John would be on-line daily, so he could track production, cost, safety and even routine teleconferences if they were in the morning (US time). The timing worked out reasonably well. With Ukraine being eight hours ahead of the US, the evenings would still be working hours. John could catch up on work and send it back to the plant during the night. John acquired an international data plan for the Blackberry, so in theory, he should be able to have a 'live' connection to the plant and not need to rely on an Internet café or wireless connection.

One specific piece of information gleaned from the visit at the Green's was Steve indicated reasonably good Internet access existed in Sevastopol. Hotels usually offered free wireless. Internet cafes, while crowded, smoke-filled and full of gamers, also provided another viable option.

Spring also brought opening of the cabin in northern Minnesota for another season. John made his only winter trip after the first meeting with Mendal, but that was now months ago.

The first family trip usually occurred over Memorial Day. The initial trip meant cleaning up after the small four-footed winter visitors. Early on, John had notions of getting every crack sealed; however, he gave up trying to mouse proof. The locals claim the rodents come with the territory, and it is a lot less frustrating to get used to them than try and fight them. He reluctantly concluded, they will find a way in, no matter how many layers of deterrents.

The other 'must do' was the first lawn mowing. Usually the ample winter snows and the spring sunshine created a nice crop of grass, along with Shasta daisies and dandelions needing their first cutting.

Memorial Day was still a few weeks away, but the family started the 'to bring the cabin' corner in the family room. It always seemed like by the time the first trip came; a large corner of the room was overtaken with things needing to go to north for the summer. Kristin had picked up a few canoe paddles at a garage sale, and the twins received compound bows for Christmas. The pile grew larger by the day.

Both John and Kristin knew the focus of the summer was likely the adoption and not spending time at the cabin. Being good friends and neighbors, Kristin let a few friends know the cabin was going to be lonely and attempted to line up volunteers to mow the grass and maintain the property in exchange for free lodging, fishing and all the canoeing one could handle.

Spring days of bright sun, light winds and just enough evening rain to keep things thriving was the pattern for May. After arriving home from work one day, a chorus of, "Daddy daddy, can we fly kites?" met John at the door. The boys discovered the kites in the basement, and after a quick supper of mac and cheese, sandwiches and fruit, the Stanton men were off to the open fields at the North Dakota College of Technology.

In no time, three kites were aloft. The prairie winds were usually favorable for flying kites; the challenge wasn't usually the lack of wind, but the excess of it. Watching these simple little contraptions hover and wave above the prairie landscape was relaxing. John loved to come out here with the boys and watch the clouds roll by as the kites danced in the sky.

The peace was quickly shattered by a cry from one of the twins, "Daddy, the kite is getting away." Sure enough, in a moment of confusion or distractedness or who knows what, Eric dropped the winder. The kite half floated to earth and half pulled into the sky. Somehow, the string tangled around the winder, so the winder was skating across the ground. Eric ran behind, trying to time a retrieving grab to the random, erratic motion of the winder; which was beginning to lift off the ground.

John mumbled to himself, "We've got just one shot at getting this." He quickly secured the other two kites to a bike rack and took off. The kite skipped and skated erratically on its way down with the winder dragging across the parking lot. As the kite gained ground; John lost steam.

Finally, upon reaching the tennis courts where the Lady Huskies were practicing tennis, a few of them witnessed the predicament and offered help and aid. They began the chase with the advantage of a head start. In the end, the kite, winder and string were all salvaged and really, none was worse for the wear. John thanked the tennis team, and once the girls eyed the cute little tater tot who released the string, they were more than happy to be able to return the kite intact.

Kites are a Great Stress Reliever

It was, however, the end of kite flying. The boys and John returned to the other two kites still aloft and safely lashed to the bicycle rack.

They brought them back to earth, packed up and went home.

Chapter 32: Leading in a Crisis

The site noticed immediate and tangible benefits from the TWI training. The application of the training brought some of the benefits, and other external influences brought change as well. Specifically, SunGrown started to ramp up hiring for their new production facility, and in the process of doing so, they picked off some of Twin Ports' best and brightest employees. "Good for them, bad for us" John said.

John did not resent this, knowing the challenges ahead for Twin Ports, but it's one of those cases when a 'person is not always just a person.' The knowledge, problem solving and abilities that exist inside some of the Twin Port's employees would take a significant amount of time and experience to replace. However, John also knew employees made decisions about their future and how best to provide for their families. It is hard to second-guess those choices. Each person decided for himself or herself the value of security, wages, time off and the type of work asked to do.

In the first round of hiring at SunGrown, the site lost three experienced maintenance technicians. The department supervisors shuffled some people around enabled by the cross training. They found between stretching out coverage a bit more, using a call-in system and viewing maintenance more as a site resource, the site could operate a bit leaner. The typical headcount number for operations was 24, six per crew. Generally, there were two in the north plant and four in the front building. Quickly the team adapted and did an admirable job of flexing based on the needs of the departments and customer priorities.

The second wave of hiring at SunGrown hit the plant a bit harder. Two people from the warehouse, one supply chain planner, two process engineers, three additional maintenance technicians and 14 production operators opted to try a new career in food production.

Several of the operators who left were those that who had invested in cross training between Glacier and Keystone, two very important products at the site. The personnel loss was a costly from a training and flexibility point of view; but, also reinforced the inherent value of the cross-training of the workers.

To balance, the supervisors ended up taking four of diskette operators and moving them to tape operations to even up the crew staffing. The TWI initiative definitely helped in the training and standardization of work between operations in the building. These were well-trained diskette operators. Hence, the learning curve was less steep, mostly due to their established skill level.

The areas of biggest benefit gained from the TWI work for the site was learning detailed systematic knowledge of the work, greater awareness of equipment, critical quality parameters, and the employees' skill in improving methods. A new set of eyes directed towards a process or a machine resulted in asking a few of the basic 'why' questions. In several cases, when a good answer couldn't be found, it made sense to change either the equipment, procedure or the way the process worked.

One of the lessons learned from customers of the site contract manufacturing business was: identify and implement the best-known method. The current best-known method was the standard by which everything else compared. If an improvement was found, it would then become the new best-known method. While this thinking was prevalent in the contract manufacturing operation; it had not been expanded to the entire plant. TWI helped draw out these differences and insure that best practices were in place and followed across the entire plant.

An ancillary benefit, which John didn't expect to see, was an emerging leadership role. John did not know if it was from the increased confidence workers had in the TWI approach and a sense they knew their equipment more thoroughly, or if they better understood how and why a process was set up as it was. The results were noticeable. TWI excels at reinforcing the Plan-Do-Check-Act [PDCA] cycle which has been a fixture in site quality training.

John truly believed people felt more empowered. Not only can they try things, but with some of the basic quality analysis tools like the fishbone diagram, Pareto analysis, histogram and run chart, many scientifically based conclusions can be reached before ever engaging a technical or engineering resource.

John was also pleased to see how the Shackelton adventures were creating their own culture. Though the sessions were winding down for the crews, John continued to hear break room talk and a few "Shackeltonisms" making their way into the plant chatter. An unpredictable and fun outcome occurred when the crews took the initiative to have a beard-growing contest for three months. Winners received prizes for style and length. Employee initiated efforts are one of the elements making the plant culture exceptional.

Leading in a crisis marked the final chapter of the training. John found it difficult to separate the crisis from the event. It seemed as if their crisis was being stuck in the middle of nowhere with no one to rescue them. If they had any hope of survival, it would be under their own power.

Eric Moore facilitated the Shackelton leadership training for the staff group. As the staff filed into the training rooms for the last session, John asked Eric how he felt things were going. Eric replied, "I have taught this now for almost two years to a variety of groups. It is amazing. When you get into the details of what is going on in businesses, academia, churches, and community organizations, there is a lot of crisis management. Not always 'the house is burning' crisis, but never having enough time, resources, planning…" He continued, "I think that is part of the reason the story resonates with so many people."

Eric continued, "It is easier to manage a crisis when there is a bit of lead time, preparation, and the process is known. What people get from Shackelton is real-time crisis management." John agreed, "Things for the crew of the Endurance seem also like they are going from bad to worse. Just when you think they might be on to something, they fall back and inevitably in a worse position than the previous. It is hard to believe Shackelton did not have a mutiny on his hands. Maybe he couldn't have a mutiny because he didn't have a ship." Eric smiled, "Good point," he said.

With the staff assembled, Eric began the training by saying, "Shackelton exhibited some memorable characteristics as a leader and ones we can emulate. Today we are going to show how Shackelton used some very simple, but also very powerful tactics to lead when everything had turned against them."

"Shackelton showed remarkable optimism and power to reset the course when needed. He had an ever-changing array of troubles beset him and the crew. First, there was the original voyage to cross the South Pole. Secondly, once the Endurance was ice-bound, the goal was to survive with the boat and complete the journey. When the ice pack crushed the Endurance, the mission was retooled yet again to survive through the winter. Upon further evaluation, he found another course, rowing in small boats hundreds of miles, hoping to reach safety, which he ended up on deserted Elephant Island, another trek in a single boat. Once the initial team reached the whaling station, it took four attempts to rescue the balance of the crew."

Eric spoke with conviction, "Friends, that is perseverance. Think of all the opportunities where a less driven and capable leader would not have had the resolve to try one more time or come up with a Plan B. Hats off to Shackelton."

Eric opened it up to the staff for discussion. Eric challenged, "What are some of the things that Shackelton specifically did during the crisis to ensure the crew remained calm, focused on the goal and ultimately led to the survival of the entire crew?"

Liz raised her hand, "It seems like Shackelton made sure everyone had a meaningful job to do." Eric added, "That is true and that is a great point for us to remember, too. If we have a portion of our charges who are just watching, what good is going to come from the effort?" He continued, "Also, if you are working towards the solution, it is a little bit harder to find time and energy to complain, right?" There was nodding across the group.

"What else?" Eric asked. Bill piped up, "It seemed like Shackelton was always an optimist and the energy and enthusiasm must have a large impact on the crew." Eric said, "There are several interesting quotes from the book about that topic. Here are two attributed to Shackelton."

> *'Optimism is true moral courage,'*
> *and*
> *'Loyalty comes easier to a cheerful person than to one who carries a heavy countenance.'*

"I know for this group, I am stating the obvious, but the tone and tenor of the leader sets the same for the entire group. Shackelton knew this and used it to his advantage." Eric said with emphasis so the words had a chance to sink in.

The group was quiet for a few seconds before a question came from the back. It was Steve, D crew supervisor. Steve said, "How come none of the crew felt betrayed? All indications are that this was a tough adventure, but I would think there would be a tendency to blame, even if it was after the return."

Eric said, "Steve, great question. I think you have hit on another element of how Shackelton led. This does not apply so much in a crisis as throughout the story. If you remember, Shackelton made some interesting promises at the beginning along the lines of low wages, long hours, bitter cold, and darkness. He did not promise an easy road and riches, did he?" Steve nodded at the insight. Mary Ann chimed in, "What struck me was that he did everything he expected of the crew as well. Even though he was the leader and there were some crummy jobs, he did his part."

As John sat in the row and listened to the discussion, he reflected on this "crisis" he had been managing the past few months. John called it a crisis because he knew and understood the stakes, as did his leadership team. The broader staff had a lesser understanding of the potential impacts. John thought to himself, "How do I stack up against the Shackelton standard?

John ruminated on the basic concepts in his mind: summarizing options, meaningful jobs to do, optimistic leader and truthful. John thought he had done well on the meaningful jobs. More initiatives existed now than any other time in the history of the plant. People performed their 'day' job, and most had additional responsibilities equating to another at least half-time job.

John probably fell a few rungs on the optimism ladder. John reconciled, "I am not a charismatic leader who can rally people to a great cause. I am an engineer who can put together plans that hopefully can avoid an even larger crisis."

As far as truthful, with those John could trust with sensitive information, he believes he has been truthful. He couldn't disclose all the information which was awkward and not the way he would prefer it to be. Down deep, he hoped the actions and the efforts demonstrated a deep care and concern for the organization and the plant viewed John as someone doing everything to create a strong, successful and healthy organization.

How do you beat the odds? Shackelton did it in the early twentieth century by rallying a raucous crew of sailors to survive months in the arctic. Could the same be done at Twin Ports?

John thought to himself, "Can we really pull this thing off?"

Time will tell - remained the only certainty.

Chapter 33: The Park

As spring morphed into summer, more and people ventured outdoors. John's family was no exception. On this night, after work and dinner, it was obvious Kristin needed a break, so John loaded up the five kids and headed to the park. With two in the bike trailer and the twins and Seth on their bikes, the family wheeled over to the park. The park was really a beautiful place. Tonight, the sky was bright blue, no wind and the temperature hovered in the high 60s, a perfect night for playing and exploring. This park was one of the reasons John loved living in Twin Ports; this was a true slice of America – one that is receding, but small-town values and life are still an important part of what makes us strong.

It is the people and the history that shapes a town and Twin Ports was no exception.

Twin Ports Municipal Park

The city leaders revealed a stroke of genius when they established this pristine spot, setting it aside as green space for the community. John was a history buff, so as the kids were playing, he wondered what it must have been like in the early days in Twin Ports. A hundred years ago - there must have been a constant flurry of activity on the river. The towns straddled the river, one in Minnesota and one in North Dakota. They also sat at the confluence of the Red River of the North, Bois de Sioux, and the Ottertail River. This is a region rich in frontier history. Just a few miles to the north lay Fort Abercrombie. "The Gateway to the Dakotas," as it is called. Fort Abercrombie was the first permanent United States military fort established in what was later to form the state of North Dakota.

It was also the only post in the area attacked by Sioux Indians. The siege lasted six weeks during the Dakota conflict of 1862. Minnesota Volunteer soldiers operated the fort when area settlers sought shelter there. The regular U.S. Army soldiers withdrew during the Civil War and replaced by the Minnesota Volunteer Infantry. Today, the fort has blockhouses at each corner and is protected by a palisade. This was not the case during the siege but these defensive structures were constructed soon afterward.

The fort guarded the oxcart trails used during the fur trade era, military supply wagon trains, stagecoach routes, and steamboat traffic on the Red River. It also was a supply base for several gold-seeking expeditions across the Dakotas and into Montana.

Now, it is a place of rest, relaxation and beauty.

First, John took Mark out of the stroller and placed him in one of the baby swings. He loved it. He was on the swing for probably 20 minutes before John returned him to his stroller. John continued his multitasking by watching the other kids out of the corner of the eye.

Seth interrupted the relative quiet. That little monkey managed to climb up to the top of the bars and could not get down. Caroline

Mark

was putting rocks in her mouth, and Mark had fallen asleep in the stroller. John gave them the five-minute warning and before time was up, they twisted their dad's arm to go the long way home and stop by Dairy Delight for ice cream. John agreed on the condition of no fussing when it was time to go. They were all troopers and complied with their end of the bargain.

The entourage paralleled the river riding on the path built on the earthen dike and slowly made their way down to Dairy Delight. This business was a treasure in Twin Towns. It was a wonderful old-fashioned ice cream store with friendly help, cold ice cream and lots of fried food. By this time, Mark was wide-awake and waiting for his treat. Two Silly bars, two ice cream cones and one chocolate chip cookie sandwich were inhaled by hungry, dirty and tired kids.

The group walked their bikes along Main Street until the street sign showed Seventh Street. They then turned north and biked five blocks to their yellow house on the corner. It occurred to John his kids might never truly know their street address as the entire town knew their residence as the yellow house on the corner.

The caravan arrived home just as the orange sun slipped behind the western skyline. It became a little cooler and it felt good go get back into the warmth of the house. Due to the ice cream stickiness, it was appropriate to do a quick washcloth clean up before John brought the kids up for bed. The twins successfully negotiated one Andy Griffith episode on TV.

Just as the whistling tune of Andy began, John popped open the laptop to log in and see how the plant was doing on a beautiful early June night. The diskettes department was running well; north building operations was only running two of the three tape lines and these were also running well.

John took a quick peek to see if there were any critical emails. Seeing nothing, he decided anything else could wait.

Chapter 34: Another Trip to Headquarters

John left with two things to accomplish on his trip to the Twin Cities. He ruminated back and forth on what to do about the letter/legal agreement Doc supplied a few weeks ago. He needed to resolve the dilemma first; and secondly, review the plan with Doug for his time out of country.

Doug was a good boss in the sense he was not averse to allowing this type of 'life' adventure. Honestly, John rather expected him to say no, which would have meant John took vacation along with a leave of absence or some other arrangements to allow for the adoption. John later learned Doug adopted two children of his own from East Asia. John reasoned that probably explains Doug's soft spot for adoption.

After listening to the Shackelton training and thinking about it, John decided his course of action on the legal document. He was going to be forthright and provide Doug with the information allowing him to take the next steps. Thinking through scenarios, John could anticipate one situation where Doug or someone else may request this to be buried or claim it doesn't exist. John resolved to not allow any outcome where the agreement did not get a full hearing. Not only would that be wrong morally, John knew Doc had the facts.

John left on Sunday night for the Twin Cities. The meetings started at nine in the morning, but John never did well with the early morning drive. The last time John drove early, traffic stopped between St. Cloud and Maple Grove because cattle broke through a fence and were freely roaming the interstate. It is amazing what a few stray cows can do to interstate traffic. It was blocked for miles and it was after 10:30 AM when John finally arrived at headquarters. John vowed this could not happen on this trip.

Driving at night, John worried more about deer darting across the road. So far, he had been fortunate. They stayed away from him, and John managed to stay away from them. Seth, Mark and Caroline were already in bed when John said goodbyes to the twins and Kristin. John told the twins they were the guardians of the house and they better gather their ammo and have their slingshots and BB guns handy, ready to knock out any bad guys. They laughed and promised they would keep mom safe.

Before leaving, John told them he was looking forward to the trip to Ukraine together. It was going to be a grand adventure, and they were going to see so many new and different things and eat crazy food and get to see their new sister and maybe even brother. Kristin told the twins about Sergey, and they were excited about another little brother in the picture. They adored Caroline, so both John and Kristin knew they would do well with Viktoria and Sergey. John had come to terms with the fact there might be two coming home; and was at peace with the decision.

John kissed Kristin and headed out to the Ford Taurus. As John turned east to cross over to the interstate, John inserted a Bruce Springsteen CD. As the disc played, eventually it arrived at the track titled "My Hometown." John listened for the words of the third verse:

> *"Now main streets whitewashed windows and vacant stores*
> *Seems like there ain't nobody wants to come down here no more*
> *They're closing down the textile mill across the railroad tracks*
> *Foreman says these jobs are going boys and they ain't coming back to*
> *Your hometown . . . "*

Haunting lyrics and exactly the scenario he was trying to avoid. did not want Twin Ports to suffer the same fate that hit the textile mills, the television manufacturing industry in the upper Midwest and continues to wreak havoc with the Rust Belt. John thought, this battle is too important to lay down arms without a fight. His adopted hometown, way of life and the security of families, is ultimately what he was fighting for.

The rest of the drive was uneventful. John pulled into the Wingate Inn at exactly 11:15 PM. Most of the time, the trip proved neatly predictable. John could leave Twin Ports around 8:00 PM and in just a bit over three hours; he would arrive at the hotel; his home away from home for two nights.

Since John arrived on Sunday night, he scheduled a meeting with Doug for 8:30 AM the following morning. Doug agreed to meeting John before they kicked off the two- day review. He thought it was the best time to have the tough discussion on the agreement he was carrying in his briefcase.

John slept restlessly. He was not sure if adrenaline or Doug's reaction to the papers or just the general feeling he was running about 100 mph on a treadmill with no getting off. The alarm rang at 6:15, so sometime between 11:45 PM and 6:15AM; John did get a little sleep.

John showered, shaved, dressed and visited the "free continental breakfast." Always a highlight to get cereal, maybe some plastic-like eggs and a yogurt, and call it breakfast. The coffee was notoriously bad even for hotel coffee. Usually a trip through Caribou on the way to headquarters was necessary, and today was no exception.

John drove to the corporate campus, just a few miles from the Wingate and parked in the visitor spot. John reasoned he qualified, because he was a campus visitor. As John badged in the front entrance, he saw a familiar face, his hiring manager, Don Cole. John had not seen Don in probably ten years but instantly recognized him. They exchanged some small talk, with a quick update and agreed to not let another ten years go by between contacts.

The Northern Pines Technology corporate campus was built over time, starting in the mid-70's, around the same time as the Twin

Ports plant. The campus continued to expand with the most recent addition a new Technology & Research Center, which was on the north end of the complex. Doug's office was in the operations wing of the Copernicus buildings. The major buildings were named for scientists: DaVinci, Galileo, Copernicus, and Edison. Copernicus held manufacturing, purchasing, supply chain and logistics.

John arrived a few minutes before 8:00 and found an empty desk in the cube farm adjacent to Doug's office. John fired up the laptop and waiting the required three minutes for the software to navigate through itself and the security protocols before he saw the familiar login screen. John opened email and scanned; not too much from the weekend.

Production numbers were good. The site did have a near miss, safety incident in the general molding area over the weekend. An oil leak on a hose sprayed a mist of oil all over the general molding area; yuck – what a mess. Thankfully, no one injured in the actual incident or the subsequent clean up. Another reason to upgrade to braided hoses – reduce the opportunity for a pinhole and the lost time and waste associated with cleanup.

At about 8:25, John walked over to see if Doug was ready. He was at his desk, eyes carefully scanning a report on the screen. Doug invited John in to take a seat. John had been in his office before, but today, John's eyes scanned the bookshelves and the pictures and the mementos placed carefully on the shelves. John saw Doug's two children who looked like early teenagers, photos from vacations, and a few product samples dotted the shelf. John was not sure what he was looking for, he had been in this office at least a dozen times, but it was always interesting to see a glimpse into the occupants' personality and values through their office decorations.

The meeting began with some small talk about the drive down and the upcoming plans for summer. This was a good entre for the adoption plan discussion. John began by thanking Doug for his support on the adoption front. He acknowledged Doug was going above and beyond what was expected or probably allowed. John continued and told Doug he appreciated the flexibility. John prepared a dossier, with week-by-week detail including steps he was going to follow for checking in with Doug and with the staff at the plant.

John designated Jeff as officially in charge. Jeff would have temporary access to the Oracle approval process as delegate. Jeff was a logical choice as he had a good sense of plant operations. He could rely on the production managers for details. Jeff's tenure and connections made him the most senior manager at the site as well.

Jeff was going to be gone for a week in July and Mary Ann agreed to cover during that period. Jeff was taking a trip out to the Black Hills with his family, so he was not going to be totally unavailable. Between Jeff and Mary Ann, the plant would be well covered. The others on staff agreed to pick up a few of the extra duties and cover for John during community activities and meetings on an 'as needed' basis.

Diane and John would be in regular contact, and she knew how to reach him day or night. Doug said, "This is going to be a grand adventure for Kristin, the boys and you. You are doing a good thing and take time to enjoy it too." Doug added that he and his wife didn't have to travel when they adopted; the children were brought to the US by the agency and they met their child at the airport. Every country has their own way of doing things. John quizzed Doug whether that was a benefit or not in orienting their new children to the US. Doug said he wished he could have seen their orphanage in Asia mostly to better understand their culture and history. Doug ended with, "Maybe someday we'll travel there with the kids."

John was thankful today's technology allowed him to stay in touch with the plant and still be involved in key decisions even though physically, he was going to be half a world away.

John cleared his throat and said, "Doug, there is something else I need to talk to you about." Doug said, "Yes, go on." John began, "I had coffee with Doc, you remember him, right? Anyway, he was telling me about the early days of the plant and the delay in starting up the plant and the impact on the town. He got on a roll, sharing his stories from the early days." Not exactly knowing how to bring up the letter, John simply said, "Have you ever heard of an agreement between the city of Twin Ports and our company or anyone by the name of Harris Thronson ?"

Doug said, "No, and who is Harris?"

John continued, "Doc told me about an agreement made when the plant first opened, a set of conditions agreed to by what is now Northern Pines Technology and the city of Twin Ports. I think back then it was called MN Consolidated or something like that. Anyway, Doc informed me of a document or contract which had been signed by the city of Twin Ports and our Management at the time. I followed up on this and went to Plains Bank where the site has a safety deposit box. I found this."

John handed him the letter and watched his countenance as he read. John could see the color drain from Doug's face and his jaw clench ever so slightly. Doug read the letter, carefully set it down on the desk and said, "Who else knows about this?" John answered, "Doc and me are the only two that I know about."

Doug thought for a long while, looking directly past John's shoulder.

Doug asked John to keep this in confidence. He was going to follow up with legal counsel from Northern Pines Technology to see if anyone knew anything about this. Doug carefully folded the letter and placed it in his desk drawer.

John was a bit surprised Doug was not angrier or visibly shaken, but he put on a game face and they walked down the hall to the conference room where the monthly meeting was waiting.

Chapter 35: Infinite Meetings.

The monthly agenda was adjusted due to the finance and supply chain managers participation at a separate planning session offsite. Doug modified the agenda so the plant reviews were up first this month, beginning with the media plants. John listened to his peers talk through their results. They must have been in collusion on their presentations, because all three of them mentioned the impact of currency and exchange rates on the cost of raw materials, particularly those coming out of Japan. The yen was at two-year high against the dollar, so the strong currency caused the cost of the materials to rise. In most of the media formulations, there is not the luxury of having a second source of materials, so the only true option is pay the price.

In the world of coating, other than capital equipment, the largest cost component is raw materials. With the speed and width of the coating machines, labor is a relatively low input cost. This dynamic was going to be interesting to watch if Mendal Industries ever got a chance to scale up these machines. Even though labor content is relatively small, if a firm does not have knowledgeable and skilled labor, one can generate a lot of scrap in a short period of time. In addition, if the maintenance staff can't get the machine to run, trouble lies ahead as well. These were complex machines and not for the faint of heart.

John scanned his notes and results as the presentations were beginning to drone on. He glanced at Doug. He seemed to be distracted which was to be expected, especially after John dropped the bombshell he did a few hours earlier. Doug was preoccupied with his notes. John could see him scribbling and working three pages at a time.

John jotted a note to make mention of the 'leave of absence.' He previously shared his leave information individually, but now it was getting close enough to share a few more details and how the plant was going to be managed while he was away.

When it was his turn, John did the usual metrics; sharing great results. The site broke through $0.08 in diskettes for the first time. The other managers knew this was a big deal, but probably could not completely fathom the magnitude of effort that went into carving half a cent out of the unit cost of a diskette. John shared, "We had the benefit of good volumes. Overall plant spending was down slightly and when you spread lower spending over more units, good things happen to cost." It was a relatively easy presentation to make.

A quick explanation on the OSHA incident rate of 3.0 versus a goal of 1.75 was needed. The site unfortunately suffered a cut hand in the packaging area requiring stitches, so there was a full court press now to continue to emphasize safety and making sure people are always putting personal safety ahead of all else. Even though this wasn't serious, it was a good reminder to stay focused on all aspects of safety.

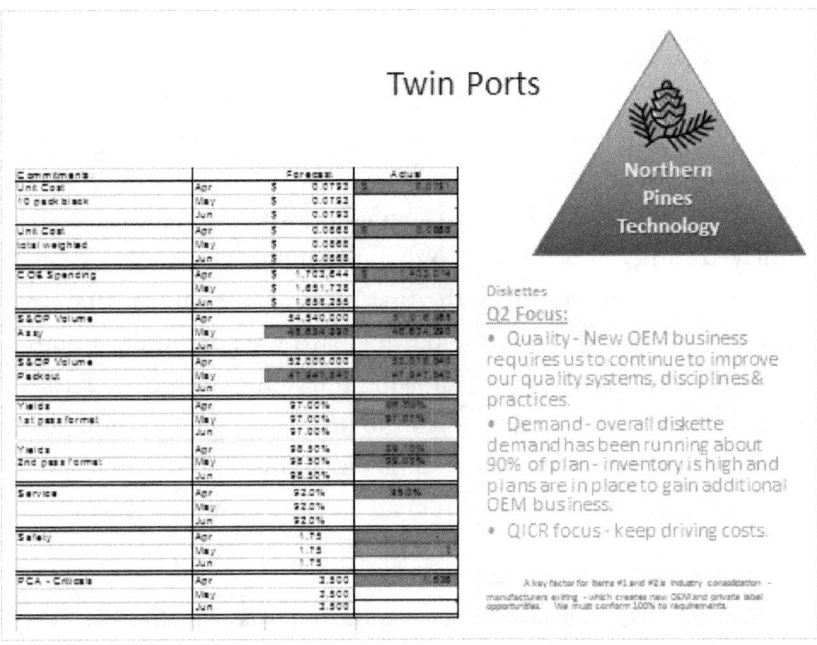

John closed the presentation with the fact that sometime in the next month or two, he, his wife, and twins would be traveling to Ukraine to adopt either one or two children with special needs. John shared the motivation and the fact that these children grow up with absolutely no hope and no future. John said simply, "We want to give them the gift of a forever family."

The presentations ended at about 4:45. Doug shared he had a surprise for his direct reports for the evening. He managed to get the Northern Pines Technology Suite for the Minnesota Twins/New York Yankees game starting at 7:05. The news was met with high anticipation; John hadn't seen a major-league game in ten years.

This was the last season for the Twins in the Metrodome, as outdoor baseball was returning to Minneapolis soon. Doug said he could drive down and the group agreed to meet in the hotel lobby at 5:45, allowing enough time to get down to the stadium, park and see warm ups. John was looking forward to the food and fun. It was going to be a good night at the ballpark.

The suite lofted above the first baseline and was well apportioned. All the food was brought in as well as drinks and snacks. The suite had seats watching the game as well as a nice reception area where the food was located. The Twins ended up winning 7-5 in a solid, well-played game. It was 4-4 into the 9th inning. The Yankees went up with a solo home run from the first batter. When it was the Twins' half of the inning, they did it the hard way: one walk, a bunt which was overthrown at first, allowing the runner to score. Torii Hunter, hit a hard drive right down the first base line and somehow it got mishandled in the outfield resulting in an inside the park homerun. The Yanks did not even get a throw to home. It was a great way to end the game and night.

After Monday night's headliner event, the Tuesday meetings were routinely dull. With the reversed agenda, Tuesday included supply chain, finance and R&D updates. Getting current information from these areas was always helpful in managing site costs.

John was also interested to hear if Doug had learned anything from Legal Counsel. It wasn't until lunch when John had a chance to ask Doug who said it was under review.

The meeting ended about 2:00 PM and timing was fine with John. Several coworkers booked dinner time flights back home. John could leave now, miss the rush hour through the northwest part of the cities and be home right around suppertime.

Once John passed Maple Grove, he set the cruise on 75 and didn't turn it off for 153 miles later, when it was time to exit and head west to Twin Ports.

John was thankful that he had been candid with Doug even though it wasn't easy. His conscience was clear. John remained interested to see what the legal experts would figure out about this agreement forged almost 30 years ago by people who are now dead.

Chapter 36: Bad News & Travel Plans

Kristin called John at work on Wednesday. She was so excited her words ran together. "John, John we had a call from the adoption agency, just a few minutes ago! Our dossier was submitted and accepted this week in Ukraine! This is a huge thing and I can't even begin to say how excited and how much work I must do and this big step forward for us! Next is a travel date." John managed to get a word in quickly and asked, "now what?" She said, "Usually most families are traveling a few weeks after acceptance."

After the initial excitement waned, her mood and tone changed and John could tell there was good news and not so good news. John's 15 years of marriage provided a sense of knowing when something else was going on. She said, "It has become apparent there is a problem with the paperwork for our dear, sweet, little Sergey. If this is not resolved, he will be unavailable for adoption."

John immediately knew the news was a very hard for Kristin to take. She had such a tender heart towards Sergey; and if they do not adopt him soon, he would invariably be sent to a mental institution. His life and future there would be very uncertain. He may be available again or maybe never; life is painfully uncertain for orphans.

Together, both Kristin and John believed it would take a miracle, but that is exactly what they are going to pray for. Despite the bleak outlook for Sergey, John and Kristin chose to believe the impossible. This has been and will continue to be a journey of trust and learning about faith.

The twins plotted how best to support the adoption as well and decided to set up a cookie stand on the driveway. When John arrived home from work, he got another full dose of excitement about the news of the day as well as the fact that Eric and David had managed to pull in $8.50 on their cookie stand.

Budding Entrepreneurs

When John walked in the house, it was obvious dinner planning had slipped through the cracks, as everyone was so excited about the new developments and the sale of cookies. The aroma of good food coming from the kitchen was very absent. John suggested they take a picnic down to the park so together they packed up a few basics and drove by Kentucky Fried Chicken for the main course.

This was one of those memorable moments as a family coupled with a beautiful summer evening. Kristin and John watched the kids play, talked about the trip and speculated of a time in the not too distant future with seven kids. Much of the discussion centered on whether they were they up to the task. In a few moments of logic mixed with clarity, John reasoned, "We are surviving with five – two more can't be that much more work – can they?"

Relaxed summer nights represented the best Twin Ports had to offer and provided warm memories to last all winter. John loved the vibrancy of a college town; however, when the students cleared out in the middle of May, it was always nice to enjoy the extra peace and quiet that enveloped their small and docile corner of the world.

At the park, the kids played hard, and when it was time to give the five-minute warning to ramp down, there were ready. No pushback tonight; the news of the day and playtime tired them out. John and Kristin packed up and walked to the Suburban. John eased out of the parking spot and pointed the Suburban onto the road for their destination a few blocks west. He let the family out and shoehorned the car between bikes, scooters and a stroller in the garage.

Further news followed a few days after the first call indicating the Ministry received the dossier. John and Kristin Stanton were granted an appointment at the Centre of Adoption at the Ministry of Ukraine for Family, Youth and Sports [abbreviated SDA for some unknown reason] in Kiev, Ukraine at 10:00 AM on July 22nd for their official referral. The date was non-negotiable; this is what they have been waiting for.

Kristin showed John her updated blog post sharing her thoughts and feelings with the latest news. *So, obviously we have known about this upcoming trip for months....but now all of a sudden when it's here I can hardly believe it is happening. I am waxing between absolute panic at all that I have to do to get ready and complete fear of all that is ahead with brief interludes of calm, interspersed with desperate cries of help to the LORD.*

This week I am focusing on finishing cleaning up from the sale a couple weeks ago, (i.e. putting back together closets, attic, basement, garage, etc...), making a million phone calls - setting up all the fall dentist, dr. appts, etc... that I would normally be scheduling in August, getting a haircut, ordering books and cds for the trip, ordering school materials for the fall, bringing the cat in for annual shots, getting a shot myself, making tons of lists of all that I have to do, emailing massive amounts of people for various reasons, building 2 beds (pictures will eventually follow), ordering plane tickets, finalizing the details of childcare for our younger children while we are gone. And so on and so on.... (of course, my significant other could write a list that was equally as long!)

I have figured out a pretty decent system to keep it all straight. I bought a notebook with 3 sections. Section One has lists of all the stuff (in categories of course) that we will be bringing. Section Two has one very long 'to do' list. Section Three has miscellaneous. Every night before bed, I fill out an index card of all that I need to do the next day. So, the following morning I rise bright and early and tape the card to the forehead until its done...not really but I do carry it around all day until it's done!

It's just plain crazy. Who knew planning a trip for a family of 7 to go in all different directions would be this much work!

Next week will consist of packing, packing, and packing....

The following week (the week before we go) hopefully will just consist of tying up all the loose ends.

Tentative schedule: Leave July 19 for 4 to 6 weeks! YIKES ! That's a lot to pack for !!!

Chapter 37: Everything Must Have a Plan

Most of the staff were out of the office Fourth of July week. The plant shuts down for preventive maintenance during the long weekend. A few employees from the facilities and maintenance crews worked doing activities which could only be done when the power and utilities were off.

For the Fourth this year, the family opted to stay in town; mostly driven by the amount of work to prepare for travel. A general feeling between excitement and panic vacillated within John. There was a lot to do.

Visiting the attorney and drafting temporary transfer power of attorney to family and friends demonstrated just one item on the long list of time- consuming tasks. John and Kristin desired their friends and relatives the ability to handle any medical emergencies and make decisions on the children's behalf if they could not be consulted.

The Stanton's attempted to manage some sense of ordinary during this crazy race to get ready for travel, one non-negotiable was celebrating the Fourth with Twin Town fireworks. It's tradition.

The town put on a good show, mostly because the way they did fireworks was unique. Many towns use the local park and then set up fireworks on an island or shoot from a distant shore allowing the lake to become the stage. The river isn't that big and there isn't a lake within the city limits. Without that option, the fire department shoots them off from the park. The onlookers sit very close to where they fire the rounds from, so the fireworks go off right above the crowd. John had never seen anything quite like it. The fireworks seemed so close that you could almost reach out and touch them. Perhaps not the absolute safest approach, but a spectacular sight none the less.

The family brought a big blanket and intently watched the aerial action. If snacks and earplugs accompany them, the kids remained happy. They also get to stay up late; and when one is young, who doesn't like to stay up late eating snacks and watching things blow up?

The family arrived home with tired kids, and simply put the smallest in their beds with clothes on from the day. The older ones stumbled around and brushed their teeth, changed in jammies and headed off to bed.

The alarm rang early; John left the house at 5:30 AM; knowing the amount of work to be accomplished in the next two weeks was more than he could manage during regular hours.

As he sat down to make yet another to-do list, he reflected on the journey. Like many of life's journeys, the outcome, destination and how you get there are less than clear. Now, even with the stress, John was enjoying every day of the adventure. He knew he was right where he needed to be; both at work, at home and of like mind with Kristin with respect to the adoption.

As he turned his full attention to work, he was looking forward to being gone and seeing how the plant does without his presence. Part of the hidden motivation for the leadership training with the staff was to push them to step up and lead.

He wanted to see how they did on their own. John reasoned with the training and experiences of the last six months they should be ready for additional autonomy. He fully expected it to be a good growth experience for all.

One of the projects John hoped to work on during the time away was additional research into products Twin Ports could make in their contract manufacturing area. The area was established almost ten years ago when there was gap in new products stream. It worked out well for the site. The facility sold its core and distinct competencies;

offering those willing to pay a significant competitive advantage. It complemented the work of Northern Pines and provided adjacent areas for the tooling and engineering functions to do some advanced technology scouting.

Financially, the 'side business' accomplished several things. Primarily, it had to be profitable. With that baseline, the site could apply shared overhead like warehouse, supply chain, HR and quality across the contract manufacturing business. Previous managers used it as a bit of a buffer from some of the fluctuations of the data storage business. The contract manufacturing arena had its ups and downs, but it was a good thing for the site and something the staff knew they had to maintain and grow to keep Twin Ports operations fully utilized.

John wanted to create a list of potential customers which could be visited over the next few months and see if the site could secure new business opportunities. An area of interest for John was the medical device market or at least providing components that would go into a medical device. There were some close parallels between data storage and medical devices; namely, very tight tolerances, no margin for quality excursions and reliability had to be quad 9s or 99.9999%.

Interweaving contract manufacturing and Northern Pines work also subtly made the process of peeling off one business more difficult. John's rationale concluded if the site is locked into a manufacturing contract(s), those generally have time out clauses that at least require providing six to nine months of notification for suitable arrangements for manufacturing can be made by the OEM. Maybe it was a longshot, but now, John needed all the advantages he could collect.

Looking back, nice strides in training resulted in increased flexibility of the operations. The initial work between Keystone and Glacier had gone well. Supervisors liked it because scheduling was easier. Supply chain loved it, because they could make to order on the two lines and maintained the flexibility to run Glacier for half the shift and Keystone the remainder. The master operators and maintenance were probably impacted most with additional shutdowns and startups. Either these can go well or if there are many issues, it can be a bit challenging. The groups continue to learn and adjust.

The first item on John's agenda for the day was an 8:30 AM meeting Mary Ann, Grant and Jeff. They were completing final planning for John's absence. John also wanted a chance to review the content of the recent site review at headquarters; so they had the most current information on plant performance.

This meeting contained a surprise element as well. Until now, John had not shared Doc's agreement which John subsequently discovered at the bank. For several reasons, John thought it important the three senior managers at the plant knew this information. As John relayed the story of his discussion with Doc, their interest obviously piqued.

He disclosed to the group the information shared with Doug. John said, "Doug brought it to the Northern Pines legal team for review and it was under review at present." After many questions; yet fewer answers, John ended the conversation saying, "You know precisely the same information I do right now."

All agreed it was going to be very interesting to see how the legal team at Northern Pines would process this information. Of course, no one could know if an agreement signed 30 plus years ago had any merit or standing today. Bottom line, it was out of their hands. John knew the people gathered in his office had a passion for the plant and its people and loved what they were doing. If there was anyone who had the best interests of the plant at heart, it was this team. Somewhat offhandedly, John said, "If you guys can come up with a solution while I'm gone, that would be great." Little did John know this nudge, some of the last words that he spoke to this team prior to his departure, would start more than a few things into motion.

The last day before travel, Diane arranged for a lunch, which John appreciated. The staff had also taken up a collection and together donated $550 to help defray the cost of the adoption. It was hard not to get a little emotional when John thanked them for their thoughtfulness and for sharing in this journey.

In a moment described as surreal, in less than 24 hours, four of the Stanton's were beginning the adventure of a lifetime. The other three remaining stateside would have their own adventures as well.

Packed & Ready to Begin the Journey to Ukraine

The final day was too busy to feel anything other than the weight of a million-item to-do list. It was a rush to the end, and thankfully, friends came to help with the kids and allowed the travelers to focus on packing and preparing for travel.

The drive to the airport was filled with excitement. Arrangements had been made for friends to pick up the car at the airport and return it to Twin Ports later that day. It was only a 45-mile drive to Fargo and the family was well aware their time together was short.

Goodbyes are tremendously difficult; especially considering not knowing when and under what circumstances the return trip would come. Scenarios ranged from a few weeks to a 1-1/2 months. No probability around either outcome was known.

Tears were shed when it came time to say goodbye to Seth, Caroline and Mark and how these three little precious lives would be missed during the trip. Thankfully, technology bridged some of the gap; however, there was no substitute for the feeling of a small hand reaching up for a hug or a chirpy little voice wishing everyone a happy day and good morning.

With final goodbyes uttered, the travelers began the routine through security and the waiting process for the flight to Minneapolis.

The planning was done, the work just beginning.

This trip would change the family forever; but much more importantly, it would save the precious lives of two children.

Chapter 38: Money Laundering

July 19th was windy, hot and muggy. Later in the afternoon, powerful thunderstorms brewed over eastern South Dakota and western Minnesota, so the plane sat for over an hour on the tarmac in Fargo waiting for clearance to take off. The flight to Minneapolis took only about 40 minutes. Thankfully, despite a late landing, Delta held the outbound plane on the ground. The weather wreaked havoc with all the flights in the upper Midwest.

This adventure was the twins' first flight. They were fascinated with the 'on demand' video systems, music, and games. The flight attendant came around and asked if they would like anything to drink or eat. John encouraged them to enjoy all the amenities; international travel still has a few perks.

An aspect of the trip not largely thought about entailed finances and the payments of steep, adoption expenses overseas. Ukraine operates largely on a cash system. US currency is valued highly. However, the currency must be perfect with no evidence of counterfeit or tampering. If it is not perfect, people assume it is adulterated and effectively unusable. The Greens tipped John off on this subtle point and he was thankful for the information. The adoption arrangement included the need to pay the facilitator for her work, as well as for food, lodging, drivers and all other expenses. John's best estimate was a total cost of $14,000, plus a little buffer.

John put a request in at Plains Bank and Trust earlier in the summer. He was going to need $15,000 in $20s and $50s. It was a good thing John started early as the tellers hunted for several weeks to find clean, crisp bills with no disqualifying marks.

In Ukraine, there were banks and money changing stations in many locales; however, there was no option to wire US funds, so John travelled with cash on his person. Half of it was in a money pouch tucked into the cargo pants pocket and the other half tucked in another pouch around his neck. John was not used to being a 'mule,' but there were no other options or alternatives. He took little comfort in knowing this method is what people before had done as well. Just thinking about the worst case made John shudder.

In addition to personal belongings, which consisted of a heaping pile of suitcases, Kristin and her friends bought up blanket sleeper- type jammies during the post winter and early spring sales. The bags included over 100 pairs of pajamas crammed into every available nook and cranny of available suitcase space. The pajamas were a gift for the children of the orphanage to provide warm bed clothes for the cold winter. Between four people, a mountain of suitcases, duffels and assorted packages accompanied them as they arrived in Kiev.

In general, the travel went smoothly. Layovers were short and flights took off and land on time. Other than being weary from the hours of travel and very little comfortable sleep, the journey was off to a good start.

Upon arrival – it wasn't immediately apparent where to go – so when in doubt, the best course of action is follow the crowd. Using this strategy – the crowd moved through the arrivals hall and to baggage claim. Another group began moving down a corridor and eventually topped in a large smoke-filled room with a low ceiling. Lines were beginning to form in front of a row of desks.

John queued up the line and waited for his turn; finally, their time came, the agent asked in broken English what needed to be declared. John said, "Just US dollars." The agent asked, "How much?" In a hushed tone, John whispered the amount. The agents mouth curled a sly smile under his thick mustache. He said, "Let me see." John did not really like where this was going, but he had no choice? John fished the pouch from his pocket and the one from around his neck and opened them up for inspection; half thinking this may be the last time he ever sees the money.

The agent looked in and chuckled to himself. He didn't say anything, took out his stamp and loudly slapped the mechanical device down on the four passports and the declaration form and said, in a loud voice, "наступного"; the only logical assumption was this meant "next", exactly what he wanted to hear.

John breathed a sigh of relief; they were safely in Ukraine with $15,000 in cash and the whole family was thankful this part was done. Their worst fear was being singled out for additional questions or scrutiny.

Once passing customs and immigration, and moving towards the arrival hall; all eyes began looking for Mariya Petrov. Mariya was the assigned facilitator and was going to be the voice, the guide and in most cases, their brain for the next few weeks.

The family had no idea who to look for short of a sign with the Stanton (or some variant) written on it. Eric spotted it first over on the left side of the airport exit area. His eyes found a cardboard sign with "Stanton" scrawled on it. Finally, after months of waiting, the moment to meet Mariya had come. Both John and Kristin knew she was their key resource in a successful adoption. After eye contact was made, she dropped the sign to her side.

The family had to trust her judgment, instincts, and instructions because there was no other choice. Others counseled and warned them Ukraine was not the place where any English-speaking someone would thrive by going 'solo.'

After a quick hello, she hastily ushered the luggage and travelers out into the bustling Kiev airport parking lot. Mariya was a middle-aged woman, well dressed and styled. Her English was very good, and she moved between Russian and English seamlessly. Once underway, she barked instructions to the driver in Russian and then turned her attention to the guests to engage in pleasantries related to the travel.

The first thing the twins noticed through their tired eyes was the nature of the written language, actually more like markings. None of the characters even looked familiar. David commented, "How do you even know what something is? It all looks like gibberish." Eric noticed a yellow sign and said, "Billa. Look, I can read Russian!" Billa happened to be one of the few examples where familiar letters are not mixed in with the Cyrillic characters. Billa would become a very familiar sign as the store was one of the main grocery store chains in Ukraine, reasonably priced and well stocked. They agreed it was going to be a fun challenge figuring out what signs and billboards actually meant.

The driver and Mariya were having an animated discussion up front. The driver was a younger man, perhaps 25; with slicked back hair, wearing a dress shirt and jeans. The Mercedes van traveled for probably ten minutes before it pulled off into a shopping center. Mariya said in very understandable but slightly broken English, "We are going to stop here for a few minutes. This is a where we pick up needed items." After we entered Billa, Mariya said, "Come, follow me, we get some supplies."

The first stop was to visit the currency exchange, and John pulled out the first crisp US $50 bill and gave it to the clerk. The clerk inspected, front and back, held it up to the light and looked for some defining features. After scrutiny of the watermarks or threads or whatever she was looking for, it was deemed good enough to exchange for Ukrainian currency. Hryvnias and kopeks would be the new currency. Rough exchange rates were between five and seven hryvnias to one US dollar. The $50 translated into 340 hryvnias. He trusted the translation was, at least, close to right and took his new currency and transferred it to his regular wallet. All of this felt a little overwhelming and confusing for John, especially coupled with jet lag and the need for a soft bed and shower.

Mariya did the shopping, because past the very basics, it was difficult figuring out what was in some of these packages. After picking up some muesli, milk, cheese, summer sausage, bread and water, the tired travelers returned to the waiting van. It was hot and dry and fortunately the driver had the common sense to leave the van running with the air conditioning on.

One strange question Mariya asked related to the type of water they preferred. In the rush of the store and weariness of the traveler, John assumed the question meant with gas or without gas and simply muttered a "yes." It wasn't until later at night John realized the question was not about fizzy water, but rather his yes chose some type of strongly infused and undrinkable mineral or salt water. John made a mental note of the brand and vowed to stay far away from the potent, salty elixir in the green bottle.

Mariya told the driver what they presumed to be directions; and the van snaked through streets, neighborhoods and even a few alleyways. Eventually their trip ended outside an older, nondescript six-story building, which was their temporary apartment, home for at least the next few days.

The appointment at the Ministry was not until Tuesday, so the family surmised at least three nights would be spent at their current location. The apartment was located one block off a major thoroughfare in Kiev. The little that was seen of Kiev so far on the trip in displayed a modern city with lots of traffic, many people and stores of all types and sizes.

A Soviet-era store called GUM was located on the block closest to the apartment. GUM was now thoroughly modern; however, it had the look of a department store from the 1960s. The other noticeable feature was the prevalence of high work cranes. The skyline was dotted with machines lifting materials to buildings rising from the earth. If not for the Cyrillic alphabet symbols, it would be hard to discern if they were in Paris, New York or any other modern mega-city.

The short stay apartment was on fourth floor, requiring a harrowing ride up a very old elevator. John was a bit skeptical based on the vintage of the elevator, but reserved judgment on the apartment. John reminded himself, "We have to trust Mariya."

An unplanned, but pleasant surprise, the apartment was very nice, modern, and looked furnished from IKEA. Maple floors, simple but very stylish furnishings, thin panel TV and many of the amenities common to a European flat. The view from the fourth floor made the ride in the freight elevator worthwhile. The boys were thankful that they did not have to lug the suitcases, duffels, backpacks and briefcases up multiple flights of stairs to their home-away-from-home.

Even before the dust settled, Mariya said, "We need to talk, now." She shared with the family the most recent information available on the status of the appointment, the situation with Sergey and options for the next few days.

Neither Kristin nor John felt in the mood for a long, emotional discussion after the journey and being awake for 30-some hours. However, from the tone in Mariya's voice, this was important, so both commanded their senses to be at full attention. They needed to understand for themselves the situation with Sergey. Mariya started, "For Sergey, we have some, how do you say it, clearness, no, no clarity." Mariya continued to explain in halted terms, "We do know for certain the boy who goes with the name we were given last January is not available now. There is problems with lost paperwork; and months will happen before new paperwork is created."

As harsh as the information sounded, especially to a sleep deprived brain, Mariya made the outcome very clear, which was in a sense what both had hoped would happen. The result was not what either John or Kristin wanted, but after receiving and processing the information; they now could begin to process the next steps. Mariya went on to explain, "There is some confusion about the photos, so between the photos and the name, we understand that his paperwork has been misplaced or lost and that he is not available for adoption." Mariya continued, "This boy you call Sergey, he may or may not be at the orphanage, we cannot know. It is all unknown and until we are actually able to see the little boys in person, we will not know."

John knew this was a significant blow and very disappointing to Kristin. Both had talked much about this and agreed if possible they were going to try to verify the identity of the little boy set on their hearts many months and miles ago. Kristin told Mariya, "If we can find him, we will." Mariya countered, "We don't know if this is even possible."

Mariya continued, "Since you are approved to adopt two, you will be showed pictures of another child. You will have to decide if you are willing to adopt this child in addition to the girl you call Vika."

Mariya said, "I give you advice, even if you don't ask. You need to think about challenges of adopting out from two different regions and orphanages. Although scenario is doable, it is very difficult. There will be much travel, disruption and more cost, depending on distance between locations. You also will have to work with 2 court systems and all is very time consuming."

Mariya went on to explain what would happen at the Ministry and what the rest of the week might be like. She offered to take the family sightseeing on Sunday, but John politely declined. She could tell from their facial countenance what was really needed was sleep. She talked for another 20 minutes, while both struggled to stay awake. Finally, after what seemed like an eternity, she said, "I leave you to get sleep. The area is safe, stay on the main streets and John I call you tomorrow." She handed John over a small Nokia phone and wrote down her cell number and she was out the door.

Finally, it was just them, alone in a faraway place.

Chapter 39: Week 1 in Ukraine

Three objectives topped the list for the first week in Ukraine: arrive safely, schedule the appointment at the Ministry of Ukraine for Family, Youth and Sports, abbreviated SDA and meet Vika. Mariya returned on Sunday morning earlier than anyone would have liked. John compared her to a whirlwind or tornado in some respects. She was focused, driven and a dervish of activity.   As a facilitator for the adoption, the attributes were good, because if she was slow and lackadaisical, it would have sent a troublesome sign. She seemed to have a very good handle on what was needed, what was coming up and was determined to help the adoption be successful.

She reviewed many of the same things from just twelve hours earlier. A hazy memory lingered from the night before; however, a repeat was probably a good thing. She continued, "The SDA appointments could go very quickly or they could consume several hours, one never knows." She drew out her "u" in consume in a way that Eric and David thought was moderately funny.   More like consuuuume.

She was preparing John and Kristin for the types of questions asked. She rattled off a list of commonly asked questions.   Some of the favorites Mariya said, "why do you come so far to adopt child?, are you sure you can handle another child?, how will you communicate with child?" And the oddest, "You are not going to sell this child, are you?"

As Mariya would say frequently, "One cannot knows", referring to the questions which will be asked by the administrator.

In the back of John's' mind, he hoped if they answered a question in some way that was not consistent with what the Ministry expected to hear, Mariya could redirect or translate in a correct manner.   John did not think that was going to be an issue. She said, "Stranger things have happened, but I help youuuuu." Again, a drawn out "u" provided fodder for two squirrely boys to snicker about for days to come.

Mariya was in like a tornado and out the same way. She must have realized the family didn't have all their wits yet due to the jet lag, because after she reiterated most of what had already been said earlier, she said, "I leave you alone. You need rest. Many days, busy days ahead." She smiled, made sure the provided cell phone was turned on and left.

Kristin and John needed some time to talk through the Sergey dynamic. It didn't come as a complete surprise, but now there appeared to be an element of finality. The discussion centered on the need to talk through whether they wanted to pursue another child. If so, girl or boy? What type of special needs can they take on? The same orphanage or different orphanage? All of these decisions seemed right about Sergey and now, they were back at square one; wondering if they should only adopt one or two. There was a lot to process in the next 48 hours.

Moreover, another unknown element played somewhat into the decision. They possessed limited capability to care for a child with a serious medical condition. John reasoned, "We are going to have our hands more than full with seven kids, so we need to be realistic about our ability to manage all this." Both realized they needed to pray for guidance. They went to a passage in Isaiah that Kristin found, it read, "I will give you hidden treasures, riches stored in secret places, so that you may know that I am the Lord, the God of Israel, who summons you by name."

In a way, this whole thing was about searching for their hidden treasure. They did not know who or where, but both John and Kristin believed to the core of her being they had been told to take a step of faith and find this hidden treasure somewhere in Ukraine. What that meant or what it looked like, would truly have to be revealed to them, just as a treasure-hunter finds their riches.

The next two days were fun, but also filled with some anxiety, based on the number of questions yet to be answered. The family walked the streets of Kiev, toured local sites and did plenty of soul searching as well.

The SDA appointment was at 10:00 AM on Tuesday, July 22. That was 4:00 AM (Central US) time. They knew they would have people thinking about them, and praying for them as what faced John and Kristin was the need to make a life changing decision in the span of less than an hour. As Mariya explained, "There is not a think about it for several days option, SDA expects immediate answer."

John and Kristin arrived at the SDA building via taxi with Mariya and the boys. Mariya sat up front leaving the four of them squished into the back of the dated Lada. This did not seem to bother anyone and they could feel the springs under the frame bottom out at every bump. The drive was short, but took a route past an ornate cathedral and a park like area. As they wound through a rather hilly section of the city, the architecture changed. It went from city modern to a more stately, academic type campus area. The building housing the SDA was anything but a typical, Soviet-style, government building. The location was equally impressive in an area with many trees and a ravine in the back – not that this was that unusual for Kiev, but it was distinctive.

It reminded John a little bit of an old east coast prep school with the ivy-covered walls and stately architecture and structure.

The group climbed a back stairwell to the second floor. They walked down the hall and came to a small office alcove with a heavy wooden door. Hallways framed either end, the tiled floors were white, but worn with age and wood doors with transoms lined each side of the hallway.

So, this is where life changing decisions are made.

The First Appointment

Mariya greeted the receptionist and conducted a lively discussion. Most Ukrainian discussions could be described as vigorous and animated. It was a level just below an argument. John heard only a "dobroye utro" which John would later learn is a friendly good morning greeting. John had heard "privyet" also as a greeting, but had yet to learn the difference between the two exchanges.

They family was ushered into a waiting area and almost immediately Valeriya Breznekov came from a side office to greet them. The twins waited in an anteroom while John and Kristin were asked to step inside the deputy director's office. They immediately noticed in her arms was their dossier and an additional binder. Kristin was very thankful to see their dossier traveled over 6,000 miles. They were now reunited with a set of papers which had taken hundreds of hours for her to create.

All the preparation and work came down to this moment in time.

Both John and Kristin felt the weight of the decision they were faced with. They knew inside the binder were backgrounds of children, parentless children surrounded by hopelessness. John and Kristin could only do so much, but which one to choose?

Where is their hidden treasure?

Valeriya asked a few basic questions, "How was your trip? When did you arrive? What have you seen in our lovely city?" John and Kristin responded with short answers, but based on Mariya's interpretation, she must have embellished the answers as some as her explanations took three times longer than their brief responses. Through smiling and friendly tones, they tried to remain complimentary of the people, culture, and experience thus far.

After the brief introduction, Valeriya began the business at hand. Mariya translated as Valeriya spoke. "The purpose of this visit is for the SDA to provide a referral to adopt either one or two children. Your petition to adopt has been accepted in the form of your dossier and you are now being given a referral (or referrals) if you opt for a second child."

Valeriya then said, "It is time to understand what we want to do." Kristin explained their desire to adopt Sergey and Vika, as counseled by Mariya. Valeriya said, "Vika is available and her paperwork is all in order. Sergey, not so much. His paperwork was lost and it is impossible to replace. He is not available". It sounded so cold and terse, but John and Kristin expected this exchange. As counseled by Mariya they asked, "Are there other children available to adopt?" Valeriya replied, "Da," which at this moment they understood as yes.

Valeriya reached for her binder and slowly began to flip the pages, in a way so the faces are only seen to her. It was hard for both not to extend their neck to try and see the children. John thought to himself, so much mystery and randomness. This was how referrals worked in Ukraine. The irony struck both Kristin and John.

This woman was going to change the life of some random child parked in a Ukrainian orphanage without hope or a future. In a worldly way, this child was about to win the lottery. He or she would be adopted by a family, have a place in this world and be cherished and loved, all because the deputy director's hand stopped on a specific page. John whispered a prayer for divine guidance, as he knew this was as significant for them as it was for the child under consideration.

She paused at a few pages and then spoke to Mariya. Mariya interpreted for us, "Valeriya would like to know if you would like to go to the same orphanage or if you are open to a new orphanage." They talked about this and based on both cost and common sense, they reasoned it was most practical to find another child from the same orphanage. This would reduce time, travel, court dates and many other potential logistical nightmares.

Valeriya held out the book and pointed to a page. Kristin and John both looked at the tattered page and the picture. It was a young boy about two years old. He was fine featured, small, smiling and appeared to have Down syndrome from the visible features. Valeriya said "he is mobile, good- natured and was a quiet little boy. No known medical history." John was unsure how she knew that from the information on the page, but he didn't challenge.

John looked at Kristin and she looked at him. John could see in her eyes the same thing John was thinking. The boy was only two years old, which is too young for their family dynamic. John and Kristin wanted a companion for Caroline. No words were spoken, but in their hearts, wrenching as it was, both knew, this was not the one.

Time suspended for a few moments.

Valeriya took the book back and looked further. She paused and glanced at a page, then continued. Finally, she handed the book over and said, "Da or Nyet? The girl's name is, "Anastasia Rebakoyen."

The photo showed a little girl with a petite, inquisitive looking face. It was a hard to see if she was a boy or girl, based on the features and haircut. She was lying on a blanket on her tummy, her head up off the blanket much like a turtle. The moment John looked at the picture, it reminded him of a photo of Caroline which looked almost identical. In fact, John was struck with the uncommon pose. Very few parents probably have the same photo of their babies. Many pictures are taken in strollers, swings, on a blanket, but this photo is not that common, especially in a child with Down syndrome where muscle tone is often a significant issue. Her head was up and the back curved, and the facial expression was one of inquiry. Mariya chimed in commenting, "Anastasia is at the same orphanage as Vika."

John did not need to look at Kristin. They both knew the search was over.

John said, "This is the one, we have found her and she has found us." Kristin whispered into John's ear, "Anastasia is our hidden treasure. Exactly like the verse said."

In a surreal way, it was obvious to both John and Kristin a miracle had just taken place. Two little girls were going to beat the odds. Their lives, as well as the entire Stanton family, were changed forever.

The weight of the decision was now over; Viktoria and Anastasia were going to be their daughters.

The next step was unceremoniously riddling with mind numbing paperwork, which was finished with animated Russian and an hour of typing; a noise not commonly heard in the US anymore, but very common in Ukraine. With the work completed, John attempted to thank Valeriya and the others in the office with a "spasibo," his first attempt at Russian. John was unsure if he massacred the pleasantry or not, but there were a few smiles from the women working in the office.

As the family walked out, Mariya was already two steps ahead and beginning to talk about the next steps. "So much to do and so little time. We will travel to Kharkov maybe that same night," Mariya chattered on. She continued, "Visit our girls and then we have decision about whether to 'accept' the referrals."

All this sounded simple, but John would later learn it took many steps to make easy tasks happen in Ukraine. This was a precursor to getting the court date set and nothing in Ukraine is simple.

If Mariya said something, they missed it as they literally bounded down the stairs. In hindsight, they didn't ask questions about Anastasia. They ascertained she had Down syndrome and that she was in the same orphanage as Vika. Unknowns included medical history, family history, capabilities or anything else.

John and Kristin both knew Anastasia was their new daughter as soon as they saw her picture. The wonderful outcome was light poured into the dark, making the treasure hidden no longer, but visible and found.

In those moments, it was easy to miss exactly what transpired. Something very deep was revealed. Not a fact, but a whisper, a revelation showing truth in the promise.

> *"I will give you hidden treasures, riches stored in secret places,*
> *so that you may know that I am the Lord, the God of Israel,*
> *who summons you by name."*

Chapter 40: Meeting Hidden Treasures

Mariya dropped the family off at the apartment and all agreed the first celebration dinner was in order. It had been a good day and from their list of three objectives, two were complete. The family had been in Kiev for three days and felt comfortable walking around the immediate area surrounding the apartment. Government buildings, commercial office buildings and retail stores punctuated their slightly more familiar neighborhood.

Through initial exploration, John and the boys found a large underground mall called City Centre. Located up on street level was the ubiquitous McDonalds. All three boys missed a taste of home. This satisfied a culinary longing, and besides, it was a good reminder of life in the US.

The Beauty of Slavic Architecture

The family dined on the universal taste and cuisine of McDonalds and talked about the day. The outcome had been bittersweet. They talked about the difficulties and Kristin said it best, "I went with a hope that we would be able to take Sergey home with us, and his loss is still very raw." All felt the loss and worried about a future for Sergey.

David chimed in, "I am super excited to meet Anastasia and you know, that is maybe the way our family was meant to be." John thought to himself, "Pretty insightful for an 11-year-old boy. Yes, this is exactly the way our family is supposed to be."

John checked work activities daily on the Blackberry, but finding a good place to sit down with a laptop or desktop to create blog posts or other correspondence was a bit more challenging. Upon leaving the US, a small email group had been pre-arranged with friends. Information was sent out to the primary group and then the recipients forwarded it to the broader group. Kristin also started a blog she intended to keep family and friends updated with current news. Both were anxious to use this technology to share the significant events of the day. They knew family and friends were waiting for an update.

John had only been gone from the office for two workdays, but it felt much longer. Perhaps the fact he was half a world away warped the illusion of time. The trusty Blackberry was at least keeping him connected with the world of Twin Ports, and John knew anything he needed to be involved in would come across as a phone message or email. It was amazing from a technology perspective. John could be involved in the intricate runnings of a complex factory from half a world away.

Mariya caught up with them via cell phone later at night and informed John train travel would not be possible. The next opportunity to get to Kiev would be by air travel. She announced, "We will leave Kiev on Wednesday night for a 90-minute flight to Kharkov. With any luck, on Thursday, we will get to meet our girls!" That was good news.

Flying in Ukraine is an event embedded in an adventure. In the US, one assumes the safety, maintenance, skills and the entire system has been tested and found to be robust.   In Ukraine, John thought maybe two or three of those elements were not on the checklist. Ukraine carried numerous small airlines with creative names such as: Air Urga, Motor Sich Airlines, Odessa Airlines, ChallengeAero; and the twins favorite, Air Anastasia.

After repacking everything and reversing the process of moving in; the family was ready to travel to Kharkov. The flight was supposed to be 90 minutes but seemed to last much longer. John did not dare look up the safety record of Aerostar Airlines as they were flying in an airplane John was positive the FAA would not have let off the ground. The plane was a Russian-built plane and looked like a Ford tri-motor from the 1930s. John could not tell if this was an Antonov or Ilyushin or some other Soviet manufacturer.

The Stanton's had a reasonably good capacity for adventure, but this airplane did a fair job of taxing their sensibilities. They knew at the end of this flight they were one-step closer to meeting Vika and Anastasia. The outcome resulted in a safe arrival in Kharkov late on Wednesday night. The plane landed sometime after 11 PM; wheels, wings, and motor all attached, another safe Aerostar Airlines flight.

Arrival on terra firma was uneventful and all were thankful to be on the ground. Due to the late hour and general state of the Stanton's, they only passively noticed the Kharkov airport was much different than Kiev. Kiev was modern, well-lit and apportioned with chrome and glass. Kharkov appeared to be fifty years back in time. The chrome and glass were replaced with wood and tile. The building looked more like a scene from Casablanca than a functioning airport.

After collecting luggage, Mariya called on her phone and summoned Andre in his trusty VW van to ferry the weary travelers through the dark streets of Kharkov. Andre Valiskiov was a middle-aged man; dark hair with piercing blue eyes, a bushy mustache, and a broad smile.

Andre's long van wound and twisted through narrow streets, past a few large orthodox churches, over a river, through some other neighborhoods and finally pulled up beside an old apartment building. Mariya announced, "We are here! Chubarya Street #6. Home for the next few weeks!" Andre assisted in unloading the final belongings, still including the bags full of pajamas that now had been hand carried through three airports, up numerous flights of stairs and were just 20 kilometers from their intended recipients. Kristin and the boys followed Mariya and Andre up a wide but tread worn stone stairway. Hard to know if it was dumb luck or planned, but the apartment was on the fourth floor, this time without the benefit of the freight elevator.

As Mariya opened the door and turned on the light, the appearance of the apartment looked, as if it once was home to the Czar. This three-room apartment, complete with kitchen, living room, bedrooms, balcony and outfitted in garish, gaudy, regal decorum. It was quite a sight, but at the time, all were thankful for a place that cost the equivalent of 30 Euros/day and met basic needs very nicely. The only drawback – no Internet either wired or wireless, which was the lifeline back to family and friends. Finding reliable connections to the outside world would have to come soon, but later.

On Thursday morning, Mariya was able to ring the orphanage and arrange for the first visit. After a vigorous pep talk, she blurted out, "We may visit in the afternoon, today." John whispered to Kristin, "After nine months, six thousand miles and hundreds of hours of paperwork, we are literally hours away from meeting our two new girls. Nervous?" Kristin nodded.

Mariya returned to her phone again, presumably to arrange with the driver, Andre, from last night. She spoke to Andre differently than the driver in Kiev. In Kiev, she used a much stronger, more directive tone. With Andre, she spoke in a more conversational way. Mariya explained, "Andre is going to be our main transportation for the next few weeks. I have used him before and found him to be reasonable and dependable, I think you agree, No?" Of course, these were two attributes which most agreed with John, especially the reasonable part. Mariya said, "Sometime I teach you how to use the subway, but anywhere transport is not possible via subway, Andre will be your driver".

Mariya explained, "The orphanage is located outside of Kharkov – perhaps 20 kilometers." This was a surprise because John thought they would have some freedom to visit anytime; however, this appeared not the case. Mariya explained, "There is a bus line, but it hot, dirty and they run sometimes on time and sometimes not so much. I worry about your safety." John was up for an adventure, but for the sake of safety and avoiding a multistep process of bus travel, he could live with the cost of private transportation, especially if the bus was anything like flying. For the trips to the orphanage, John agreed to pay the 75 hryvnias /day for the driver.

After a quick morning of getting organized and trying to stay busy, the family was finally ready to make the first trip to Zelani Guy orphanage on the outskirts of Kharkov to meet their two new daughters.

Kristin penned the experience in her blog that evening:

"It was an incredible day. It hard to even to put into words all the emotions that I have felt today. Our girls are beautiful. Victoria was very afraid at first, but after a short while, she relaxed. Anastasia was much more brave and interacted with us more quickly. Victoria is much like Annie - particular, determined and a little mother hen. Anastasia is more relaxed and laid back. She was also very tired and almost fell asleep on the bed. We have learned that Victoria and Anastasia are their given birth names. We will likely use these as their middle

names. In the orphanage - they are called Vika and Nastya"

Vika expressed some fear and anxiety around us; Anastasia, not so much. It was hard to understand and process what these little girls must be thinking. Here come some people they have never seen before, speak a funny language, and suddenly, are interested in them.

Despite spending a few hours with them, their cognitive abilities were not obvious in this setting; however, the lawyer for the orphanage said that both girls seemed very smart. Mariya also commented on their capabilities; especially Vika, complimenting her on her speech and language. Anastasia did not say much, but her eyes were expressive. Other than being very tired, she certainly was interested and aware of her environment.

First Photos of Viktoria, aka Vika

All in all, a good first visit. Mariya explained, "You must decide, we have to decide to accept our referral by the end of tomorrow and then the adoption could proceed to the next step." The family had a small conference and before leaving that day, the decision was made. John communicated to Mariya, "We want to proceed with the adoption of Anastasia and Viktoria; we want them to be part of our family."

After conferring with Mariya and the staff, it was decided the best time to visit the girls was in the morning when the weather was cooler and they were more alert. It was not as if their days were full, but they have their routines and all agreed it would be best to maintain as much continuity as possible. Their afternoon activities were not fully explained; but they must have included a mandatory rest time.

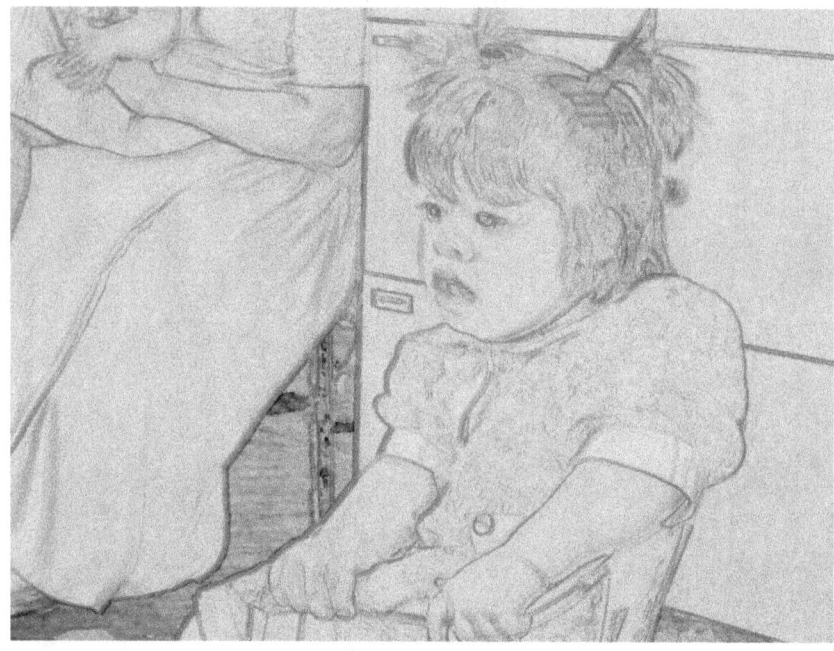

First Photo of Anastasia – aka Nastya

The people John and Kristin had discussed adoption with encouraged them to take it slow, especially at first. Don't expect a warm response. This was good advice, because little by little, each visit, the girls warmed up just a bit more. It started with very small steps. It was somewhat hard to fathom, but these beautiful children rarely felt the touch of another human being.

Their mission: establish some common interest and allow the girls to become comfortable gradually. Some days were better in terms of affection, coupled with times of apprehension, fear and uncertainty.

Some of the common activities filling the time together included: soap bubbles, playing with a beach ball and lots of drinking from water bottles. The girls loved to carry around the Russian/English phrase books, and in fact, cried when they had them taken away. John did not know if they had ever seen a book before. They were enamored with books. Holding them and flipping through the pages provided a high level of entertainment. John suspected it is possible books were not allowed, or available. There was a unique fascination on the part of both girls with books.

To keep things simple – the family shortened their given names to Vika and Nastya; which resembled what the orphanage worked called Viktoria and Anastasia.

Once there was some trust established between Kristin and Mariya, Kristin began to ask questions. Mariya explained, "Orphanage workers are paid some of the lowest wage jobs in the country. The workers are almost always women, except for the head doctor and the maintenance worker."

Kristin asked about care and Mariya continued, "They are not affectionate with the kids, in a few instances there might be a brief touch; but nothing that would be considered outright affection. From what I see so far, this is one of the better orphanages with good care." Mariya surmised it helped the surroundings were more rural as the workers valued their jobs, even with the low pay because there were few alternatives.

John concluded they were doing the best they could with provided resources, which was not much.

The site staff asked to meet with the Stanton's early on, probably to ascertain intent and figure out why anyone would want to adopt children with special needs. The medical director's office was cluttered, partially with papers and partly with mementos cluttering the horizontal surfaces. The office reeked of smoke, an ashtray overflowed with partially smoked cigarettes. Perhaps the Surgeon General's warning had not yet reached the outskirts of Kharkov.

After introductions and a few basic questions about the motivation for adoption, the medical director began to explain, "The children at the orphanage are collectively known as invalids. Their parents have abandon them, mostly because of their defects." All in all, it was a disturbing discussion. These children truly are some of the least of the least, in the eyes of this doctor and society. Both thought it odd no distinction was made between those with physical challenges or mental challenges. These children were known by their government, simply as invalids.

John and Kristin were prepared to hear this, but seeing it first hand was heartbreaking. The regressive mindset characterizes the sad irony of having a disability in Eastern Europe. First, one is abandoned. Second, labeled; and third, the label drives assumptions. These three factors create the reality these children are not important. They are isolated, given nothing, physical needs are barely met at the most basic level. They are left to the cruel hand of time. At the prescribed time, they move through the next phase in their paltry, planned life: the mental institution, or the street.

The whole system was set up to provide barely the minimal of physical care. Nothing is done to ensure the children are able to learn, live and love and grow to their full potential. These children happened to be born in the wrong place at the wrong time. It was John and Kristin's hope even their visit to Ukraine could begin to change hearts and minds. When they look at these children, they are not invalids. In fact, nothing could be further from the truth. These children are beautiful and deserve a chance to have a life, complete with a family to love them and care for them.

Being at the orphanage generated deep emotions. This was the place that John and Kristin had thought of hundreds of times, but could not fully envision in their minds.

Mariya remained at the site to take care of some additional business. She said she would catch a ride with one of the workers who goes back to the city. She could then hop on the subway and make her way back to the apartment.

Andre was waiting just inside the gate, with the vehicle pointed towards the lane, away from the orphanage. At first the drive was quiet. All were lost in their own thoughts of how awesome it was to finally meet Vika and Nastya after so many months of thinking, praying, wondering. Now they had a picture of what their new children and sisters looked like. It was relieving and tension filled, both at the same time.

John looked at the twins. They were somber, he wondered what they were thinking. They now clearly understood firsthand how not everyone grows up with the benefit of a family to love, food to eat and someone who will always take care of you.

Even though they did not know it at the time, the Stanton's quickly settled into what would be the routine for many weeks to come.

Chapter 41: Week 2 in Ukraine

The next step in the journey to bring Viktoria and Anastasia home was to formally accept the referral, which was done quickly and well ahead of the deadline. Even though this was done verbally, as with almost everything in Ukraine, there was a form and forms automatically required a visit to a government office, which required payment for services and on and on it went. Perhaps this is a vestige from the days of Communism; endless paperwork was involved for even the simplest transaction.

Mariya communicated the acceptance back to Kiev and immediately began working with the local officials to secure a court date. The first available date was one week away. It was a bit disappointing the date was still one week out, but Mariya spun it as a positive move. She told us, "Because if we could have our court date, there is mandatory ten day waiting period before we could leave the country." John quickly did that math. In the country one week, so another week for court, ten days for waiting and then a day or two to wrap up immigration issues should put a return in about 24 or 25 days. Not a record, but an efficient trip, John thought.

The daily routines continued with the goal to strengthen the girl's bonds of acceptance and trust. They quickly endeared themselves to their new family; or at least enjoyed strangers coming to play; the truth probably was somewhere in between. One consequence of the growing attachment was departing became harder and harder. One of the first Russian words Kristin learned was "zafstra," which meant tomorrow. It was a challenge to know if the girls had any concept and understanding of time, but it was the best explanation available. The Stantons thought zafstra or tomorrow would be a good word to leave with the girls. Whether they understood or not, it offered hope and did not mean goodbye.

After just a few days it became heart wrenching to leave them and go through the process of explaining tomorrow would come. Impossible to recall all the ways they tried to reassure them of their return. The girls' reaction was always the same. They would cry and cling to Kristin and John's legs when leaving. They were not sure the girls were in love with them as much as they certainly enjoyed the food, the playtime and the attention these strange people were providing for them. Either way, parting became a difficult emotional detachment each day. It was not hard to imagine they felt confusion, insecurity and perhaps even the beginning of a sense of loss.

Certainly, they experienced complex emotions for children whose life had been largely emotionless. In their institutional setting, they quickly learned emotions are meaningless because no one comes to comfort, sooth, or care for their needs. Even though they were only four and five; they were very much alone, and they knew it.

Eastern Europe offers a range of quality of care for orphans. The primary reason orphanages exist is social services are nonexistent and almost all families are unable to care adequately for children born with special needs. The stories the Stanton's heard and the evidence presented before them daily confirmed that to be true.

If a baby is born with a birth defect, the parents are encouraged to simply leave the child at the hospital. Doctors tell them they have given birth to an invalid and they should leave this child and return home and try have another baby. Common birth defects include Down syndrome, spina bifida, malformation of limbs, AIDs and fetal alcohol/drug dependent babies. Largely from a lack of cultural acceptance and support, children with disabilities and medical conditions are almost always left to the care of the state.

There is no safety net for parents to care for their children within a home. The culture largely doesn't accept it, and there is no help available in the form of education or services. Unfortunately, much of the additional burden is financial. Wages are low and it is common for several generations to live together in one home in a very limited space. Caring for a child with special health and developmental needs is very difficult with strained resources and no external support.

During the time John and family were at Zelani Guy orphanage, they observed the orphanage car come in several times with a nurse carrying a newborn baby. A very somber signal there was a new resident at the baby house.

The newborns are initially transferred to a baby house where they are placed in a crib along with other children. Generally, once they are mobile, they will transition to a grupa. A grupa is a small unit of eight children; they eat, sleep and are cared for as a unit. The ages of children in a grupa are perhaps between two and three through age six. Depending on the facilities at the orphanage, some children will transition directly from the baby house to the grupa and other times they are transferred to another orphanage.

The orphanage housing Vika and Nastya outside of Kharkov is an institution; it is the only world they have ever known. As babies they were never held, rocked or comforted. The girls and the other children learn self-soothing behaviors of rocking motions, sucking their thumbs or tongues or whatever else to provide a perceived level of comfort. All are treated as invalids and assumed to have no capabilities to grow learn and develop.

There is no stimulation and no touch; not having love, care and attention is a heinous form of passive abuse. For children, so much development occurs when babies and toddlers exploring their worlds. These lives are deprived of both the exploration and knowing and learning boundaries, safety and appropriate affection. These learnings, when they come at a later age, also come with many challenges around the areas of trust and behavior.

Disease or viruses can run through an orphanage and severely impact children. Based on the diagnosis, there is no treatment other than isolation. Pneumonia is common as are other dysentery-related diseases.

When a resident of the baby house reached an age between five and six, they transfer to a mental institution that include residents up to age 18. These institutions of horror have been featured on the news and in documentaries. The fact these places still exist in the twenty-first century is a crime against humanity.

Beyond the institution, at ages 16-18, they are released to the street, unprepared, vulnerable, scared and unable to care for their own needs.

It is common knowledge many of the children who are sent to the mental institutions simply die. It is impossible to know for certain, but between the physical and mental challenges these individuals have and lacking a will to live, many simply give up hope. Dying is easier than living.

The problem? Too few voices for those who cannot speak. This reality ripped at John's heart every time he walked through the doors of this orphanage. Why do children have to live in houses of death, which are cold and inhumane in every respect?

There is little stimulation to help the children pass the time. No education and positive influences exist to challenge the young minds. The boys often remarked during the time they were with Vika and Nastya, they did not see the other children even playing with toys. They had some toys, but the Stantons surmised the children probably did not know how to play, because no one had ever taken the time to show them.

During the summer months, the children would travel out to the orchard and sit on chairs. The more energetic ones were tied to their chairs while the quieter ones would just sit, staring blankly.

In perhaps the most depressing fact Kristin learned during the entire trip, one of the doctors who spoke broken English indicated that the children were medicated, mostly to control behavior. By asking some questions and conducting additional research, Kristin learned the children were given sedatives as a calming influence. It is impossible to know exactly if their true self even existed. As the doctor explained, "The sedatives are used to get them to sleep and keep them from being too crazy."

Mealtime reinforced the daily monotony. They were served soup, bread and a thick dark drink that may have been a vitamin/medicine mix. It was never fully clear what the thick beverage contained. The orphanage staff planted a large garden within the walls of the complex with beets, carrots, cabbage and other basic root crops. The soup was made in the kitchen at the far end of the complex and hand carried to the different dormitory/barracks.

The boys always were amazed when they observed mealtime. The children managed to eat piping hot soup at record pace. The workers were strict about mealtime; no monkey business and there must have been a limited time, because even after the girls came home, they would shovel food in their mouth like they were racing against the clock.

Kristin commented wistfully, "when our girls get home, I want to have a big round table, where we can look at each other, spend time eating and enjoying each other's company."

One day, during the drive back to Kharkov, Eric asked, "Why can't every child simply have a home and parents to love them, meet their needs and care for them? Is that too much to ask?"

John answered, "Eric and David, it is even worse than you can image. Over the past 40 years the United States competed with the USSR to be the ultimate global superpower. By spending money on bombs, missiles and military might rather than working to end suffering and promoting a home for all children. Even recently, politicians in Russia have used their political might to reduce the number of international adoptions driving a further chasm into the goal of every child having a home."

Vika

John finished with, "We can't do something to help everyone, but I am so glad that you guys have a heart for other children and were willing to open up our family to adding more sisters. Just think, your cookie sale helped us get here."

Eric and David smiled, but it was short lived, they obviously had a lot to work through in their minds.

Truth sobers the soul.

Chapter 42: Weeks 3 and 4 in Ukraine

Mariya had been on the phone a very long time when she announced, "There has been a change. We will not be able to have court this week; the judge has to conduct a large criminal mafia trial." Both John and Kristin appeared dumbfounded and bristled at the delay. They were in the outpost of Kharkov on the northeastern edge Ukraine, and the judge takes on the trial of the decade to try to rid Ukraine of corruption.

The delay was trying as every delay is one more day of separation from family and home back in the US. It caused immediate confusion, disappointment and questioning whether they were in over their heads.

The other element starting to creep into John's thinking was the fact in August, like most of Europe, things would likely 'shut down.' It is common in many European countries to have extended breaks during the month of August, when most of the population is on holiday. John knew, if the adoption isn't done by the 15th of August, while still two weeks away, decisions would have to be made.

John was already thinking about options to cut down on time, but each was expensive. John didn't mention it to Kristin, but he had already received a rather serious email from Doug asking about a return date. He began to think about what scenarios would cause him to head home and then come back to court and finish the adoption. Then there was the ten-day waiting period.

At John's request, Mariya still checked the court docket daily without success. There was no ability to petition or to influence any judges' schedules. John and Kristin gathered the "be patient and wait" message as they learned only a few judges are available to hear the adoption petitions.

Mariya had already explained to them the judge's lowest priority in their caseload were issues such as adoption. They just didn't have the excitement and challenge as a criminal trial. The docket would have to be nearly empty before most judges would take on such a trivial and simple matter as an adoption.

The wait felt arduous along with complete sense of helplessness. There appeared to be nothing they could do to influence the timing or direction of the events at the courthouse.

One of the items not yet taken care of was the delivery of nearly 100 pairs of pajamas for children ages three to eight. Kristin and her friends made it their mission to buy as many pairs of new pajamas as they could find to leave behind for the orphans.

Kristin asked Mariya how best to handle this gift. Mariya suggested she make an appointment with the orphanage medical doctor who functions as the operational director as well. Mariya did this for Kristin, and thankfully helped her understand that beyond the gifts, the orphanage expected a financial donation. This had not been mentioned, but at this point in the process, it did not surprise either of them.

Mariya scheduled the meeting for 1:30 on Thursday afternoon. On this day, Vlad took the responsibility of the prearranged driver, Andre must have been busy. Vlad's approach to driving proved interesting. When needed, he crossed lanes and wove through the oncoming traffic. Anytime Vlad maneuvered a close call, he crossed himself, as if to thank God he survived. When Vlad drove, all four Stanton's silently prayed for a safe arrival.

After lugging two suitcases packed with pajamas over 5,000 miles, they were very soon to arrive at their final destination to be presented to their intended recipients. The day held a bit of irony as the delivery day's temperature nearly reached 100 degrees F. The children were mostly running around in underwear or shorts and very few wore shirts. However, in six months, the warm fleece will feel good against the chill of winter.

The visit with the chief doctor was cordial. It was their second time in the smoke-stained office and John knew enough to ask basic questions about number of children and complimented the director on their care, even though there wasn't much to compliment about the facility. They also handed the director a donation in the amount of 1,500 hryvnias to the orphanage.

They hoped and prayed the money would go towards food, supplies and things directly benefitted the children, but there certainly was no guarantee. The medical doctor was genuinely grateful for the pajamas and said in very broken English, "Winter very cold and clothes help keep children warm." Both John and Kristin smiled and thanked the doctor as they left to go back into the dry, hot August sun.

As John and Kristin headed out the door, the director followed them and again sincerely thanked them for the monetary gift and the clothing. He then made the comment, "In the greater society these children were not seen as valuable and rather a burden and their lives are not worth half a hryvnia."

Much had transpired in the past few days; and there was a need to update those back home on status. There were several positives, the pajamas were delivered, everyone was healthy, Vika and Nastya continued to enjoy the time with their new family.

On the negative side, the prospective court date loomed large.

One item remained elusive was a reliable Internet connection. Their apartment did not have service and despite searching all around the neighborhood, there was little to be found. The local McDonalds, about four blocks from the apartment provided somewhat spotty service. The twins surmised the spotty service may be due to the number of people hanging around outside – probably drawing on the minimal available bandwidth to watch videos or play games.

Farther away, John found several Internet cafes. These were small, crowded, dank and often the seats occupied exclusively by hard-core gamers. They sat shoulder to shoulder and the noise of simultaneous games created a difficult environment to work or concentrate. At any given time, these were full and the lights and sound of a rousing game of Doom or Slayer from the adjacent carrel were not highly conducive to thinking.

The cafes did not allow one to use their own machine, so the setup was more for gaming or general web surfing. To log on, one had to recall the similarity of English keyboards and assume the ENTER, SHIFT and CTRL keys were all in the same location. None of the Stanton's ever really did figure out the Russian keyboards. Many of the keys were the same but not all, creating a slow and frustrating typing experience.

The Aurora Hotel provided the most reliable Internet service. The hotel was modern, European-style and included a small restaurant and bar off the lobby. The hotel was in a nice neighborhood three blocks off the main street of Pushkins'ka. It was one half mile away from the apartment and offered good service and a relaxed atmosphere. Techno-electro-dance music pummeled from MTV, but the noise could be toned down with earplugs.

John found if he ordered a Diet Coke and the nut sampler, he could work, eat and be left alone for over two hours. Aurora became his new 'work address.' Other than the frequency of Katy Perry solo "I Kissed a Girl" every thirty minutes, nothing distracted John; it was a good environment and suitable for email and checking in on the plant. Due to the time difference between the US and Ukraine, John would often walk to the Aurora after dinnertime and an evening walk and work until late in the night.

Summer evenings in Ukraine are lovely; the hot temperatures recede and the residents move outside to the parks and promenades. Street performers and artists demonstrate their talents. Kharkov contained many unique landmarks, parks and areas with their own reminders of life under Soviet rule. The Stanton's made it their mission to find and explore as much of Kharkov as possible.

A common after supper activity included a family walk to the nearby park or a trip up to Svobody Square, the second largest open square in Europe. Often concerts, magicians, book fairs and other interesting life occupied the square. This summer, the city trucked in sand and artists created complex and beautiful sand sculptures enjoyed by the residents of Kharkov. Another exhibit travelled through and showed the aftermath of WWII and the German occupation of Kharkov.

Early in August a traveling exhibit displayed an overview of Ukraine's history, a proud, but sad story. During Stalin's reign of terror, there were numerous campaigns to create hardships for the average Ukrainian and silence intellectuals, artists and others promoting freedom of expression. The country has seen more than its fair share of turmoil, bloodshed and death. The exhibit was a reminder to all of the evil man can inflict on fellow man and provided good discussions with Eric and David on the horrors of war.

While an evening walk may cover new ground, the trip home followed a common path. The route traveled down Teatal'nyi Lane to an old gutted out building resembling a school, turn left and walk Chubarya Street # 6. If water needed to be purchased; the closest shop, and the most expensive: Moscow Deli was at the end of Teatal'nyi Lane. By this time the twins were usually tired, so John was left to build bicep strength by carrying the litres of drinking water the rest of the way home.

The family enjoyed the buildings, the shops and the freedom to meander about the streets. Mariya reminded John often about safety, but precautions were taken and none of them ever felt threatened or targeted.

Nastya

Reminders of bureaucracy and inefficiency were easy to identify. Early on, the boys and John realized the need of a frying pan to supplement the cooking utensils in the apartment. In the first two weeks, Mariya accompanied them and provided direction in customary buying practices, but as they became more familiar with the neighborhood and emboldened in their navigation, the boys and John decided to shop on their own. Their ability to recognize certain types of shops improved over time; and confidence increased daily.

When in need of a pan, the boys and John headed over to a store at the end of Teatal'nyi Lane, by their favorite pizza restaurant.

The boy's recollection of shopping included the following steps.

First step, shop around and find what you are looking to purchase. Stand by it and flag worker to help. With no Russian-speaking capabilities, this means using the 'point and nod' method of communication. The clerk then goes to another area of the store, finds the merchandise, and presents the merchandise back to the buyer for approval. Buyer then inspects and decides the merchandise is acceptable. Once done, the store merchandise goes one way and the buyer goes another way to pay for the agreed upon merchandise at another location in the store. While away, another clerk takes the goods and wraps them very carefully. Finally, buyer presents the receipt at the door, just before leaving and the goods appears. Buyer leaves with purchase.

Certainly not the most efficient way of doing business, but one of the quirks of Ukraine and enjoyable to experience. When they returned home, the packages were gift wrapped, either for giving or to open as a present to yourself. In this case, the 'present' was put to its planned use, making grilled cheese sandwiches.

During the family's tenure in Ukraine, daily shopping was a way of life, much like the locals. A local drug store conveniently located near the apartment made it easy and cheap to get the necessities. A bakery kiosk baked wonderful fresh bread daily and for literally a few hryvnias, a bountiful assortment of all types of bread was available.

The groceries for the family mostly came from Billa, known for the yellow and orange bags. Billa was always a fun experience. They seemed to have a disproportionate number of aisles set aside for crackers, cookies and goodies. The boys would linger in the crackers, cookies and goodies aisle and look for treats they had not yet tried. All were very tasty.

Billa stocked all the staples and a huge selection of stiff Russian drinks, mostly vodka. During the time there, they did not see much evidence of drunkenness, but there was certainly an abundance of cheap liquor.

Billa also sold vernake in the freezer section, a local dumpling filled with everything from meat to cheese, to veggies to fruit and jelly. It is the all-purpose Ukrainian food and both tasty and filling.

On the not so bright side, Billa gained a reputation in John's mind for some of the surliest cashiers in the city. They would get visibly tense if one fumbled to find correct change, which they demanded, but only if one could access all the coins and bills without holding up the line. John was one westerner who never really did figure out the fine art of finding exact change under the thick, watchful eyebrows of the Billa cashiering staff.

Another favorite hunt involved finding second hand stores. Kristin discovered several nearby mostly due to necessity. Most of them were in a basement level of a building, so being below street level and crowded; they felt like a cave. John acquired a sweatshirt at one in a nearby neighborhood during the first week of being in Kharkov. Despite the summer heat, mornings were cool enough to need an extra layer.

And finally, on days when the Stanton's felt adventuresome, there was the open-air market. Everything was available at the market, mostly in its rawest form. Boar heads, freshly killed chickens, organs from cows were proudly displayed and available for purchase.

John enjoyed getting out in the early morning for a walk. It was quiet and relaxing to see the street sweepers with their straw brooms cleaning the debris from the previous night's activities. Downtown Kharkov was clean, at least in the morning, which made for nice early morning walk and pleasant surroundings. The parks were well kept and provided a beautiful respite from the rest of the city.

Convinced she could do no more in Kharkov to influence the court dates, Mariya left the family for a few days to go back to Kiev and work out some additional details. Although it was not said, it did not seem like things were going well. Delays continued, and now without a target date for court; the family was in flux. In calls with Mariya, every day, a different variation of the story emerged to the point it was tough to know what to believe.

The morning routine continued as a constant, with no firm date for court. All enjoyed spending time at the orphanage visiting the girls. Vika and Nastya enjoyed this immensely and the activities aided in the bonding process. The visits never ended well and frankly that was the most difficult part; breaking two little girls' hearts whenever it was time to leave. It was now obvious a true bond of affection was developing by these routine visits.

The afternoon routine generally involved some type of sightseeing. The locals seemed to indicate this period to be an especially hot and dry summer for this region of Ukraine. The apartment was not air conditioned, but often finding a subway, mall, library, shopping center or museum afforded the chance to get at least a temporary break from the heat. During this year, temperatures commonly rose to 100 degrees plus with a few days topping 105.

In the evenings, the boys watched the Beijing Olympics but the feeds were Russian, so the twins were a bit disappointed they missed the cool stuff like diving, and instead, caught weight lifting and dressage, which they certainly deemed less interesting parts of the competition.

Mariya returned after five days in Kiev. During the time she was gone, fighting broke out in Georgia and she was very concerned about the regional aggression. Her family region is Sevastopol, the same area where the Green's went to adopt Sergei. Sevastopol is strategically very important to Russia as they share a naval base. Mariya reasoned if Russia could jump in and intervene in a sovereign state's affairs as they did in Georgia and South Ossetia, why not in Sevastopol?

Mariya looked worried. She was clearly bothered and preoccupied by the Soviet aggression. She did not speak much about life under Soviet rule, but one could only surmise the Ukrainian people were enjoying their current freedoms much more than living in the Soviet regime.

Mariya continued her daily phone calls and trips to the courthouse. Often, she would stop on the way back from the orphanage and speak with the court schedule administrator. She left the Stanton's to wait outside; often Andre would accompany her inside the courthouse. It was difficult not to wonder what went on inside the building and in these private discussions. Mariya would disappear for 20 minutes, and then emerge. The boys would try to read her demeanor before she announced the outcome.

The courthouse building was uniquely non-Russian. The entire building was dedicated to legal activities. The courtroom was on the second floor of a very old building halfway between Kharkov and the orphanage. The building's placement seemed odd. It sat a good ten kilometers outside of the city limits, not near anything except a stagnant pond across the road. It was difficult to tell it was a courthouse from the outside. It could have been an office, small factory or even a storage building.

Days slipped by and it was hard to not get discouraged, as there were many days without success. She was persistent, however, and somehow John knew the persistence would pay off and that thought kept hope alive. There was no plan b.

During one longer visit and wait outside this nondescript building, the boys watched a local try to carry (and subsequently drop) a goat on the trail to the stagnant pond, also affectionately called the swimmin' hole. An interesting cast of characters will from time to time swim in the stagnant and murky waters.

After a visit to the orphanage, she asked Andre to stop for her to check on the docket. Mariya's persistence at the courthouse was finally rewarded on Friday, August 8th.

It was that day she announced in rapid-fire words, "We receive court date for Monday, 11 of August." This was the moment they had been waiting for almost three weeks. An opportunity to stand before a judge and indicate their desire to adopt two girls and provide them with a family forever.

There was much joy and happiness in the van on the short ride back to Kharkov. The twins had smiles, Mariya had a smile and John and Kristin were relieved this roadblock had finally been removed.

Kristin's blog that night read shared the joy they all felt:

> *"As of early morning, things looked very bleak...the best information we were getting was a situation where we might not get a court date until late August or early September!" Mariya went on to describe later in the morning at the courthouse, a series of events "fell" into place. Mariya was able to work out the situation for us to have our court date this Monday! There is still a 10 day wait after that before we can pick up the girls. And of course, after that there will be time needed to get the girls new birth certificates, passports, visas, health exams etc... but Mariya says, we have date!*

Chapter 43: Week 5 in Ukraine

On Saturday morning, John took his early walk and stopped with his morning coffee to people watch. A large ominous statue of Lenin towered over him and Svobody square as well. John pulled out his trusty Blackberry and scanned the first email from the plant's automated data reporting. The Daily Monitor, contained the major production lines and feeder lines with last day output, week to date and month to date.

John concluded Twin Ports seemed to be holding its own over the past month. He scanned down and reviewed two other notes, both a bit cryptic. One was from Diane and another from Jeff. Both conveyed the same information. Jeff wrote to tell John that Doug had been up at the plant for an unannounced visit yesterday. John was reading this on Saturday morning, so that meant Doug had been at the plant yesterday. He just showed up, Jeff said. That wasn't too unusual as Doug owned a lake place farther up the road in northwestern MN; maybe he decided to swing by on his way up the lake. John emailed back asking Jeff for details. Given that it was morning in Ukraine – he knew the note would reach Twin Ports at late on Friday night. John would not hear anything until later.

On the walk back to the apartment for Saturday morning breakfast, John reflected. The adoption proved a true test of patience. When one roadblock was removed, it usually meant the next barrier was not yet visible, but lurking nearby. Not unlike Shackelton's journey – it was one step forward and two steps back.

Other than schedule delays, they were pleased with Mariya's work serving as their: translator, facilitator, guide and legal advisor. She treated them very well, and her skills at navigating the convoluted system were apparent and appreciated. John and Kristin agreed this whole event was a venture of trust and faith. They learned they must trust her, as she is the only one who capable of figuring out the details and the next steps. She cared genuinely about the welfare of the family and the outcome of the adoption.

Mariya loosened up a little now with a court date established. To celebrate the victory, Mariya helped the family find a traditional Ukrainian restaurant and navigate the menu. There was much conversation at their table on Saturday night about the upcoming court date, what would happen and how to answer the questions the judge was likely to ask in the most straightforward way.

Sunday was typically not a day to visit the orphanage. Andre was not available to drive on Sundays' and by now, driving with Vlad was only done in the case of emergencies. A Sunday visit did not constitute an emergency, at least not yet.

Monday morning finally arrived, another hot and dry day in Kharkov; all dressed in their best clothes and were at the courthouse thirty minutes before the scheduled trial time. Being a litigant in a Ukrainian court is a once in a lifetime experience. Especially true, if one can imagine (and if it really happened) the trial of the decade just wrapped up in that very courtroom.

The courtroom where the adoption hearing was scheduled was on the second floor. A long hallway, not unlike an old university lecture hall ended with the door to the chambers. Once inside, the room was sparse, consisting of a judge's bench with three chairs. The judge sat in the middle and the two jurors on either side on risers a foot or so below the judge. John leaned over to Kristin and said, "Just think, the people occupying these seats are charged with granting our request to become parents of Vika and Nastya.

The courtroom was a medium sized room, measuring approximately 20' x 30'. The most interesting feature was a stand-alone jail cell in the room. The structure consisted of a metal cage in the corner with dimensions about 6' x 10'. Chairs and a bench able to hold five or six people sat inside the cell. John could only guess the variety of characters who occupied the cell for their day in court.

The twins wondered aloud how and where they separated people if they didn't get along? Did the bad guys ever try to settle the score inside the cage while the judge and jury watched? Mariya cleared up the mystery by explained this courtroom had been the scene of many cases. Unruly or dangerous prisoners are placed in the cell during their trial if the judge feared, to quote Mariya, "things get how to you say, out of control and crazy."

A table and podium occupied the middle of the room. During Mariya's pre-hearing instructions, she coached John to stand and move to the podium when the judge began to ask questions.

Having two eleven-year-olds in Ukraine was largely a good idea; however, curiosity got the best of the twins. They had to look inside the jail to get their photo snapped behind bars. Mariya told them to be careful because only the police possessed keys to the lock. Although it would have been funny to lock Eric and David in the cell, John imagined the judge would be less than amused.

After a few minutes, and thankfully after the twins left the jail cell, the judge and jurors entered the courtroom. Other than the judge, jury, Mariya and the Stanton family, the only other participant was the lawyer from the orphanage. John never learned where the jury came from. It did not appear there was a formal jury selection process. John wondered if these three jurors were selected citizens or simply were found wandering around the courthouse or nearby roads with nothing better to do at that moment in time.

The adoption process at the courthouse took several hours. More paperwork and forms and more trips up and down the stairs aligning details occurred. After a few hours, Eric had to use the restroom. John asked Mariya, "Where are the facilities?" Mariya pointed outside behind the building. In the back of the building in a shack was the bathroom, as in outhouse, which consisted of a lean-to with holes in the floor. No more, no less. An outdoor toilet for use by all. Judges, lawyers, defendants, men and women, it didn't matter. All used the common outdoor toilet.

Kristin recalled the details of the day in her blog:

> *"It's been an incredible day! Amazing things happened for us today! We left for court at 8 am this morning. Our facilitator had told us that court is different in every region. Sometimes it is very informal and lasts as little as 15 min. or sometimes it is very formal and very official. Apparently in our region, court is about as formal as it gets! She spent quite a bit of time prepping us the night before so we knew exactly what to say. The entire session lasted an hour and a half! They repeated all the official information in great detail numerous times.*
> *Both John and I were asked several questions. Most we were prepared for. Aside from all the official legal questions (which of course they asked John), they asked 3 main personal questions; (I fielded the first two questions. John got to field the last one.)*
> *1)Why would we want to adopt 2 children with Down Syndrome? (maybe they think we are crazy?) Answer - because we desire to have sisters for Caroline to grow up with, which are like her. (although our*

ultimate reason is because the Lord set this in our hearts and we want to
be obedient to Him, the answer we gave above is the one they can
understand)

2) How on earth will I be able to mother 7 children, 3 with special
needs? (of course John added the "on earth" part, but I am sure they
were thinking that) Answer - very supportive husband, older children
who help with the younger children, very supportive and helpful
grandparents, aunts and uncles (this in particular is a huge point to
make with Ukrainians, they are very pro extended family), very
supportive friends in our community, excellent source of healthcare
professionals, therapists and educators, a huge network of fellow adopting
parents of children with special needs(Yeah, Reece's Rainbow!) and of
course the Lord!

3) How will we communicate with them, not knowing any Russian? (of
course John could've pulled out the tattered, but trusty Russian Phrase
book, but I don't think that would have impressed them.) Answer - sign
language of course!   - the universal language.

Kristin mentioned it, but the Ukrainian court system definitely
receives an award for repetition. Every time a name was mentioned,
the birthday needed to be stated, too. The judge was very methodical
about reading every detail.   John repeated the request to be the
adoptive parents of Vika and Nastya to the court twice and it was
repeated back three times!

The court appearance lasted one hour and thirty minutes.   The time
went by slowly, as it was difficult to see if the outcome was favorable
or not.   – The judge repeated several times the actions the court was
taking deemed to be in the best interests of these children. Kristin

and John thought this was a good thing. Vika and Nastya remained back at the orphanage with no clue that people who now had grown to love them were working very hard to make their lives infinitely better.

By the time the proceedings finished, the judge not only granted the rights of adoption to John and Kristin, but proclaimed the change of their official names from Viktoria Shatova and Anastasia Rebakoyen to their new names:

> Katherine Victoria Stanton
> and
> Emelia Anastasia Stanton

Again, in Kristin's words.

> *"In the end though, it was obvious the prayers of our family and friends had gone before us into this very courtroom! Despite our earlier nervousness, we both felt relaxed and at peace about all we needed to say. And when the final court decree was read to us while we stood (which by the way took at least 20 minutes, repeating everything that had already been repeated at least twice), they were very happy to grant us our request of adopting our 2 little sweet girls!!!! And...they amazingly issued us an "urgent court decree"! This is very, very rare and we consider it a miracle on behalf of our girls and us! There is still a 10-day appeal period but we don't have to "wait" the usual 10 days before starting all the rest of the paperwork. This was huge because normally the 10-day waiting period is a period of no work; in our case, because of the urgent court decree, we could begin with paperwork, visit the embassy, have appropriate doctor visits, secure Ukrainian passports*

and all the other items that take time. There is a shot we could be traveling home on the 11th day."

It was obvious from the court decree that Mariya assisted in a significant way to grant the "urgent" portion of the court decree. Mariya did not describe in detail her words; however, she must have created an emergency requiring the girls be granted freedom from the orphanage and an expedited trip back to their new home in the United States.

With the court decree finalized and issued as urgent, the dollars doled out to Mariya were worth every penny. Without her, none of this could have happened! She moved bureaucratic mountains. So many other details remained, but having court done, the ten-day waiting period waved and the ability to focus on the next boulder ahead made them feel like finally there is momentum and forward progress.

Mariya needed to track down the information for Nastya's passport. She planned a day or two before needing this information, but it was critical for her to have it before they could move forward. John told Mariya, "We need to know to know by the middle of this week if I need to change the return tickets." Mariya responded with the standard and now familiar, "Da."

After the morning in court, Andre drove everyone to the orphanage for a short visit with the girls. It had been a long and stressful morning already. They were thankful to see their girls, now officially a part of the Stanton family. They prayed the next steps would be more straightforward than the virtual wringer they just survived.

The girls were oblivious to all the legal work which had just been completed. They were happy to see these strangers again, and play with them, eat snacks and enjoy the undivided attention. John and Kristin began their orientation as parents by providing the girls with an introduction and transition to their new names.

Viktoria became Katie-Vika and Anastasia would be known as Emie Nastya. This should help with the transition – as at least they will hear a familiar name in conjunction with their new name.

Being optimists, both Kristin and John hoped the hard work over. After all, it seemed straightforward to finish the remaining activities. The two primary tasks were to secure Ukrainian passports and finish paperwork for the return to the states. The final activities would occur at the US Embassy in Kiev. Working with Americans again would be a welcomed change from the bureaucratic labyrinth Mariya led them through the past 35 days.

John continued his nightly routine at the Aurora, arriving about 8:00 PM and leaving sometime between 10:30 and 11:00 PM. Fortunately, John fulfilled his end of the vacation arrangement by working four hours per day and using four hours of vacation for the balance. The extra time was needed to accomplish all the work required to successfully adopt two children from Ukraine.

On this Monday night with the relative high of the court appearance and forward progress, it was time to hop on the proverbial emotional roller coaster again. John's upbeat mood quickly tempered with a note from Doug. Doug finally received a legal opinion from the Northern Pines Technology lawyers on the agreement between the

City of Twin Ports and Harris Thronson, Chief Legal Counsel of MN Consolidated.

It was the opinion of the legal team at Northern Pines Technology this was a valid legal document, and in court, would be enforceable. The footnote was that even if it was not, the court of public opinion would not favor Northern Pines Technology. The perception of a big business trying to screw small town USA by negotiating out of an agreement was not palatable. The executives believed both the shareholders and image of the company could be irreparably harmed.

Doug's note read on to say based on this opinion, he was unsure what the next step relative to Mendal Enterprise was going to be. Any type of payment would completely negate the net present value of the calculated financial benefit. There were high-level meetings going on at headquarters to figure out a plan. John could tell from the tone and tenor of the note, Doug was angry. It was tough to read whether he was angry with John or at the fact that he had to deal with bringing this unpleasant news forward.

John reasoned, it was better to find out now than have this come up in the news or through some due diligence by the city of Twin Ports. John surmised maybe others knew about this. If this surfaced in the newspaper or through other media, it would create an impossibly complex public relations fiasco.

John read the rest of his emails. He scheduled a teleconference with the staff the next night, so he quickly created an agenda and fired the agenda off into cyberspace. He looked at the clock next to the television blaring MTV. It was past midnight as he packed up his briefcase and headed off in the late August night towards #6 Chubarya Street.

As John walked down the tree-lined streets, he reflected on the events of the past few weeks. So many delays, road blocks, ups and downs but, they must be close.

Little did he know the next routine detail was going to cause more anxious moments and lost sleep.

Chapter 44: Week 6 in Ukraine

Doug supported this trip, but John could tell from the tone of recent emails and a few discussions on the phone his patience was wearing thin. Frankly, John's was too. The uncertainty created stress, much like a spring in tension and waiting to release.

John would much rather have certainty, knowing when this adventure was going to end and when he was going to return to his life as site manager of Northern Pines Twin Ports plant. His leave was unprecedented and he did not want to give the impression he was not eager to return to his role.

At this point, even the worst-case scenario plan had him home a week ago. The frustration on Doug's part was understandable. Not only had the court date delayed multiple times, but Mariya now hinted of a new problem, with yet another minefield needing traversing: Ukrainian passports.

The issuance of a Ukrainian passport followed the same convoluted pattern as obtaining the court date. It began as a simple task, but during two days of missed promises, the issuance of the identification and travel document became another slippery slope with facts changing hourly. Both John and Kristin were a bit dumbfounded, because passports are issued every day, weren't they?

The girls', for some reason, took a strange turn.

The most disturbing piece of information Mariya communicated happened midweek during their sixth week in country. On Wednesday evening, Mariya informed John, "John, you sit down. I have very tough news. I spoke with my contact at immigration office and he told me the entire passport system is going down for technology upgrade." That was the bad news. The good news is, "Do not worry, because the new computer system would be up again the following Monday."

John sat in stunned silence. His muscles tensed, his body numb. John admitted he was no software installation expert, but he knew enough about computer hardware and software upgrades to deduce this type of upgrade would not happen in a few days. This, coupled with the weekend in which the system was to be down was the equivalent of the United States Fourth of July, John imagined the parties, revelry, consumption of vodka and the lack of work done on the aforementioned computer system, would dampen any attempts of completion. How in the name of Stalin would this work be completed when the country was on a three-day bender?

John's emotion turned to fury, and unfortunately, Mariya received the uncoiling of the very tightly wound spring. "Why is this the first time anyone is telling us about this?" John roared at Mariya. "Do they have a backup plan?. Mariya, what are we going to do?" Once again, learning in Ukraine, all things seemingly logical or rational were not. The simple is difficult. The difficult is impossible.

At this point, John yelled, "Mariya, we have now been in the country for over 40 days. I am out of time off and need to return to the US. Another trip back to Ukraine would be $4,000 more dollars that we really didn't have budgeted, as well as time. Mariya, do you understand, we are desperate!" Mariya felt empathetic and helpless as she was only one person and moving a grinding bureaucracy took a small army.

The discussion ended as quickly as it flared; nothing else could be said. John knew she was doing everything in her capabilities to bring this to closure. He was angry, frustrated and simply wanted to be in control of a situation well outside of his ability to influence. John had enough, he hastily unbolted the three locks on the door and flew down the steps to outside. He just wanted to get away; anger and frustration flowed to the surface. He stared at the vacant shelled out building down the street he had lived on for the past six weeks and wanted to be anywhere but here.

Not knowing she had followed, he turned around and she was waiting. After extended silence, with both looking only at the cracks in the sidewalk she asked, "John how much money you have." John told her, "$2100 USD."

She said, "I don't like to do this, but John, I think we are going to have to. It is the last thing we can try. We need to see if officials will accept an expediting fee to move this along."

In short, a bribe. It had other terms, but it was a payment in exchange for specific actions on a specific timeline; outside of the operating norms, which most rationale people would call a bribe.

She pulled out her cellphone; dialed a number and conducted an animated conversation. Then, she mapped out instructions for John. John was to take a magazine with an envelope inside to an office building in Kharkov. A manager would meet met John there. Say nothing, ask no questions and this person would take John to the deputy director on the second floor. Mariya continued in hushed tones, "There, John, you will wait, and you then will be ushered into the office. At this time, John, take the magazine with the envelope containing cash inside it and place it on the desk."

John asked, "Then what?"

She simply said, "You leave."

Mariya arranged the exchange for the next day, over the noon hour. John slept restlessly, tossing and turning all night. He did not tell Kristin or the boys about the new plan. It was clear in his mind he was going to be bribing a public official. He was pretty sure that could get him into a heap of trouble, but after rationalizing this is probably how business is done in Ukraine, he had a semi-clear conscience about the plan.

Morning came without a trip to the orphanage. Routines were now suspended; the focus was on getting out of the country as quickly as possible. After a nervous, somewhat unproductive morning, John began to execute the plan Mariya outlined.

John followed the steps, to the letter. By now, he knew Kharkov well enough to take the subway to the nearest station adjacent to the government office building. He tucked the magazine under his arm and held it tight, not wanting the cash-laden envelope to fall out. John switched between arms, careful to keep the open side facing up. Before walking into the building, he discretely opened the magazine to confirm the cash stuffed white envelope was still there.

Just as Mariya promised, the handler met John and escorted him around the back way, bypassing the elevators to a set of very well-worn marble stairs. They navigated the hallways and turned the corner on the left side, straight to the deputy director office. John waited in the anteroom, eventually ushered into the director's office. As detailed by Mariya, John placed the magazine with the envelope of cash on the desk and waited briefly. The aid dismissed herself. The deputy director looked at John, looked at the magazine and gently slid the magazine to the side of the desk. The envelope dropped into the desk drawer, out of view.

The director continued to look at John, saying nothing and slid the magazine back across the long desk. A slight wave of the hand signaled John to exit. John muttered "spasibo" in his best Russian, walked to the leaded glass door, turned the heavy iron nob and exited.

John never felt so relieved to be done with something in his life. Oddly, his steps did not seem lighter as he walked back to the subway station. Either he had just wasted a large sum of money or he had to trust somehow this risky and strange plan might actually work. He chose the latter – so every step away from the office represented one more step towards freedom for himself and his family.

The 'drop' transpired on Thursday afternoon prior to the long holiday weekend. John felt depleted, as he knew nothing would happen until Monday. Even then, the news could be bad. John spent most of the weekend in mental gymnastics, relieved the 'drop' was a completed, but also weighing the probability of success. He was also contemplating the latest moment he could pull the trigger on the family to returning home. His deductions landed on Monday night. The timeline would barely leave room to purchase tickets to Kiev, fly to Kiev, and take care of any business at the embassy to return to the US. Flying took the better part of two days.

The residents of Kharkov embraced the holiday weekend much like the US celebrated the Fourth of July. Parades, fireworks, concerts, food and festivities filled the city. The fun and lively celebrations represented a relatively new event for the citizens of Ukraine. While the US celebrated its 232nd birthday; Ukrainian independence did not come until 1991. The fledgling democracy celebrated its 17th birthday in grand style. The revelry and openness made it equally festive and sweet. The proud citizens of Ukraine set aside 24 August as their day of freedom.

The boys especially enjoyed the pageantry of the independence celebration. The Ukrainians, who are good people suffered significantly under oppressive dictatorships. So many of the buildings and statues from the past remained present in their daily lives. The freedom celebration was a reminder of all that had changed.

As John walked around central Kharkov and watched the parades, the crazy notion of waiting for a simple passport struck him again. The timing of the incident made the debacle more incredulous. The idea that Ukrainian authorities scheduled to upgrade the passport system over the holiday and have it up and running again on the Monday boggled the logical mind.

John speculated maybe half the workers would not be at work on Monday, nursing themselves back to health after all the festivities.

He was concerned the other half may not even remember their place of employment.

The situation looked bleak.

Mariya busily chased around Kharkov on Monday morning. Two things needed her attention with no obvious pathway to success. First, the passports, second, a final attempt to contact the parents of the children being adopted to provide them a copy of the court decree. The ideal adoption situation is a final release of parental rights, however Mariya assured them there are other ways around this detail.

The ten-day waiting allows parents a final opportunity to reclaim their parental rights. John and Kristin discussed the oddity of this approach, as most of the children were left at the hospital at birth; years ago, with no attempt at contact. It was strange to think some change of heart would occur at the very last hour when suddenly, parents show up to begin care for their abandon child. However, they learned and reasoned not everything in Ukraine was logical.

The ten-day waiting period is only waived in situations where the health of the child is at risk, meaning the family will be taking them and leaving the country for immediate medical care. Sobering, but some adoptee's medical situation is that tenuous.

Without the signed parental release, Mariya needed to demonstrate good faith in finding the parents versus their actual signature Mariya remained quite consistent in her opinion once the passports arrived, it would be time to leave.

Through a series of events, the parental release was secured for Katie-Vika several weeks before. The Stanton's met Vika's parents and grandparents; and spent an afternoon in conversation at the orphanage. They were a unique family as they continued to maintain basic contact, periodic visits and show concern for their daughter. At birth, they made a very difficult choice, knowing they could not take care of a child with special needs. They loved their daughter and granddaughter dearly. They wanted Vika to know although they could not meet her needs, she was loved.

The visit with Vika's family took place at a time when Mariya was not able to assist John and Kristin with translation. Between the use of sign language and the phrase books, the families held an effective conversation. Kristin learned the grandmother and grandfather, mother and father and another set of parents all lived in a home that was perhaps 30 feet by 30 feet. They recognized their own inabilities to care for Vika and very concerned about her welfare. They wanted their precious daughter to have a better life and were supportive of Vika's adoption. They knew they would likely never see their daughter again, but also, they knew she would be loved, cared for, attend school, and have the best medical care available. They felt profoundly grateful. Kristin was especially grateful they could make this connection and promised to keep in touch.

Anastasia's parents left her at the hospital after she was born with no evidence of contact since March of 2004. Mariya needed to obtain an official birth certificate stored at the hospital in which she was born. The orphanage's connection to the hospital established the first link, but since Anastasia transferred to Zelani Guy orphanage, the director was not sure what paperwork was available.

Eventually, Mariya tracked down Anastasia's information. She was born to Viktor and Sofya Rebakoyn on 5 March 2004 in one of the neighborhood hospitals in Kharkov. From there, Mariya's search for Viktor and Sofya began.

Just before noon on Monday, Mariya called John and Kristin at the orphanage with the most astounding news. She received word through her contact at the immigration office the passports for Vika and Nastya were available for pickup. While both John and Kristin were elated with the news. However, they would not believe it until they could see the passports for themselves and hold the documents in their hands.

After a quick trip by Andre back to Chubarya Street #6, Mariya met John and the family outside the door on the grass covered boulevard. She had a big smile on her face. She handed John a manila envelope. He looked inside. By some miracle, there were two official aqua colored Ukrainian passports, one for each of the girls. John hugged Mariya as this was truly a miracle. How all of this happened, John will never know. He could not fathom a divine bribery, but somehow the events of the last 72 hours had shaken loose the hardest of politicians and triggered actions during a complete system shutdown during a holiday weekend.

All John could see was the evidence, but a million small pieces needed to come together to bring these documents into his hands. The arrival of the documents was nothing short of a miracle. Securing the passports led them one step closer to bringing the girls to their forever family and home.

The family's six-week separation from Caroline, Seth and Mark seemed like a lifetime. They were tired of Ukraine and ready to go home. Today, Mariya was full of good news.

She located a document at the birth hospital for Emie-Nastya. The document gave her the final piece of information needed to ensure the adoption would not be contested. Finally, everyone could see the Kharkov portion of the adventure coming to a close.

Mariya even hinted it was not out of the question she could finish arrangements in the morning in Kharkov and the whole family could get either an overnight train or afternoon flight from Kharkov to Kiev. Wednesday and Thursday's schedules filled with going to the Embassy for paperwork and to the medical clinic for a physical before the children released to travel to the US. A dizzying pace but the entire family could see the finish line and were prepared to do anything it would take to expedite the return trip home.

Mariya immediately left for Kiev to prepare for the next phase of this journey. She felt comfortable with the family to navigate their way back to the orphanage, finish the paperwork at the orphanage and get to the airport – all in the next 24 hours.

In fact, until every milestone achieved, every boulder removed, it seemed one more thing always loomed. John did not think he could relax and let down until the wheels of the KLM 747 would lift off Ukrainian soil to begin the journey home.

The plant and his normal life in Twin Ports seemed a very long time ago.

Chapter 45: Westward Bound - Heading Home

With passports in hand, John and Kristin could legally take the girls from the orphanage. Prior to that time, the government of Ukraine was the designated custodians and legal guardian. Final custody would be granted in Kiev with some additional paperwork and final documents from the SDA and the US Embassy.

What a change from a mere 24 hours ago! Yesterday, when they went to the orphanage, the status of the passports was uncertain, unknown and seemingly hopeless. Now just one day later, Kristin is a whirling dervish of activity with dresses and shoes in hand, presents purchased for the staff and all other details swirling around in her head being converted to immediate and swift action.

The day was bittersweet. It was a day too long in coming. Katie-Vika and Emie-Nastya were getting ready to leave the only home they had ever known with two new people who were officially their parents, but practically, little more than friendly strangers. It was indeed an odd mix of feelings.

The girls could immediately sense today was not business as usual. Normal morning routines included a walk around the orphanage grounds, snacks and playing. The girls had come to expect and enjoy their playtimes, freedom to explore the orphanage and other fun things these strangers allowed them to do. Often the twins would play on the swings or teeter-totter. Sometimes the girls would run between the boys with John and Kristin each taking a side. Other times, the routine included sitting on the bench eating a cracker, cookie or fruit snack.

Today, it was all rush. There was no time to play and a normally relaxed schedule was timed to the minute. In a matter of minutes, the girls were dressed, goodbyes said to the caregivers and doctors and staff, gifts given, last photos taken, and gear packed into the car.

They were leaving Zelani Guy orphanage forever!

The girls excitedly and willingly waved bye and said, "Paka, paka" to everyone, which was "bye bye" in Russian. Neither girl looked back or hesitated. Kristin whispered to John, "Do you know what an amazing and miraculous feeling it must be for them to leave this place?"

Their lives changed forever because four strangers who called themselves mama, papa, and brat (brother), showed up at their orphanage in the middle of Ukraine six weeks ago. Suddenly, these precious girls were saying goodbye to everyone and everything to travel to a strange land. John felt odd taking them. It must have felt even stranger for them to be seeing and sensing so many things as never before. Their new life as a loved and cherished member of a family was just beginning.

The night before, Kristin reminded John, "On this journey, it seems so many times we have been brought to the edge of the unknown and just been told to have faith and trust. We continued to be at the edge of the unknown, even up until the last minute." John also reminded her, "So many times during this adoption journey we have just been asked to wait until the mist clears and the next step is known. That feeling of walking without seeing is scary and often lonely; but it is a step towards belief and letting go of the things that hold us down."

This started as a journey of faith and will end as a journey of faith.

So many emotions packed into this day. As the orchard and the rough road disappeared under the tires of Vlad's Skoda, yet another series of paperwork waited. Mariya seemed to have a handle on the stops required along the route. Both John and Kristin knew the balance of the day was going to be stressful. With Vlad as the driver in his small car, space was tight.

The entourage of John, Kristin and two daughters (maybe having their first car ride since their original trip to the baby house or orphanage), the orphanage lawyer (who spoke about as much English as John spoke Russian), Vlad, and Natalia (another orphanage staffer who didn't speak any English), who Mariya hired to assist with paperwork. Five adults and two additional children stuffed into a car that was tight with five small adults. The overloaded sedan drove back into Kharkov to finish the legal paperwork at the courthouse and local Board of Custody.

Because both John and Kristin knew this was going to be a hurried day, they opted to leave the twins back in Kharkov and not go to the orphanage. In hindsight, this was a good call – because it was not evident where two more bodies would have fit in Vlad's car. John was surprised Vlad allowed all these people into his car because it taxed the suspension system. Natalia was the opposite of petite. The group reasoned with some semblance of logic this was a short trek back into Kharkov and while crowded, the trip would not take too long.

John and Kristin were told both the girls were potty trained, which was true in a sense. However, when you are four or five years old and everything is new and while sitting in a car with your new mama and papa, and you have not gone potty since morning, you suddenly get a case of the diarrhea; any sense of control goes out the window.

Almost on cue, both girls went from a pleasant demeanor to one of agitation and pain declaring "kaka." Suddenly, it smelled really bad. John grabbed the driver's shoulder, pointed to Nastya and declared with a sense of immediate urgency, "Kaka!" Vlad instantly panicked and slammed on the brakes. The Skoda screeched to a halt and Vlad hopped out of the car and hurriedly pointed John over to a clump of bushes adjacent to the road. The unspoken message was quite clear, "Get your new children out of my car before they ruin it!"

Between wipes, Ziploc bags and a fresh pair of shorts, it was possible to get the girls back to a state allowed to ride in Vlad's car again, temporarily.

Just a few kilometers down the road, both girls had the same issue and accident, again. John and Kristin were somewhat prepared for the first one having bought Pullups and wipes. After all, these were children number six and seven, so both were quite comfortable with things coming out the south end of a child. But after the second time, the "be prepared" had turned into "you have got to be kidding." There was nothing to do but endure until the ride was over.

Fortunately, not long after the second potty accident, the group arrived at the apartment on Chubarya Street and Kristin was able to bring the girls inside to be cleaned up. Vlad, John, Natalia and the orphanage lawyer hurried to the office buildings to finish paperwork before the offices closed for lunch. Also on the to do list was purchase airplane tickets to begin the trip back to Kiev and ultimately home.

John came back to the apartment late in the afternoon. He called Kristin earlier to let them know to start packing. They were on the 7:10 PM flight to Kiev. Upon John's arrival, the family hurriedly finished packing and transported loads of suitcases down the stairwell. Vlad drove the crew along the now familiar roads to the south, but rather than turn west to the orphanage, Vlad turned east to the Kharkov airport.

Vlad dropped the Stanton's off at the front entrance of the aging airport, and Natalia helped John navigate the check-in process. She pointed to the ticket counter, showed John and family where to wait and then bid them goodbye. Natalia turned, walked down the stairway to the outside and left with Vlad.

The Stanton's were now on their own to get back to Kiev.

Due to delays and other unintelligible events, what should have been a short wait at the airport began to drag into a longer delay. John constantly ran after Emie-Nastya while the boys and Kristin guarded the luggage pile and tried to keep Katie-Vika entertained. Finally, after what seemed like an eternity, the airline ushered passengers into a more contained waiting area. MTV was once again blaring techno-dance videos into the preloading area, but by this time, no one cared – all were one step closer to home.

The summer sun set as the plane lifted off from the ground. All the troubles of the last six weeks seemed to lift with it.

It was time to turn attention to something other than the troubles of Kharkov. Outside the oval window, the scenery stunned. People refer to Ukraine as the breadbasket of Russia. Flying above the wheat, corn and soybean fields, the title fit. The last rays of the summer sunset played on the fields below only in a way appreciated from the air. The patchwork of crops below left little doubt to the fertility of the region and work ethic of the people.

The family was ready to storm Kiev, meet up with Mariya and finish the sprint to the finish line. Several unexpected blessings ensued during the short hop from Kharkov to Kiev. Amazingly and notably, both girls loved the airplane! Mariya warned sometimes motion made the kids scared or even sick. That was not something they needed now -- two little girls all of sudden airsick with their newly minted parents. They chatted, snacked, drank water and played with their magazines! David and Eric taught them how to sign airplane and they continually repeated it.

It became obvious very quickly children with Down Syndrome were not a common sight to the average Ukrainian. The family of foreigners with two 'invalid' daughters received many cold questioning stares. John was certain many people wondered why they had these two girls in public. Did they not know they were 'invalids'? At this point, John didn't care what others thought.

By the time the plane began its descent into Kiev, it was dark. Because of the domestic flight, Mariya met the travelers on the tarmac. Mariya prearranged a different apartment several blocks from their initial dwelling. Thinking back, only six weeks passed, but it seemed much longer since the family's July arrival in Kiev.

The shuttle driver brought the luggage up to the apartment via the elevator as the family began to settle in. Ideally, John planned this stay for only three nights. Mariya did well. The flat was nicely furnished, a bit larger than the previous place and offered what had been elusive in Kharkov, the Internet. Kristin pulled out her laptop, furiously tried to post pictures, update her blog, email with friends and communicate the plan for the next several days and homecoming.

Restless best described their first night together as a family. John took Emie-Nastya in one bedroom, and Kristin and Katie-Vika in another. The boys slept on the floor in the living room area. Emie-Nastya took forever to go to sleep, as did Katie-Vika. John slept on the floor – but could feel near constant motion from the little girl in the bed above him. John and Kristin thought the girls should have been exhausted from the activities of the day; but for these girls, fatigue did not translate into sleep.

Morning came too quickly. Mariya dictated the schedule. The girls needed examinations by a doctor to complete their physicals for immigration. The clinic handling physicals for adoptees was in a hospital complex in a new area of Kiev. The grounds included a small play area for kids. The girls' eyes widened when they saw the play equipment. Getting them past the equipment to see the doctor proved very difficult.

John asked Mariya to translate to them 'play later', but they didn't seem to understand. John finally picked up Katie-Vika and brought her into the examining room, sobbing. Little did they know; this outburst was a precursor of things ahead. Again, the stares greeted them as they walked the steps up to the clinic; past more 'looks' in the waiting room.

The doctor was professional and cordial; she spoke English well and provided them an informative and enjoyable visit. Katie-Vika developed a rash on her torso, so the doctor prescribed some first aid cream to alleviate the symptoms and reduce the urge to itch.

Mariya built in a little rest time for the family, back at the flat. She assured John after the clinic visit and physicals, the rest of the day was free time. Mariya resumed her natural flurry of activity, running to several different government offices to take care of things on behalf of Katie-Vika and Emie-Nastya. Now on her home turf, everything was very familiar and Mariya was well connected.

She let John and Kristin know after the doctor appointment, "We go out tomorrow after lunch to the American consulate to do more paperwork. If the girl's visas are issued tomorrow, then you done! If not, then on Friday and to your home on Saturday!" Those were the best words the entire family could possibly hear.

John felt remorseful for his tone with Mariya earlier in the week, stress and tension levels were high. During a private moment, he apologized and thanked her for all her assistance, expertise and support during the adoption. With eyes misty, she said, "John, what you do for these children is the best; they have no hope and no future here, you are the hero here." John hugged Mariya and brushed away a tear in his eye as well.

Kristin immediately went into mom-mode and with fresh access into a live Internet connection, she took advantage of the situation, writing the things on her mind the first 36 hours after acquiring these two new daughters.

"Thank you all for your continued support and encouragement! We are learning by the hour about our girls — especially regarding the allergies

*the orphanage Dr. said she had. We were told she was allergic to sugar -
like candy?, and red fruits and veggies? She woke up this morning with
very puffy eyes, and as the day has progressed I began to see hives and
some rash. I have no idea what it is if it is something we are feeding her?
This is what we have given her since she came to us: bread, crackers,
bananas, cherry yogurt, milk, noodles, cheese, chicken broth, potatoes.
Do you really think it could be an allergy to the cherry in the yogurt?
The Dr. this morning gave her some children's Claritin - which I gave
her after lunch - but I'm not really seeing any improvement. (The Dr.
also said no more yogurt, fruit or veggies for now, but wouldn't bananas
be ok?) I also brought children's Benadryl with me - but I wasn't' sure I
should give it to her, not knowing how she will react. If any of you out
there have some advice please - I would appreciate it. We don't know
this area well - and for now we are limited on food we can find and cook.
I feel like all I'm giving them is bread and noodles but I don't know
what else to do. Thanks!"*

The first family trip out with the girls made a lifetime memory for
John. As parents of adopted children, John and Kristin needed to
learn much. They realized the huge translation and transition
between reading about adopting orphans and actually parenting two
orphans. They learned quickly to be the girls' throttle and regulator.

For example, playing outside for any length of time became too
stimulating for them; too much to take in. To put this into context,
these two little girls rarely had been outside a space of about one acre
tucked in the Ukrainian countryside. No boundaries or an
understanding of personal space compounded their special needs
issues. Adding to the complexity, they reside in a culture that treats
them as invalids hid from the rest of the world.

Here they were, two girls out with their parents in public, being
treated to the things that all children with a family experience a

hundred times or more. Overwhelming was an understatement. Kristin and John attempted to meter out what the girls could take and 'dose' it appropriately for them.

John remembered the looks, the stares, but frankly, he did not care. He and Kristin were doing what they were called to do, and they were doing what they knew to be right. He wished he could yell so that everyone would understand, "Even though these two are still strangers to me, they are my daughters and I am infinitely proud to be their father."

On Thursday night, the party of six went up to Freedom Square in Kiev, the site of the 1991 peaceful Orange revolution. The girls dipped their hands in the fountain. They would have taken off their clothes and taken a swim if allowed. John watched fondly the joy and delight on their faces. It gave him a memory he would treasure forever. Much like the memory of the Indian children on the roadside, this memory is forever written in his mind.

In the moment, they were doing what they were called to do.

John's pride stretched to his two eleven-year-old boys, who had given up half their summer to participate in this adventure. The boys grew up over the past six weeks. They witnessed very important things and realized not everyone owned a nice home, had access to plenty of food and the love of a family. Both parents were thankful they made the choice to bring them. Their maturity and patience daily reinforced this decision.

John had not checked into the plant in the last week. Too much emotional drain and time at a premium kept John from work. It seemed odd to be this disconnected after staying very close to things for the first five weeks while in Ukraine. John reasoned this was more like his true vacation anyway. The plant would be fine, and he needed to focus on his family during this time anyway. He hoped the plane ride back brought an opportunity to catch up on email and reconnect with Twin Ports again.

Friday dawned with another harsh dose of reality. Being mildly sleep deprived since Tuesday; John and Kristin were learning of the girls' hyper stimulation in almost any situation. Because of their environment, curiosity and lack of control, the girls cannot self-regulate emotions. If allowed too many new things, they didn't function well. It was impossible for them to successfully process all the input stimulus and come up with an appropriate response. A meltdown was inevitable; an important thing to learn, and a fine balance to strike.

It made for a very long day, and together, they geared up for the travel day. It was made sweeter by the knowledge of their children and home lies in wait at the end of air travel, and this became their saving grace.

Suffice it to say, Friday turned into the longest day ever.

Again, in the words of Kristin,

> "Hmmm....have I mentioned what a loooooooong day this had been in this tiny apartment with 2 very dear but very crabby girls? Not much stuff here to get into - just a few suitcases of clothes, card games, a few books, some diapers, some baggies, 3 remote controls (which are useless as we've unplugged anything resembling a piece of electronic equipment

except the computer) - so not much stuff and the place is an absolute disaster! I can't even imagine what these little tornadoes (who are experiencing freedom for the first time in their lives) are going to do in conjunction with the other 2 little tornadoes (Mark and Caroline) when they all get together back home again! Hence...the gating every door in sight.

We have taken turns going out today for sanity runs. (since the girls really cannot be out walking we tag teamed watching them) Earlier in the afternoon John took the boys for some last-minute groceries. (water of course, eggs for breakfast, a loaf of yummy Ukrainian bread, frozen pizza for supper, and bananas and noodles for the girls.) John took the boys out after supper tonight. They walked up a hill to a huge famous monument in Kiev - some big statues and a massive arch. From that vantage point you can look over almost the entire city of Kiev. We talked a bit, reminisced about our time here - just the twins and John. John said it was cool. He told them sometimes it is hard to believe we are here in Ukraine, doing what we are doing. If you would have told me a year ago that we would be standing on a high hill overlooking the city of Kiev, just about to travel home with 2 newly adopted girls with Down syndrome, I would not have believed it in a million years.

David said, "It seems like it's taking a million hours to get through this day." Eric said, "I just want to be home."

Today's nap was mostly a bust...Vika slept about an hour but we don't think Nastya slept at all. Which of course, all adds up to the longest day feeling....Our only hope there is that we can get them to bed really early? We hope our interpretation of girls who are incredibly tired and overstimulated translates to "incomparably crabby". . .) is accurate,

347

because we are out of guesses.

Now, the other big news that we have is actually an announcement from David, "I lost the first molar in the great country of Ukraine!" - obviously, more bragging rights with friends!

Thank you for praying for us tomorrow as we travel. We will be flying and maneuvering the airports of Kiev, Amsterdam and Minneapolis / St. Paul on our way home to Twin Ports.

The entire family geared up, knowing it was going to be a long and stressful day.

One can only imagine after being gone for six full weeks how anxious everyone was to get back home. However, another great adventure was about to begin, being back with the rest of the family, starting new routines, traditions and roles as a family of nine.

Chapter 46: Homecoming

The trip home went surprisingly well. The family predictions ranged from terrible to a disaster; however, the girls settled down and were able to focus on the new experiences, without too many meltdowns. The first leg of the journey was from Kiev to Amsterdam. A three-hour flight and despite trying the girls did not sleep. The team of six navigated Schiphol, the Amsterdam Airport with only about 90 minutes between planes, not quite enough time to get into any trouble.

Once airborne and over the Atlantic Ocean, the girls went back to their routine; they sat, watched cartoons on the screen, snacked and flipped through books. This was no small feat, considering how difficult it was to keep them entertained in the apartment.

John used the part of the flight when Emie-Nastya was distracted with headphones and a cartoon to catch up on email. He was trying to put back on his game face. He knew Tuesday would come soon, and he had to hit the ground running. John perused through the unit cost numbers, checking over production data and reviewed site metrics from the end of the months of July and August.

John studied diskette unit cost data when a conversation with the orphanage director replayed in his mind. The orphanage director, made the comment as they were leaving one of their visits, "In the greater society, these children are not seen as valuable and rather a burden and their lives were not worth half a hryvnia." John looked down at the spreadsheet in front of him. For the first time, Northern Pines created a diskette for $.07123; not yet below the stretch goal, but, a hryvnia, equaled about $0.14 US. Half a hryvnia amounted to seven cents.

The journey was coming full circle. The team at Twin Ports chased after a ridiculously low cost target for a product produced in his plant; and at the same time half a world away, the orphanage director placed societal value on the children at the orphanage and it was the same small amount.

John knew society was wrong. His daughters, were going to show the world just how valuable they are. When placed in an environment where they are cared for, nurtured and loved; they will do great things. They will learn to read, ride bikes, love their family and contribute to the greater good in many ways.

Little time remained for pondering such deep parallels, but John tucked the thought in his mind knowing somewhere and sometime, this deserved more attention.

Preparing the girls to enter the US and invariably stand in line when they were tired and most wanted to be free to just run around ranked as the immediate and daunting task at hand.

Unbeknownst to the Stanton family, the most challenging aspect awaited them in Minneapolis after the plane arrived. The international arrival area is separated from the rest of the airport, and John had to present the documents prepared at the embassy in Kiev. They were under strict instructions not to open or tamper with the envelopes. The naturalization process would take place when Katie-Vika and Emie-Nastya arrived in the US.

By this time, Katie-Vika and Emie-Nastya were in no mood to be guided. They simply wanted to run and cut loose. It took the energy of all the Stanton's to keep them corralled. Thankfully, the immigration officials, very understanding of the situation, brought the tribe of six weary travelers to a special expedited line.

They verified all the paperwork, reviewed the aqua colored passports and welcomed Katie-Vika and Emie-Nastya to their new life as citizens of the United States of America. A momentous occasion; the culmination of almost two years of effort, but frankly all were tired, strung out from travel and simply wanted the next short flight to be over so the entire family could be reunited again.

When the plane eased on one of two Fargo taxiways, John looked at Kristin and words seemed completely inadequate. Nothing could convey the collective relief and significance of the moment. John whispered, "We did it" to Kristin and smiled. This family was tired, happy, relieved, wondering what was next and most anxious to see Seth, Caroline and Mark again after a very long separation.

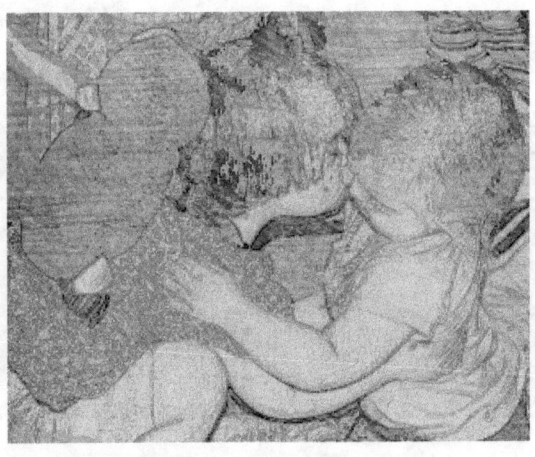

Caroline Meeting Her New Sister Katie-Vika for the First Time

No one on the flight knew what the family had been through, but after the two soldiers on the plane exited, the passengers allowed those with young children to disembark. At the airport, quite a receiving party greeted them. Friends, family and people all a part of this journey from the beginning met them. John and Kristin felt overwhelmed by the show of support and appreciated everyone who came to welcome Katie-Vika and Emie-Nastya home. Tears flowed freely, tears of happiness, relief and mostly thankfulness, just to be home.

The best and most memorable reunions were three little Stanton's meeting their two new adopted sisters. They started with tentative hugs, but all knew it would not be long before everyone would begin to melt together into a family.

Back in the USA

The next 24 hours blurred together. Driving home, unloading, getting acclimated again, sleeping, waking up and all the other details of life, but neither John nor Kristin remembered much about the first day or two. Laundry piles were high, the house was a mess and chaos slowly settled into the routine.

John wondered if shock was going through the motions and not remembering what happened. If that was the functional definition; both were in shock. A new way of life was beginning and reality hit hard.

On Monday, Labor Day, extended family left and it was just Kristin, John, and the seven kids. Kristin said to John, "I have this sinking, overwhelming feeling this decision has ruined our family. Katie-Vika and Emie-Nastya need help, but why us? What about our other kids? What were we thinking?"

John empathized with Kristin as the pit in his stomach felt raw and begged some of the same questions. It was difficult to connect the feelings with logic. Why would one go 6,000 miles away for six weeks and spend thousands of dollars on this only now to experience fear, confusion, anxiety and regret?

The feelings lingered and ran the gamut of positive and negative. The positive included all being safely back together, the accomplishment of all the adoptions tasks and beginning new routines. The negative included Katie-Vika and Emie-Nastya crying a lot, not knowing how to identify their needs, their inability to settle down at night and sleep, and the time, effort and energy not available for the other children.

Both John and Kristin tried to rationalize this as normal. The first weeks were adjusting and these feeling of regret would go away. But elements of fear and regret persisted. John and Kristin both felt a huge weight or burden and thought they split the family in half. Both asked, "Did we just screw up the rest of our family by introducing these two into the mix?"

All kinds of psychological reasons for these feelings may exist, and both might have been feeling some symptoms of depression induced by a very stressful situation, a form of post-traumatic stress disorder or something. Neither one was in a very healthy place as neither could rid the mind of the overwhelming feeling of regret and guilt, for what seemed to be lost. Both shared the feeling this decision destroyed their family dynamic, and it was gone forever, irreparably damaged.

John assumed and rationalized the idea that things would slide back into a 'normal' routine, much like in the past. A new baby comes into the home and routines are upset, but a new normal emerges. In this case, maybe the challenges awaited them were bigger, but nothing they could not handle, right? Neither John nor Kristin were prepared for the behavior issues, the lack of boundaries and the amount of learning these two little additions would put them through. John thought the girls would learn the simple things quickly; things like how to play with toys, dolls, Duplos, and other common children's toys. How hard can that be?

Reality was the furthest thing from the truth.

These girls had no concept of constructive play. Their idea of fun turned anything and everything into chaos quickly. Examples included taking every book off the bookshelf and dumping it on the floor, or opening the DVD cupboard and opening every case, letting the discs cascade onto the floor. Other common nuisances involved grabbing toys from another, physical aggression, dropping to the floor and having a meltdown, getting into the food cupboard and gorging, hiding food in pockets and even trying to run away. The backyard was fenced in, and up until now, had successfully contained all five Stanton children. It took Emie-Nastya only about a week to find a spot where the fence separated from the ground by maybe a foot. She escaped and John found her standing out in the street, totally unaware of the boundaries or present dangers.

John and Kristin anticipated the language barrier in the beginning. That was the reason Kristin and the boys worked hard during the time in the orphanage to teach them signs for "drink, eat, more, please, tired" and several other necessities. In their new home environment, a million distractions hindered language and the girls seemed to be much more emotional, having fits rather than using their sign language to tell Kristin what they wanted.

Kristin continued to do research and tied a few pieces of information together. The girls were probably going through withdrawal from whatever sedatives they were given in the orphanage. Drug withdrawal explained some of the actions, but did not make parenting any easier, as dozens of temper tantrums, not listening and emotional withdrawal by the girls characterized a normal day.

The battle raged fiercely in their minds relative to food. They ate as if wolves had raised them, stuffing their faces, stealing food, hiding food in their pockets. Suddenly, mealtime, which had been relatively relaxing and peaceful, turned into a battleground. This caused frustration for Kristin because the girls vacillated between eating everything and then being stubborn and not eating well or focusing on only one thing, desiring a meal of only one type of food.

In hindsight, the girls must have been very confused by meals that changed every time they ate, as the variety in the orphanage had to be minimal by comparison. Kristen's vision for the family sitting around a big round table and enjoying each other's company was a long way from reality at this point.

So many unexpected things could have been anticipated, but honestly, all the activity, energy, and focus remained on the process of getting these two little girls out of their orphanage and saving them from the mental institution. As parents, John and Kristin assumed the parenting would come naturally. Neither had given much thought to the integration process and all the things that would have to be adapted (or abandon) when the girls arrived home.

Kristin connected with dozens of adopted parents through support groups and other venues and quickly learned what they were experiencing was common. The children arrive at a new home, something they have never known before; and while everything is safe and has been prepared, they do not know how to process this new reality. The reality they know is abandonment, fear and to rely on their survival and coping skills, whatever they are. Their previous world was very small, regulated through meaningless routine and numbing medication.

In their past, they learned to stifle their emotions because if they cried, nothing happened. Both girls exhibited their own ways of self-soothing. Katie-Vika sat, rocked, and sucked her tongue. Emie-Nastya emotionally shut down, usually sitting with her head down and sucking her thumb.

The newfound information made it is easier to be rational about the situation; but at the time, emotions ran high, creating tension and copious amounts of stress. Those factors generated a very grim scenario for many families, especially those without support and counsel.

The best analogy John gleaned from a discussion with Dave Adams, as he and his family adopted a baby girl two years ago. He said, "It is like a game of pick up sticks or maybe a puzzle. You throw everything you know into the air and it lands in a different spot. It takes time and work to put it all back together again. Be ready, some pieces fall near where they were and some are upside down, some off the table – you get the idea." He went on, "But when it does come together, and it will, it is different, and the outcome is good."

It made no sense when Dave first said this. It did not seem like a single event could be so disruptive as to shake up the whole family, but John learned there is profound wisdom in every aspect of that statement. John relayed Dave's analogy to Kristin shortly after Katie-Vika and Emie-Nastya arrived home. The concept is one both John and Kristin clung to in the days and weeks since this crazy adventure landed two little girls from a faraway land into their family.

It was becoming evident their job was to help put the puzzle pieces together again, day by day and one by one.

Chapter 47: Reality Ranch

The alarm did not need to ring on Tuesday, September 2nd, the day after Labor Day. John heard stirring from down the hall. It was still dark, the clock said 4:15AM. He walked down the hallway to the girls' room and firmly told the girls "niplach," which was supposed to have some semblance of a firm "be quiet" embedded in it. The night was over. John was jetlagged, tired and drained, but he also knew he needed to return to the work routine and continue to fight the battle Twin Ports waged for the past six months.

It felt odd to be walking back into the Twin Ports plant after a six-week hiatus. From an 'up to speed' and data perspective, John was current, at least as of early Saturday morning, thanks to 14 hours in airplanes over the past three days. What he had not been a part of for the last six weeks was the day-to-day activities, the camaraderie and the mutual sense of fighting the battle for competitiveness and survival.

Reality hit hard and it hit quickly. Doug scheduled a plant review on Friday, so the staff met quickly to draft the outline and highlight the data each function would share. Previous leaders developed a template for the quarterly site reviews, so this was not a new event; but with John being gone the last half of the summer, he was more concerned about the rhythm and cadence of the review.

John knew Doug would be looking to measure the group and see if it acted as one team. He knew from experience it was one of Doug's litmus tests for leadership. John wanted his team to show a high level of performance, not only for his benefit but for his staff as well.

Being associated with and part of a high functioning team was always better than being viewed as a player on the farm team.

John made it a priority to walk the factory floor after he returned. Everyone knew what he had been up to, so he showed pictures, thanked the crews for their support and their great work and told them how glad everyone was to be safely home. People truly did care; a strong dose of humanity was something that made Twin Ports special.

The days literally flew by; so much to do. The first day John snuck home for lunch was Thursday. As he drove up to the house, he was reminded when they bought this house, it seemed so big.

What a contrast! Now every available nook and cranny was filled and the new struggle was to figure out where to put everyone and everything. The cars outgrew the garage, replaced with bicycles, wagons, trikes and all the other things a growing family with seven kids need! Beds were bunked and dressers and desks stashed below to maximize space. The suitcases clothes and remnants from the trip created the appropriate backdrop. It looked like a warzone.

Kristin was in the backyard with the little ones. They were swinging on the playset having a grand time. Kristin appeared stressed and upset. John could see it on her face.

The house was a total disaster from just having arrived home, trying to find room for two more people. The girls had been up extraordinarily early that morning, and Kristin had not had a free moment even to break away to take a shower. She asked if she could quickly hop in the shower and, at least, get her hair washed. John said, "Sure." That was the least he could do.

John didn't get the full dose of the morning, but Kristin summarized it like this:

> "Katie Vika, (all things considered - having spent 5 years in an orphanage) is showing signs of positive adjustment. She is affectionate towards me. She is often interacting very positively with Caroline and the other children. (playing etc...) We have a long way to go in the hitting department but I know that will improve. She seems quick to pick up words and signs - today she heard us mention cookie in a conversation and immediately began signing it!
>
> Emie Nastya is having a much harder time with all the transitions. She has many, many tantrums a day — which usually consist of covering her face with her hands, throwing herself to the floor, sobbing, then hitting and barking (I have no clue how to describe this - kind of like a yell or a grunt of UUUHH) at anyone who comes near her, or she'll throw anything nearby. Sometimes she can be just delightful and other times she does this same tantrum thing at every single change of activity. I have thought much about her and am constantly trying to analyze her — she too signs and says some words, but emotionally she is incredibly immature — kind of like a baby or young toddler? She seems to be able to focus in sometimes on repetitive activities, (i.e. — she can spend a long time drawing shapes with color wonder) but in other activities she seems to lack the ability to stay focused and is basically, constantly moving and getting into things. She does seem to like the Signing Time and Sesame Street videos and at times will sit for a short while.

John did his best to let Kristin know they were a team and in this together. Even though it was incredibly difficult at the time, things would get better. Friends were helpful and quickly understood the intensity of the challenge. Both John and Kristin realized it was humbling and hard to ask for help. Friends could see they were struggling and people would show up and take the kids for activities, wash and dry the laundry, bring meals and just do what friends do. These simple acts were appreciated more than the giver will ever know.

Adjustment was incredibly difficult, and these were only the early stages of a new and very long journey. This knowledge made the process even more overwhelming for both parents. They battled feelings of loss, despair and confusion daily, partly because neither knew if it was going to be three months, three years or longer before things changed.

When would the puzzle pieces start to feel like they were going back to where they belonged?

The twins dove back into the schoolwork at home. Thankfully, they were sixth graders and largely self-sufficient. Kristin ordered materials before leaving for Eastern Europe so they could get directions from mom, receive their assignment and then work independently; retreating to the relative quiet of their room. Seth started his first-grade material, working on reading, spelling, and simple math concepts. Kristin juggled her time between the four "littles" and keeping the others moving forward in school. She was now educating three children, entertaining four toddlers, cooking, cleaning, laundering for nine and being a wife and mother. John thought of her as amazing, talented, selfless and remarkable.

Later that evening when Dave stopped by to borrow a hedge trimmer, he asked, "So, you've been home less than a week, how are things going." John said, "To make a long story short, we were

Katie Vika and Emie Nastya Helping Rake Leaves

unprepared for the whole process of reintegrating our family. I think part of this is because there isn't really a playbook or guide. When you have a new baby who is an infant, it is easier to adjust because patterns haven't yet been formed or established. Babies are not mobile; their needs are satisfied largely by food, clean diapers, holding and sleep. When you have a four or five-year-old, the demands are much higher; and then when they have been in institutional care their entire life, it is almost like lighting a firecracker

362

and then watching what happens." Dave nodded in agreement, "Nothing is predictable, is it?" John agreed and added, "It is literally driving us crazy."

After evening activities completed, John joined Kristin on the couch in the living room. Kristin dug into anything and everything she could get her hands on, related to adoption, attachment, orphanages and special needs. Admittedly, she discovered much in those early weeks. Together they learned about reactive attachment disorder, hypervigilance, and patterns of early childhood attachment. The knowledge helped explain most of the why, but not necessarily how to fix it or if fixing it was even possible.

The more Kristin learned, the more despairing the outlook. So much brain development happens early in life, and when these patterns of abuse and neglect are established, it can take years to retrain and re-pattern the mind. When Kristin showed John the description of reactive-attachment and hypervigilance, not only did it fit, but it scared the wits out of them both. The natural question any parent would want to know, what does it take to fix it?

Kristin told John that evening her honest struggles, "We thought we were adopting a child with Down syndrome who happened to spend the first five years of life in an orphanage. Instead, we have a child who hasn't formed normal attachments due to neglect, abuse, abrupt changes in caregivers, and this dysfunction early on in life has now put patterns in place that may be with her for a long time if not the rest of her life. It is not fair. This isn't what we signed up for."

Kristin pulled up a web page she had been reading during a rare moment of quiet when the kids watched Veggie Tales earlier in the afternoon. The clinical aspects are highlighted in a definition taken from the WHO International Statistical Classification of Diseases and Related Health Problems (ICD-10)

> Reactive attachment disorder (RAD) is characterized by markedly disturbed and developmentally inappropriate ways of relating socially in most contexts. It can take the form of a persistent failure to initiate or respond to most social interactions in a developmentally appropriate way—known as the "inhibited form"—or can present itself as indiscriminate sociability, such as excessive familiarity with relative strangers—known as the "disinhibited form."

As fate would have it, the two girls reacted differently to the same stimulus. Emie-Nastya seemed to be exhibiting a whole other set of behaviors, dozens of tantrums a day which usually consisted of covering her face with her hands, throwing herself to the floor, sobbing, then hitting and making noises that sounded more like an animal than a child.

"It is hard not to think that she understands, but I don't know if it a maturity thing, or she is just confused about this new life, or frustrated because she cannot communicate," Kristin said. She went on, "I have looked into those beautiful green eyes and asked, 'what is going on in there?'"

Kristin also read up on sensory issues, common for orphans and those that are institutionalized. This is a direct result of them not having human contact. They have come up with alternate methods of soothing and comfort, but there are some things that simply help them feel safe. Sometimes the weight of blanket or being grasped tightly can provide a level of comfort beyond just the physical touch.

Kristin had the tougher end of this deal. John, at least, got an escape at work. She has the daily grind. Both agreed it was getting late and time for bed. Friday morning would arrive too soon.

Chapter 48: Cracks in the Foundation

Thursday afternoon, Doug called John for two reasons. First, he needed to reschedule the site review at the plant. Doug was due to come up on Friday and review plant operations. John confessed disappointment but knew the staff would be delighted with the extra 'day' he was about to give them.

No matter how hard the agenda was crafted to minimize disruption, the fact of the matter was an executive visit was more than a day lost. The prep time, developing the agenda and attending to details to get the site ready involved nearly the whole plant. Running the review took time, effort and energy away from the real work at hand.

Not that the reviews were all bad. They certainly provided an opportunity for sharing new information, career growth for new managers and engineers, and a two-way exchange of information and influence.

The other bombshell reason Doug called was to give John the news in advance of an upcoming press release. Doug shared Lucinda Marshall, hotshot rising star executive, was leaving Northern Pines. Although the press release would indicate she was going to pursue a new career path, Doug confirmed what was running up the rumor mill. She was being investigated by the SEC for insider trading violations during her time at Norwood.

The accusation related to purchase of stock at a vendor that Norwood was considering acquiring. While she was not directly involved in the transaction, the Securities and Exchange Commission was investigating whether she accessed and used information not publicly available. The trades were of a size and scale that caught the attention of investigators at the SEC.

John did not have the time for day for Lucinda, so her departure was the bright spot in an otherwise hectic and stressful week. Since his return from Ukraine, John had not had a chance to speak with Doug about Mendal. John used the opportunity to quiz Doug briefly on what happened in the last six weeks.

Doug stated the Vice President of Finance called him into a high-level risk management meeting. Doug was only invited to the morning session, but the objective of the meeting, from what he could garner, was the executive team was reassessing the ROI around the joint venture. Doug said the morning session was to gather the inputs from the supply chain, manufacturing, technology development and finance. The afternoon was dedicated to establishing the prioritized risk profile, identifying viable mitigation activities and making a recommendation to the executive committee (Ex-Com) with respect to probability of success and scenarios to manage the risk.

John threw a little bait out there to see if Doug would take it. John said, "It does seem like a few things have changed since the original Mendal agreement was signed. First, the Twin Ports agreement from 30 years ago. Second, I know the capital cost estimates and closure estimates have come in higher, and our plant performance has been really good. Any changes would disrupt the supply and potentially create a reset?"

Doug nibbled on the bait, "John, between you and me, I can't see this going anywhere. I have always thought it was crazy, but in this environment, sadly, if you don't use your mind and your analytical skills, you end up using your political skills. Politics doesn't lead to solutions. It leads to compromising convictions to stay employed, which has little to do with what is best for the business."

Doug went on, "We were one of the later groups to be quizzed by the Ex Com, and I don' think they intended us to see this; but Robert Loras, the division controller flashed up the spreadsheet of the risks and benefits, and all I could see was the quantity. There must have been thirty risks identified, and perhaps there were five or six on the benefits side. Not always that quantity matters, but those benefits would have to be pretty powerful to outweigh all the risks that were on that page."

This was the most candid discussion John and Doug engaged in since John was given the site manager role. John thanked Doug for the information and ended with a 'see you next week at the monthly review.'

Chapter 49: Transitions

John stressed about home and work.

It was great to be back with the team and have the adoption milestone completed. Everyone pitched in and did a remarkable job when John was absent. Production met targets and remained stable, progress on programs continued and currently the plant was doing well. All of this was highly satisfying to John. He had confidence in the team and knew they would deliver; however, people were tired and stressed.

John took some time the first two weeks to sit down with each team to assess their impact on the site transformation. He wanted to know how well the three initiatives started to change the culture and return results, and if the results were already there or if additional benefits could still be gained.

First, John met with Jeff. He set up a cross-functional group of operators, maintenance techs and one supervisor to talk about the leadership lessons.

The outcomes surprised John. These topics can be a bit squishy, but the thing that had made the biggest impact on Twin Ports was the employees made the connection between Shackelton's journey and the daily operational struggles of the plant. They articulated the mission sometimes must change depending on what else is going on, and flexibility to change the mission is key.

Another takeaway was everyone had the capacity to lead. People may be called in different ways, but everyone can exhibit leadership characteristics in their own situation; and in many cases, it is taking charge of a situation, assessing what needs to be done, agreeing on the path forward and then allowing people to do their jobs. These steps make a tangible difference.

Dan, one of the maintenance techs, shared a great example. On the Glacier line, the conveyor used to bunch up parts at times. When this happened, if someone was not close by to see it and hit the STOP button, parts would continue to back up. Therefore, between the operators on the line and the maintenance techs, they started an A3 to figure out why this was happening.

In the past, maintenance would have put a sensor on the line. If the sensor was blocked, the line would have shut down or at least alarmed. However, Dan and team took it another step further. They studied why the backups occurred and found a timing issue on the conveyor. If a signal from the PLC was not cleared quickly enough, the leading conveyor stopped which created a backup further up the line.

John was proud of them for two reasons. First, the teams exhibited leadership and possessed the initiative to take on a problem they were best equipped to solve; and secondly, they got to root cause and elimination of the problem forever. The line will never have a back up again which is much better than a sensor to tell operators a back-up occurred and stopped the line. One was corrective in nature and the other was truly preventive. John complimented the team and said, "I'll take the preventive any day!"

As John listened, more and more of these stories started to come forward. He listened to story after story of little, incremental changes that on the surface may not seem like a lot, but when an operation runs seven days a week, 24 hours a day and nearly 365 days a year, little changes are significant. The additive effect of small changes is a significant net result. Maintenance technicians are not running to fix trivial items. Therefore, the effort they spent on real problems is more impactful. Not only was a small irritating problem solved for good, people's time freed up to work on the bigger solutions.

The more important element was the empowerment these success stories provided. Those doing the work were responsible and accountable. They understood and felt a true sense of ownership. What could be a more empowering message?

John was pumped from the morning and proud of the team for the energy derived from the Shackelton training. The impact was beyond John's expectations, and if the other areas engaged even half as well, this would be a game changer for the plant.

John noticed an odd meeting on his calendar scheduled by Diane for 2:00 PM. It was not titled, so John assumed no prep was needed. John returned to his office when Diane popped her head in about 1:55 and reminded him to get down to the training room. He wrapped up work on his presentation for the monthly review in the Twin Cities and hit save on the menu bar before heading down to Training Room A.

John walked into a room with Jeff, Mary Ann and Grant and they all looked serious. John wondered if this was an ambush or something. Maybe they all wanted a raise or bonus since they had run the plant for the last six weeks.

John was soon to learn of their much bigger plans.

Grant began. He said that after they had learned about the letter between Harris Thronson and the city of Twin Ports, it started a thought. The thought was, if Northern Pines Technology could not get out of the agreement, and indeed it was enforceable, was there a way to mutually satisfy both parties?

The three senior managers talked and came up with a somewhat crazy idea. If the agreement was ironclad, and Northern Pines Technology was committed to Twin Ports for another three years, could there be an exchange? Grant explained, it would work like this, "Northern Pines Technology would allow a transfer of the ownership of the plant to the employees in lieu of having to payout to the city. The city would benefit because jobs would be maintained in the community. Northern Pines Technology would continue to get their products from Twin Ports, but not have the financial liability of a payroll, factory costs, inventory and associated operations."

Mary Ann chimed in, "In exchange, we would work with a local bank to secure financing for operations and a commitment from Northern Pines Technology for a base amount of business and the assurance the site could actively grow the contract manufacturing business."

Jeff added, "Our thought would be at some point in time, Northern Pines Technology would no longer be making diskettes, but the equipment could be repurposed to support contract manufacturing. We have been meeting, developing a plan and we are very serious about seeking an audience with Northern Pines management to pitch this."

At first, the proposal shocked John, but in a good way.

These were three people he had the utmost professional and personal respect for and knew if anyone could pull this off, it would be Jeff, Grant, and Mary Ann. The proposal showed perseverance, creative thinking, collaboration and put the interests of the people above the profits of the corporation.

Before responding, John paused as they obviously thought this through carefully and considered the impact and the potential outcomes. Their analysis showed a three-year runway was about what they needed to replace the diskette business. They could maintain near full employment and keep good jobs in North Dakota.

John could see this group was serious and determined.

He began peppering them with questions, "what is the value of assets at the plant versus the payout based on SVOP?" Mary Ann said, "book value is somewhere in the $30 million range. A buyout of SVOP would be at least three times that price, so Northern Pines Technology was reducing a significant liability for much less than the straight up buyout would cost. In short, they were getting a good deal. The depreciation would continue to drop over the next few years, and without knowing all the tax ramifications; Northern Pines could maintain its depreciation schedule and continue to reduce the financial cost to shareholders."

John asked about operating funds. They signed a non-disclosure agreement and spoken with the ND Economic Development Foundation; the Bank of ND, and a local bank about funding. They indicated with an audit of past financial records, funding could be secured to finance the ongoing day to day operations. They worked especially on cash flow so the new venture would not have all their operating funds tied up in inventory. Together they agreed upon a proposal to pitch to Northern Pines management on less inventory and shorter payment terms.

John thought the immediate operational questions were answerable, but what about the growth prospects? He asked about future growth projections. They reduced the diskette forecast annually by 15%, kept the others flat and then built in some reasonable assumptions about new business. They planned after three years, diskettes would be done and the space available for new operations with a ramp down period allowing for a phased approach as well as potentially repurposing equipment, especially the molding and metal stamping presses.

The thoroughness of their scenarios impressed John; as well as the planning and rigor they applied to the analysis. They were serious about this proposal and were willing to do what it takes to make it happen. They obviously thought and planned, because every question John could ask, they had a reasonable, data-based answer.

Finally, they filled John in on the details of Doug's visit. They did not want to worry John when he was overseas, but Doug did some digging. He asked the three of them exactly what John told them, and they answered honestly.

They thought that maybe this would strike terror in John, but strangely enough, there was a bit of relief. Deep down, John was proud of this group for their fortitude, for their vision and mostly for the fact they stepped up to lead. Each of these three had deep roots in Twin Ports and North Dakota. This was not a cut and run exercise. This was a well thought out plan to not only preserve a way of life but create jobs and hope for a brighter future.

John asked if they shared any of this with Doug, which they had not. John asked if they were ready. They indicated they were. John said, "Soon I think you will get your chance."

John went back to his desk and sunk into the worn leather chair that had occupied the plant manager's office for the past 25 years. So many leaders sat in this chair, each with their own aspirations and talents. Several went on to become division vice presidents and rule larger kingdoms. Several retired from this chair and a few had simply gone on to other adventures.

John wondered what his future would be? He wasn't worried, as most of what he had set out to do had been accomplished. He wondered, how would he be remembered?

John realized the events of the past six weeks clarified in his mind his legacy. To him, success was not defined with power and accumulation. It was about working to change lives. In fact, the more success that came his way in terms of financial incentives and influence, the more he realized he was there to help others.

John thought if he can leave an organization more stable, self-sufficient, focused on fulfillment of its mission and achieving excellence, he was happy. In short, if he could leave the organization with people, systems and tools better positioned to meet the next set of challenges; his work was successful.

Chapter 50: Review at Headquarters

For the plant review, John did what he normally did not do. He woke up at 3:30 AM and drove down to the Twin Cities in the morning, and with traffic and construction, arrived just ahead of the meeting.

John did this for two reasons. First, Kristin needed the help. Nighttime routines developed into a nightmare. These two girls, who bounded into their lives and kept them hopping all day, one might assume would be dog-tired at night. The opposite was true. Those little beans got more wound up as the evening progressed. They didn't stay in their beds, they fooled around, they talked, they got up in the middle of the night and played.

The first few times it was somewhat cute and understandable but after the third, fourth, fifth. . . infinite nights, it got really old, really fast.

One of Kristin's friends who adopted in Ukraine confirmed they had seen the orphanage workers putting the sleep sedative into the kids' soup at dinnertime. She had asked the worker through a series of signs regarding the medicine and the worker folded her hands and put her head on her hands, indicating sleep.

Since learning the kids were sedated specifically to fall asleep, not only did the girls not know how to settle themselves down, they had somewhat of a drug dependency to get them to do what their body should naturally tell them to do.

The second reason John came down in the morning was he needed some thinking time. John knew he was going to be asked some tough questions from Doug about his activities over the past nine months. John was proud of the team and the results. He had no problem defending his actions based on a principled argument about what was right for the site and their business.

John arrived at Doug's office promptly at 8:00 AM. Doug welcomed him and asked, "John – coffee?" John needed coffee, responding with "Sure." They walked to the cafeteria and traded small talk, mostly about Ukraine. Doug followed Kristin's blog, so he knew some of the ups and downs. When they arrived back at the office, Doug asked John to take a seat as he closed the door.

They sat down and Doug spoke first. "John, you have been busy, haven't you?" John said, "Yes, I have. As you know from your visit, I have been doing what I think it takes to prove to you, Lucinda and Marshall this plant is worth saving. Moving these operations overseas is a financial mistake because we are the lowest cost producer. I and my entire team believe the technology we possess cannot be effectively managed outside this plant."

Doug thought for a moment and said, "Right around the time you left for Ukraine, Melyssa Aroms stopped by the office and asked me about you." John asked, "Who is she?" Doug responded, "She was with us back at the Northland Inn in February. The rep from legal. Her name changed – she used to be McDonald, but is now Melissa Aroms." John remembered her as the one with the fancy bag.

"Anyway, she looked at the agreements signed back in the Northland Inn and could not find one signed by you. In fact, the one that should have been signed by you was signed by Clyde Champion Barrows."

John smiled and said, "Yup, that's me." Doug continued, "When Melyssa found out she had a bogus signature, she just about hit the roof. I told her not to worry. John, I have known you long enough that you are no Clyde Barrows, but it was my first clue and I did have to figure out what you were up to."

"I learned a few things about what has been going on. First, you disclosed confidential information. Second, you directly worked to disrupt the strategic direction of this company. Third, you were insubordinate. Fourth . . ." John stopped him, "I get it," John said.

John had just a minute to compose a million thoughts, and he did not know how they were all going to come out. He had not rehearsed this speech in his mind.

John started with a note of hesitancy, "This team has put their heart and soul into creating one of the best manufacturing plants in the country. To suddenly come in and tell us that this is all going away is unconscionable, and I vowed the minute I heard it, I was going to do the only thing I knew would possibly save the plant. That was to make it unprofitable to pick up and move. I don't know exactly where we are at on that journey, but I could not stand idle and watch the hopes and dreams of 400 people in my charge disappear."

Doug said, "The consolidation objective is still intact. Even though it is unlikely that Mendal will be the suitor, we must consolidate our operations. We simply cannot afford to have the infrastructure which currently exists.

The note that you produced from Mr. Thronson has created a bit of a wrinkle and the executive committee is still trying to figure out what it all means.

Delaying action is not an option. We are getting clobbered in the marketplace. We will all be out of business if we keep the infrastructure we have for another three years. If there was only some other way to fulfill the obligation…" Doug looked wistfully out the window towards the rising sun.

Doug went on to embellish more of the information he shared over the phone. "The Mendal Enterprise efforts are on shaky ground. The transition teams put together project plans to move facilities and both the timing and the costs were too high. Not only that, even with the significant labor cost advantage of India on diskettes, there was not enough labor content in the products to offset the costs of moving."

John thought to himself, I told you so.

Doug went on to say the board of directors was concerned about the risk of product supply. The analysis currently going on was a consolidation of coating plants. It was going to be reducing the three plants ideally down to one, so there was a Tiger team looking at the continued feasibility of running all products out of one facility on just one or two coaters. The leading site was the plant in Oregon since the equipment seemed to have the most flexibility. The Arizona plant had older technology and the most prudent course of action was probably to end of life these products. The California plant and Oregon were the two logical remaining candidates.

Doug did say the projections for the next three years put the division in a very tough spot. It was conceivable gross margins could drop between five and six percentage points. This would make the division at break even for profit and loss; not acceptable to the management team, the board of directors or the shareholders, so every possible angle was being pursued to dramatically cut operating costs.

John said, "I think I have something I think you should listen to. Can you clear your calendar tomorrow AM?" Doug glanced at his desk and said, "Yes, starting at 9, I can be free, but what do you have in mind?" John said, "I am going to give you some time with Grant,

Mary Ann, and Jeff because they have been thinking about the very same thing and have something you should seriously consider."

John went on to explain there had been some work done when John was in Ukraine. In fact, it was a counter proposal to letting Mendal Enterprises move the operation overseas. John outlined the basic plan, "This is based on the belief that if Northern Pines Technology is willing to leave the plant in Twin Ports, there is a group that would be interested in doing a time-phased employee owned buy-out. Pure and simple, the benefit for Northern Pines Technology is we reduce the entire expense of operating the plant, pay only for the components. The plant would continue to supply products to Northern Pines Technology, but the site would also have freedom to pursue new business, leveraging the technology and equipment that exists at Twin Ports."

John continued, "This would also get Northern Pines Technology out of the cloud of having to provide a three-year notification of closure. Northern Pines guarantees some predefined purchase of three years' worth of components and cartridges. This just provides the new enterprise a runway to begin building upon through the transition. And I guarantee this bill will be much less than the one under the existing agreement."

Doug was more than interested and John said he would call Jeff, Mary Ann and Grant to travel down tonight to pitch their plan to Doug tomorrow.

The remained of the one-hour meeting went quickly and John thanked him for the time and thanked him in advance for meeting with Jeff, Mary Ann and Grant. The plant reviews did not start until

10:00 AM that morning so John took the next hour to catch up on email and make the call back to the plant.

John dialed Mary Ann first. No answer. Then he tried Grant, same. Last chance was Jeff. Thankfully, Jeff was at his desk. He was surprised that there was an open reception and said they would pull together everything they had and be down later that night.

John called Kristin to see how the early morning had gone and apologized for a second (or third) time for being gone these couple of days. Kristin said the girls were up at 5:45 AM and she was thankful for a strong dose of freshly ground and brewed Caribou Coffee.

John took a few minutes to review the notes for the site update. John had all the data, but he also had some important talking points he wanted to cover first.

John stared at the slide.

**Twin Ports
Sept Highlights**

Northern
Pines
Technology

1. Safety – QTD – 0 incidents
2. Record low diskette cost
3. Critical Operating Expense Reduction
   - QTD – Q3: $2.0MM
4. Training Within Industry

John thought back to what he started in February, just six short months ago. At the time, he put out a crazy goal of a $0.07 diskette. John was now going to report the site was well within reach of a seemingly unattainable goal. John knew his team would reach it before year-end.

John considered how the Twin Ports team had achieved so much; several large dollar programs certainly provided the momentum to get significantly lower in cost. The aluminum shutters, the molded-in features, and reduction of materials like liners brought tens of millions of dollars in savings. When John looked over the "Blue Ox" list created back at the beginning, most of the items were operational improvements. For the product changes, the site had the technical expertise and first principles knowledge to be able to drive the improvement locally rather than rely on R&D to support.

John also thought back to the extensive use of modeling that accelerated the rate of improvement. For tooling changes at the site, designers could model not only the optimal mold design, but also the flow of plastic in the tool for various designs, the thermal characteristics so they could predict sink and shrinkage of the part and even modeling cycle time before anyone ever cut a tool and clamped the tool into a physical press.

The site was winning by knowledge and that was a powerful force when used well.

John went through the punch list on the second page

1.	Format Yield & Media @ Fcst	99.5%	up .3%
2.	D machine yield	99.4%	up .1%
3.	Reverse image - less ink	done	
4.	Shell Optimization – molding	100% w/ regrind	
5.	Kanban - one dept scheduler	$120k/yr saving	

John smiled at the last one on the list. This had been on the wish list for a while. The site ended up losing a materials control scheduler to the new SunGrown plant in June, just before John left for Ukraine. Grant asked John for a replacement requisition before he left. Grant knew where John stood. John made a deal with him. He takes the time he would spend onboarding a new employee and put that effort into working out a shell Kanban with the production cell coordinators.

The reasoning was simple. Why schedule the molding of diskette shells? John reasoned with Grant, "We know we are going to make between 50 and 55 million diskettes per month. We have historical averages on mix of colors. We knew that 75% plus was black, so figure out how many shells need to be ahead of assembly, including safety stock to avoid a line down situation and plan for that. On the colors, do the same – come up with an amount that needs to flow through assembly and then molding can self-replenish within a set of rules." Grant reluctantly agreed to try it.

Grant came back to John a few weeks later somewhat sheepishly. The Kanban was working perfectly and Grant said, "We had only stocked out once – and that was foreseeable. We had a long weekend where we had a temporary cell coordinator who had not realized completely how the Kanban worked, so they hadn't given the make order and we ran a line out for a few hours." A forgivable mistake and one that John would gladly take for a savings greater than $100,000 annually.

Grant went on to say it was working so well, they implemented a webcam for the media area. The site was getting media from the coating plants every two to three days. They put a webcam on the production floor, covering the area of the media storage. The planners in the outside plants could logon to the intranet site and check their inventory levels visually.

This saved some time for the local planners to have the cell coordinators count the media totes periodically, figure out if they were full or empty and communicate that to back to the shipping plant. A few simple rules were when the truck arrived from the coating plant, all media had to be out on the floor in eight hours, no partials. If a tote of media was pulled, take the whole thing and maintain first in first out (FIFO) and the system nearly ran itself, if the safety stock calculations were right.

The two journeys John had been on were both incredible in their own way. The plant was set to achieve goals that just six months ago would have been laughable, because they was so much distance to cover. The site was on the verge of achieving the impossible. At home, John and Kristin rescued two girls with the goal of providing them the love and security of a family. Truthfully, on that front, it was hard to see or feel any progress.

John checked his watch and realized it was time to head to the site manager's meeting.

Doug kicked off the discussion with much of the same information he shared with John in private. This was the first monthly meeting since returning from Ukraine, so John was not sure how much of this had been covered with the site managers previously. John could see the look of surprise on all the site managers' faces when Doug announced that Lucinda was leaving and Mendal was being rethought.

John heard a collective sigh of relief the Mendal business was cooling. John could see Charlie and Ray, and it looked like they were hearing this information for the first time. John could not see Tom, as he was sitting in front and he didn't have a direct line of sight. The four plant managers were not unified in much, as each tried to position their plant. John knew there was perfect alignment on this one. It was one thing to have a technology agreement with them, but to think that Northern Pines could pull off a manufacturing outsourcing project across four plants to an overseas location with complex process technology was a stretch for even the most optimistic.

John did not envy the dilemma the executive team faced. There were tough choices. This was a highly cost competitive business. Margins were shrinking and only tough questions with no easy answers remained ahead.

The finance results were not what anyone wanted to see. Sales were down, when all expected to see a slight bump in August results from the back-to-school business. Another dynamic commonly observed came between August and September with a bump in IT spending, as several of Northern Pines customers followed a fiscal year ending at the end September. None of these dynamics seemed to be present, creating a brutal month of sales.

Northern Pines bonus system comprised of three components: operating income, sales and cash flow. It was gated by sales, so missing two out of three-quarters was not a good omen for any bonus at the end of the year.

There seemed to be a downward trend each time in terms of payout. The bonus was always nice because it was a tangible reminder the actions of employees returned value to the corporation and shareholders. The outlook this year was grim.

Maybe there was a September miracle that could happen, who knows? Demand on the factory had been strong, but with all the end of quarter promos and deals, sometimes it was hard to analyze the sales and see if they had a positive effect in driving closer to the final goal. Sales may be selling, but if margin is empty, that only helps the sales number and not the operating income.

The rest of the day and a half was routine. On Monday night, Doug downgraded from steak and went for pizza and billiards instead. John guessed this was a deliberate signal that austerity was the new normal for Northern Pines Technology. Somehow, John doubted the message was universally received, but that wasn't up to him to enforce. John enjoyed pizza and a few games of eight-ball at Pins & Sticks in downtown St. Paul.

Chapter 51: New Beginnings

John met the Twin Ports team at the hotel later that evening. They excitedly showed John the entire proposal and it was impressive. John relayed additional information from his learning today and his time with Doug. They sat down in the lobby and excitedly went over their plans and who was going to say what. John was pleased with how this queued up and could not have been prouder of these three dedicated employees.

When the conversation died down, John left them with words of advice, aptly the voice of Ernest Shackelton. John said, "I have watched you guys grow and develop and we have created something very special at Twin Ports. I could not be prouder of you and your passion and expertise. Remember the words of Shackelton, as they will serve you well, 'By endurance we conquer.'" John went on to say, "I can't wait to see the outcome of your meeting and work with Doug; he is going to be blown away."

With those words, John excused himself and left to take a walk into the cool September air. The trees were just beginning to show the first signs of fall color. The days were warm this time of year, but due to the earlier sunset, nights cooled off quickly. John walked across the parking lot and across Miller Avenue. The hotel was located near a bicycle path, and John often woke up early to walk the path. The walk was somewhat sentimental, as John knew his time at Northern Pines Technology was limited.

Earlier in the day before the plant review, Doug effectively fired John. It came in words more graceful than "You're fired," but the outcome was the same. Doug let John know he was relieved of duties and removed from his role as site manager. Doug stated the obvious, "John, there will be no additional roles within Northern Pines open to you."

After almost twenty years, this is the end.

John was not surprised.

Doug explained John's termination was due to his actions back in February, essentially falsification of a corporate record. Northern Pines Technology security staff monitored all of John's communication and reviewed by legal counsel. Last month, a Human Resources panel conducted a personnel review, and a decision rendered was unanimous to terminate his employment. Through the personnel review, the consensus of the committee was John's actions had been determined to be insubordination. Oddly enough, Doug chose to share with John a lot of discussions emerged regarding his positive reputation and the contributions made during his career. The facts remained and the committee rendered their verdict: John could no longer be trusted to lead the Twin Ports plant.

Doug continued, with a wry smile on his face, "John, they concluded you were not an imminent threat to the company, so they allowed you to remain in the position for the time during the adoption and the past few weeks." Doug added, "They were watching you pretty closely, however, and daily reports generated by legal and security about your communications, summary of analysis files and phone conversations. Kind of clandestine stuff, John." Doug ended, "You know, other than running a rebellion; you lead kind of a boring life."

Doug informed John his last day of pay would be September 28th.

There would be no severance or separation; this was the end of the road.

John had time to reflect on the events of the day on his walk; he was at peace. John could understand the decision.

John mused, when I started at Twin Ports back in 1993, I wondered why am I at Northern Pines? Where is my place in this world? Now, with some clarity, he realized the answer. It was to lead and to serve the people; in his own way. Weigh every decision, decide what is best for the many competing priorities and forge ahead. His role was to help Twin Ports survive.

John served the shortest tenure of any site manager in Twin Ports' history. Although impossible to know, his may have been the most action-packed tenure as well.

John took inspiration from Ernest Shackelton. During his time as leader of the Endurance, he had many moments that tested the wills and the patience of man. John brought the story of Ernest Shackelton to the plant thinking they needed the lesson; however, in retrospect, the message not only taught them, it served as a beacon for him.

John functioned as one of the north stars to guide the way. If a 19th Century Irish explorer could bring home 28 men, certainly John possessed the fortitude to pull together a group of people to do some extraordinary things. When John began, the goal was to prove to Northern Pines Technology management the site could compete with any low-cost producer in the world. Not only had the site met the challenge, but more leaders now stood ready to move the plant forward.

John reflected on his time and the many opportunities he had to learn, grow and lead. The termination stung a bit, but he knew going in there were risks; this was one of them.

After John returned from his walk, he sat down in the quiet of his room, opened his computer and began a note that he hoped he would never have to write.

To: jalberts@northernpinestech.com; mtackett@northernpinestech.com, grichards@northernpinestech.com

Cc: dwalker@northernpinestech.com

From: jstanton@northernpinestech.com

Friends,

I will not be with you tomorrow morning when you present to Doug. This is for two reasons. First, my time with Northern Pines is short. In my desire to save the plant, my actions were deemed to be insubordinate and my employment will end soon. Secondly, and more importantly - I think there is a very good likelihood this plant will be yours in the very near future. It solves the problem of the old contract and provides other financial benefits during a tough time.

I could not be prouder to be a part of this outstanding plant and associated with the fine people. Part of this plant will live with me forever. I am traveling home tonight to be with my wife and kids. The rest of the world will find out tomorrow; I wanted you to hear from me first.

Knock it out of the park tomorrow you three!!!

js

Chapter 52: Home

On that September night, John packed up his things and started driving a very familiar road past Brooklyn Center, past Rogers, and tonight, even past the usual coffee stop. He did not need coffee tonight even though it was 3:30 AM.

As the Taurus turned west on MN 210, John looked out his right window and saw the aurora borealis, the mythical northern lights. How could collisions of particles from the sun interact so beautifully with the earth's atmosphere? The pale green, pink and red shimmered as ribbons, which slowly morphed into a curtain and changed yet again into a streamer. It was slow motion, yet tantalizing to see what came next. The show was better than anything created by man.

John arrived in Twin Ports just as the sun was beginning its rise across the prairie. He quietly opened the front door of his home. He sat on the living room sofa and watched the sunlight cast a shadow of the window on the opposite wall. The timer on the coffee pot turned on at 6:15 AM. John heard the first stirring upstairs shortly afterward, then the sound of feet coming down the stairs. First, it was Katie-Vika, then Emie-Nastya and finally Caroline. Three precious girls, each with their own futures ahead of them.

Before long, everyone except Mark was in the living room. Mark wouldn't surface for at least another hour; if past history was any guide.

The first glance John gave Kristin, his eyes told it all. She knew. Of course, the kids were oblivious and after the initial excitement of daddy being home settled down, John gathered everyone on the sofa and told them a story.

The story ended with, "Daddy is not going to be able to work at the plant anymore." The weight of the final statement hit John harder than expected. It was quiet for a minute, and then Seth asked, "Daddy, what are you going to do?"

John said with a smile, "Right now, I think I know seven kids who need a full-time dad at home." John continued, "After that, I don't know. I have many things I would like to do, maybe become a forest ranger, maybe open a small business. Who knows? Maybe I will even write a book".

With two kids hanging on his legs, John rambled to the kitchen, grabbed a spatula and exclaimed, "Who wants pancakes?"

Epilogue

Companies live and die by the decisions of leaders.

Northern Pines Technology was no different. To understand its place in a changing global economy, it hired financial analysts, consultants and business experts; all with opinions and solutions. The consensus, in meetings far away from the factory floor, it was decided manufacturing was not at the core of their business strategy. Technology and manufacturing had too much liability and not enough potential for return.

With the exit of manufacturing, the executives hired more strategists and consultants who convincing each other the way to easy money was to buy brands, leverage the strength of the brand and growth will follow.

None of this ended well. Integration of new brands and companies was difficult, the perceived leverage did not translate into real value, sales continued to decline and the spiral of layoffs accelerated. A once mighty company disintegrated into just a shell of its previous self.

Twin Ports discontinued diskette production in November of 2008, after nineteen years of continuous manufacturing. Over 5.6 billion diskettes were made by the dedicated employees of Twin Ports. Ironically, there was stronger demand at the end of life than planned and diskettes had to be outsourced from China at a cost much higher than $.07.

Jeff, Mary Ann and Grant were successful in their pitch to save the plant. They continued to supply Northern Pines with products, although fewer and fewer each year. The entire employee population rallied by using their collective skills and abilities to create true customer value. In the end, the employees are the winners; they create results which drive customer value. Today, the plant continues to use QICR and engineering principles to solve customers' problems.

The moral of this story, an excellent organization is never defined by the name on the door; but always by the people within.

As for the Stanton's, much like the analogy of the puzzle pieces – they did slowly fall into place. It took years. Today, all are doing well and many enjoyable meals have been eaten with all nine sitting around that big round table.